THE VICTORIES™

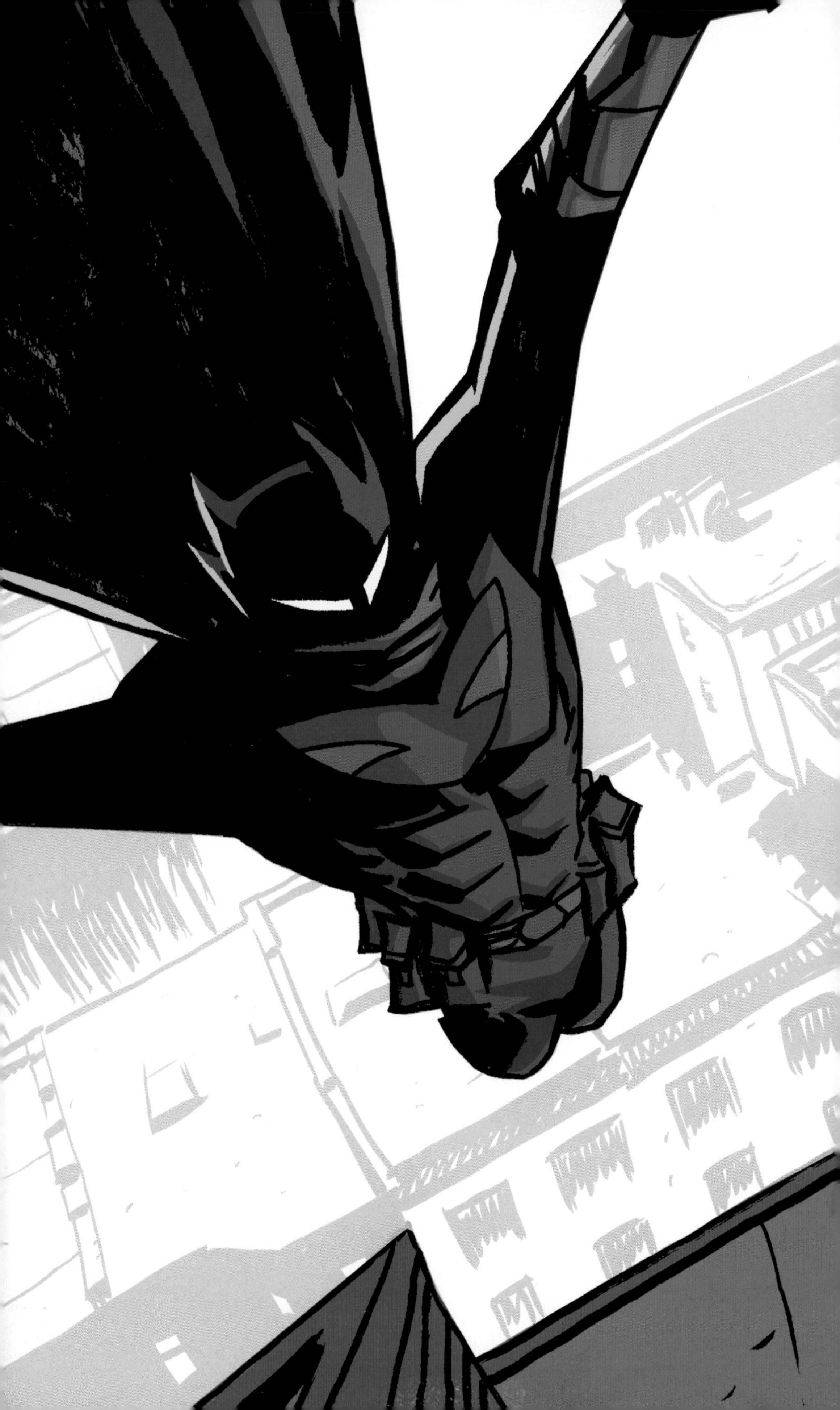

MICHAEL AVON OEMING'S

THE VICTORIES™

TOUCHED

STORY AND ART
Michael Avon Oeming

COLORS Nick Filardi

LETTERS Aaron Walker

DARK HORSE BOOKS

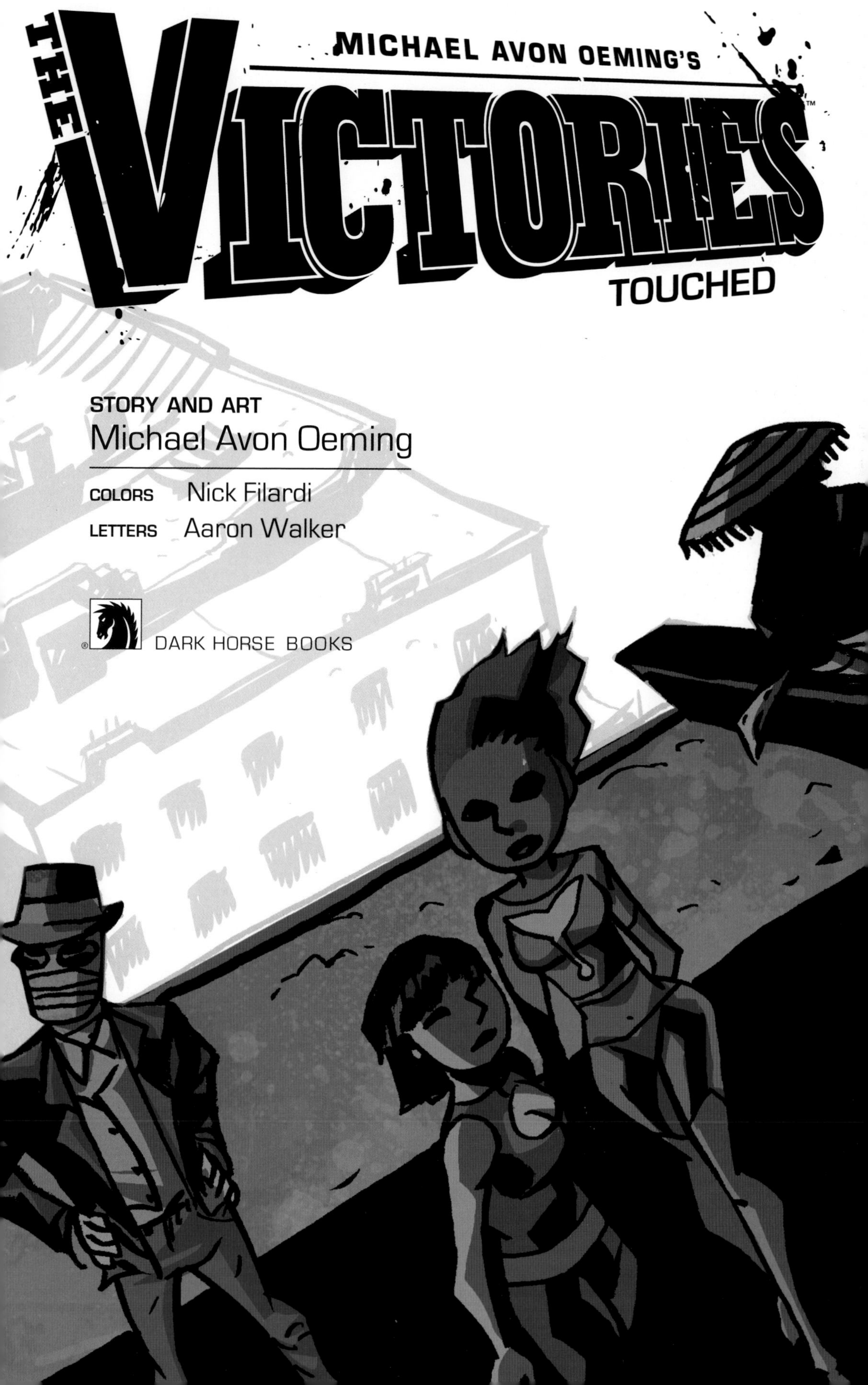

ASSISTANT EDITOR Shantel LaRocque

EDITORS Scott Allie and Daniel Chabon

PUBLISHER Mike Richardson

Mike Richardson, President and Publisher | Neil Hankerson, Executive Vice President | Tom Weddle, Chief Financial Officer | Randy Stradley, Vice President of Publishing | Michael Martens, Vice President of Book Trade Sales | Anita Nelson, Vice President of Business Affairs | Scott Allie, Editor in Chief | Matt Parkinson, Vice President of Marketing | David Scroggy, Vice President of Product Development | Dale LaFountain, Vice President of Information Technology | Darlene Vogel, Senior Director of Print, Design, and Production | Ken Lizzi, General Counsel | Davey Estrada, Editorial Director | Chris Warner, Senior Books Editor | Diana Schutz, Executive Editor | Cary Grazzini, Director of Print and Development | Lia Ribacchi, Art Director | Cara Niece, Director of Scheduling | Tim Wiesch, Director of International Licensing | Mark Bernardi, Director of Digital Publishing

Published by Dark Horse Books
A division of Dark Horse Comics, Inc.
10956 SE Main Street
Milwaukie, OR 97222

First edition: June 2013
ISBN 978-1-61655-100-1

10 9 8 7 6 5 4 3 2 1
Printed in China

International Licensing: (503) 905-2377
Advertising Sales: (503) 905-2370
Comic Shop Locator Service: (888) 266-4226

CHAPTER ONE

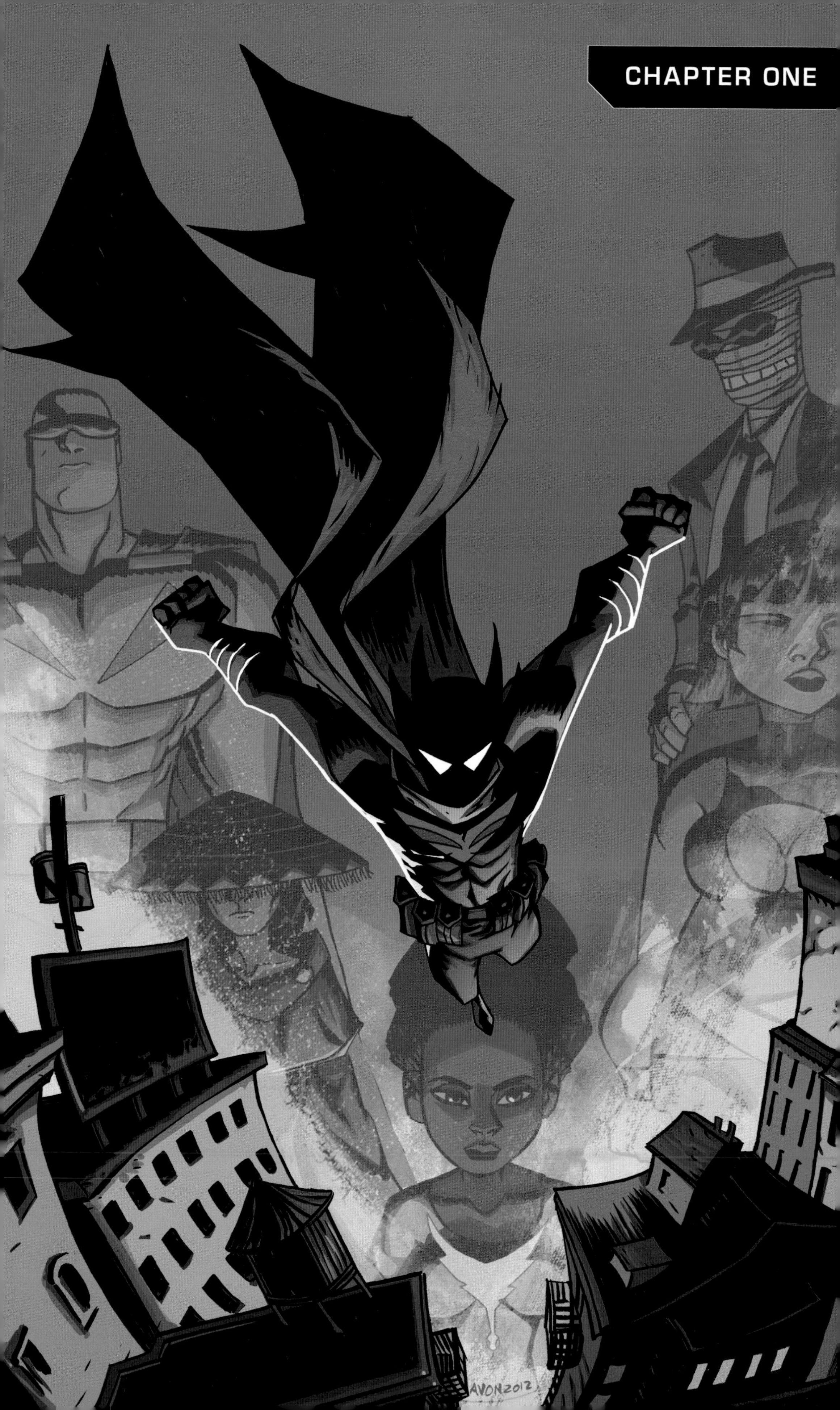

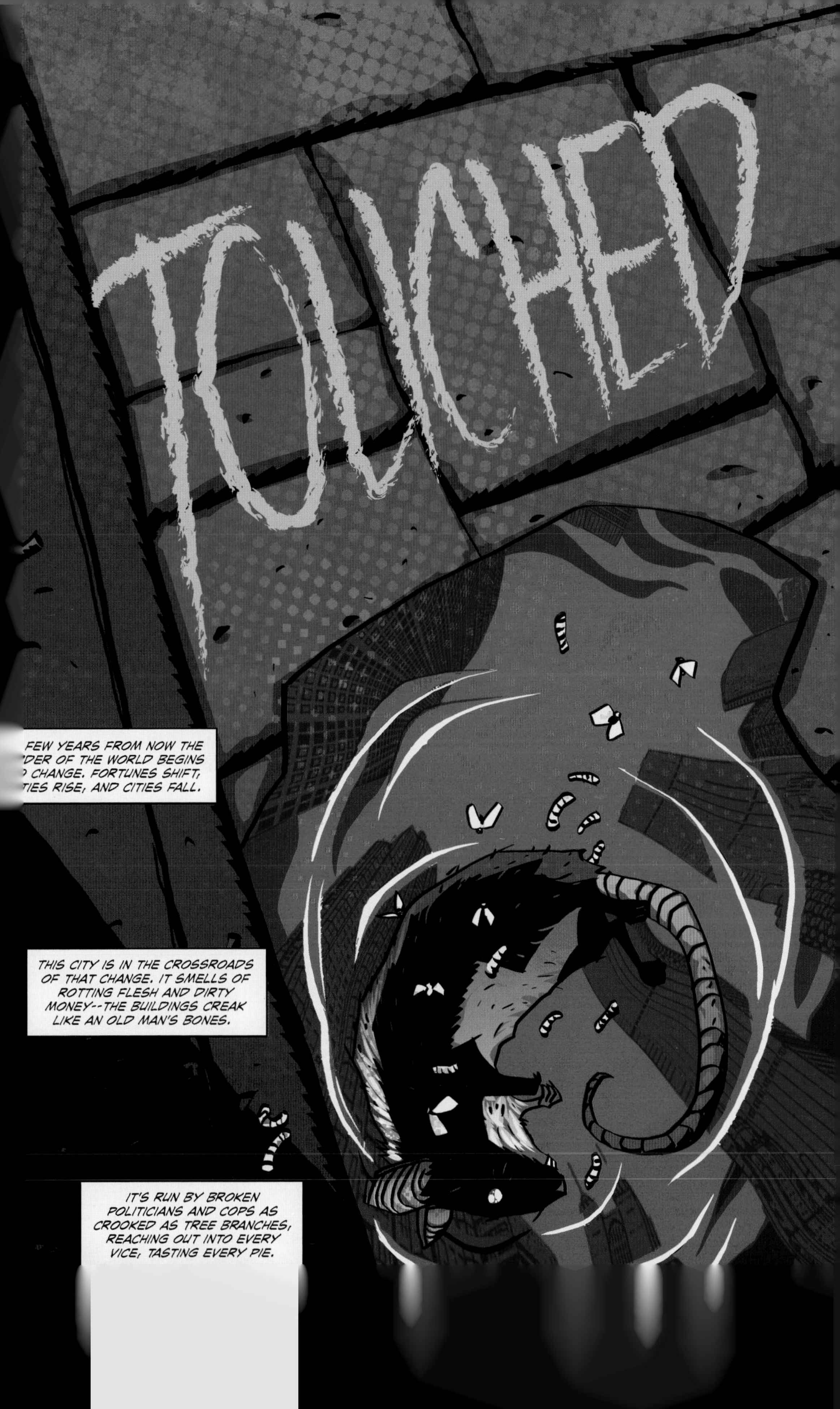
TOUCHED
FEW YEARS FROM NOW THE DER OF THE WORLD BEGINS CHANGE. FORTUNES SHIFT, TIES RISE, AND CITIES FALL.
THIS CITY IS IN THE CROSSROADS OF THAT CHANGE. IT SMELLS OF ROTTING FLESH AND DIRTY MONEY--THE BUILDINGS CREAK LIKE AN OLD MAN'S BONES.
IT'S RUN BY BROKEN POLITICIANS AND COPS AS CROOKED AS TREE BRANCHES, REACHING OUT INTO EVERY VICE, TASTING EVERY PIE.

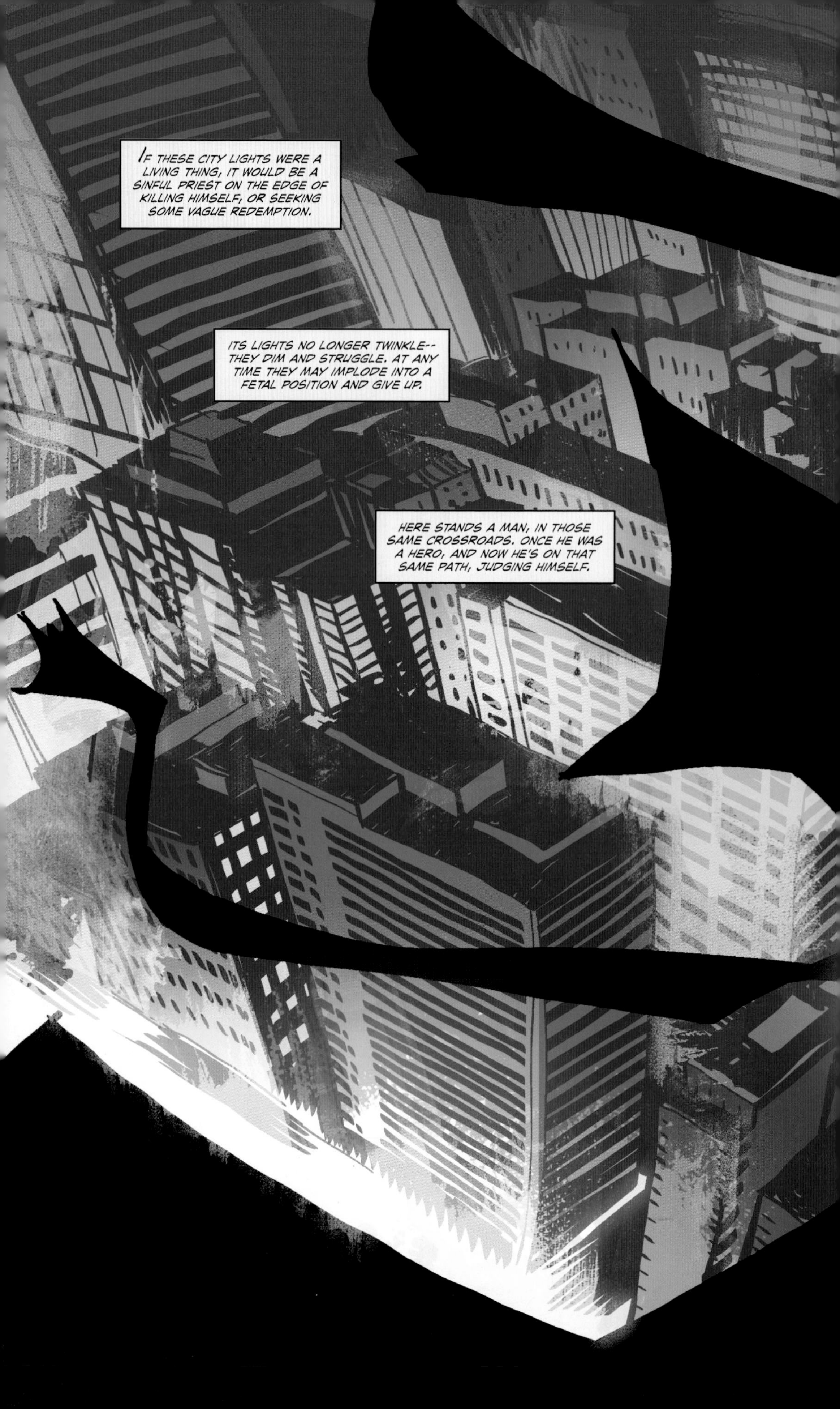
IF THESE CITY LIGHTS WERE A LIVING THING, IT WOULD BE A SINFUL PRIEST ON THE EDGE OF KILLING HIMSELF, OR SEEKING SOME VAGUE REDEMPTION.
ITS LIGHTS NO LONGER TWINKLE-- THEY DIM AND STRUGGLE. AT ANY TIME THEY MAY IMPLODE INTO A FETAL POSITION AND GIVE UP.
HERE STANDS A MAN, IN THOSE SAME CROSSROADS. ONCE HE WAS A HERO, AND NOW HE'S ON THAT SAME PATH, JUDGING HIMSELF.

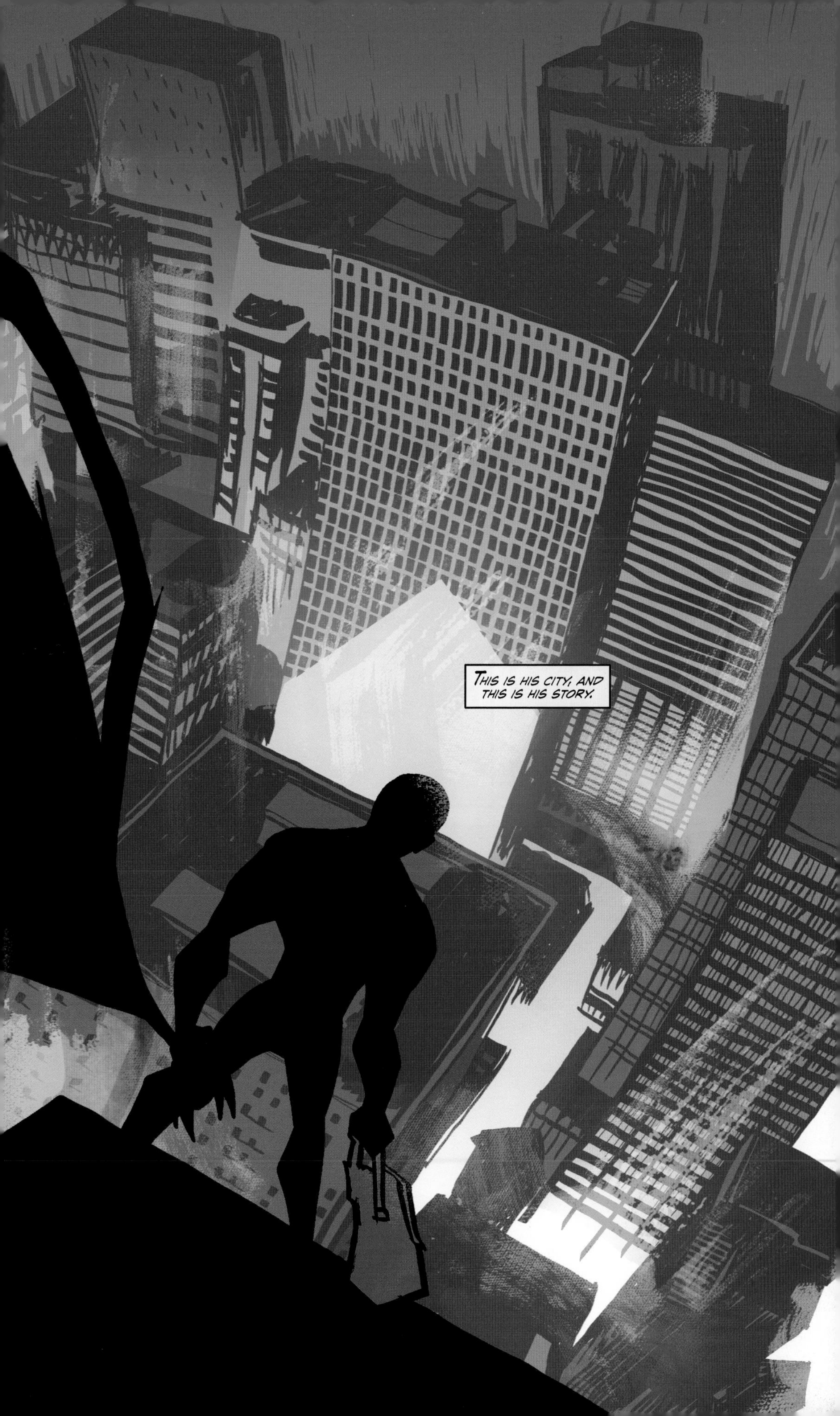
This is his city, and this is his story.

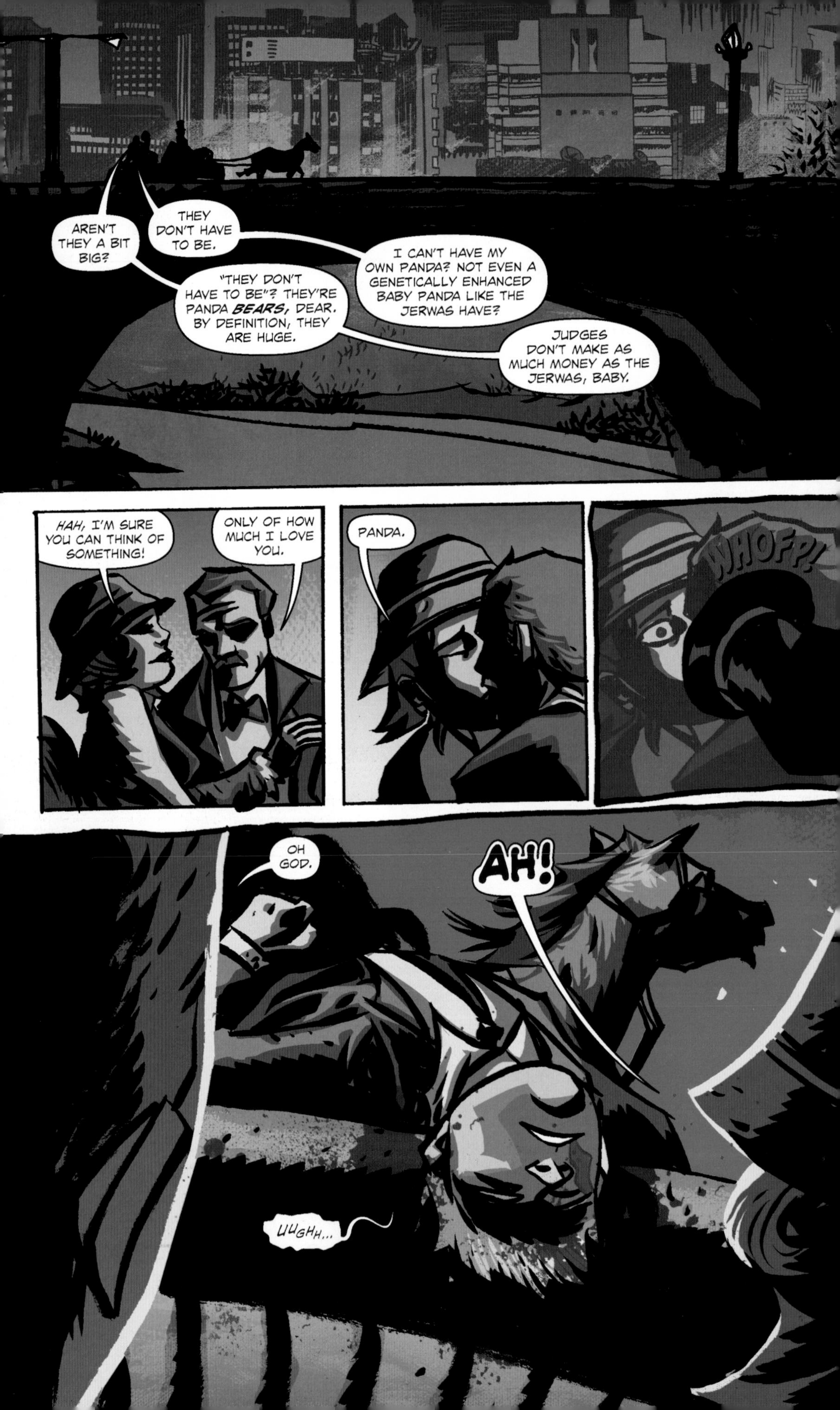

AREN'T THEY A BIT BIG?
THEY DON'T HAVE TO BE.
"THEY DON'T HAVE TO BE"? THEY'RE PANDA **BEARS,** DEAR. BY DEFINITION, THEY ARE HUGE.
I CAN'T HAVE MY OWN PANDA? NOT EVEN A GENETICALLY ENHANCED BABY PANDA LIKE THE JERWAS HAVE?
JUDGES DON'T MAKE AS MUCH MONEY AS THE JERWAS, BABY.
HAH, I'M SURE YOU CAN THINK OF SOMETHING!
ONLY OF HOW MUCH I LOVE YOU.
PANDA.
WHOFP!
OH GOD.
AH!
UUGHH...

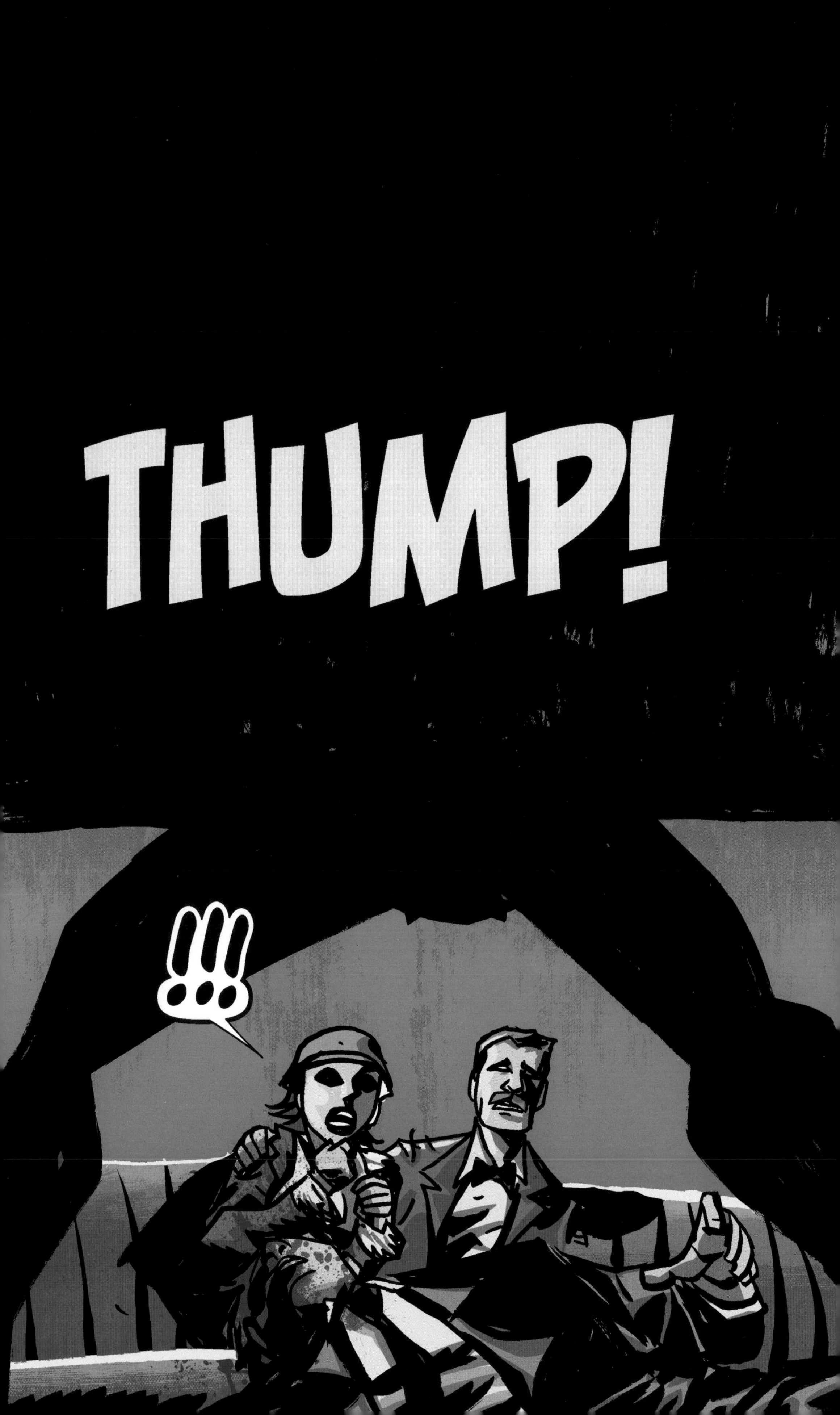
THUMP!
!!!

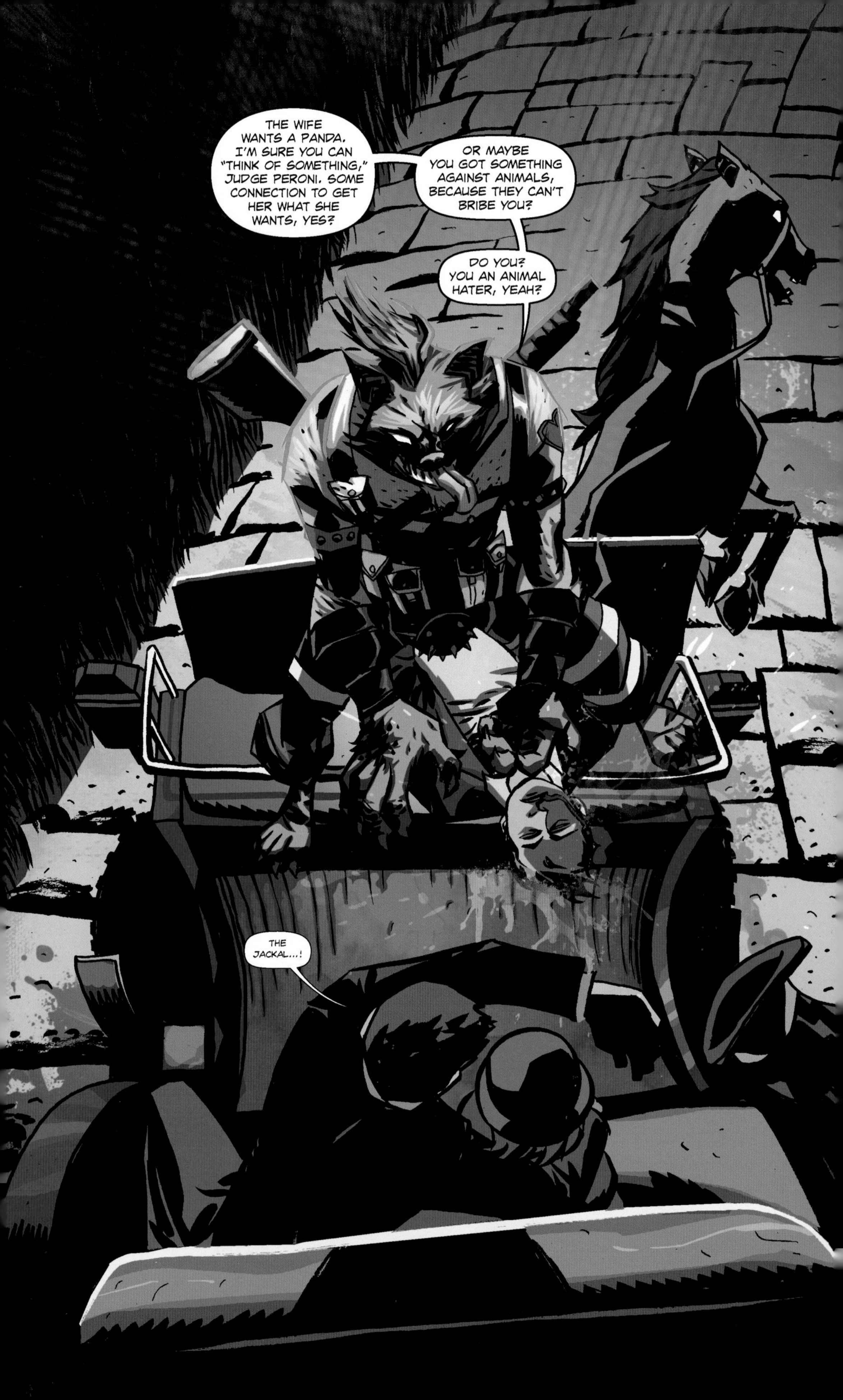
THE WIFE WANTS A PANDA. I'M SURE YOU CAN "THINK OF SOMETHING," JUDGE PERONI. SOME CONNECTION TO GET HER WHAT SHE WANTS, YES?
OR MAYBE YOU GOT SOMETHING AGAINST ANIMALS, BECAUSE THEY CAN'T BRIBE YOU?
DO YOU? YOU AN ANIMAL HATER, YEAH?
THE JACKAL...!

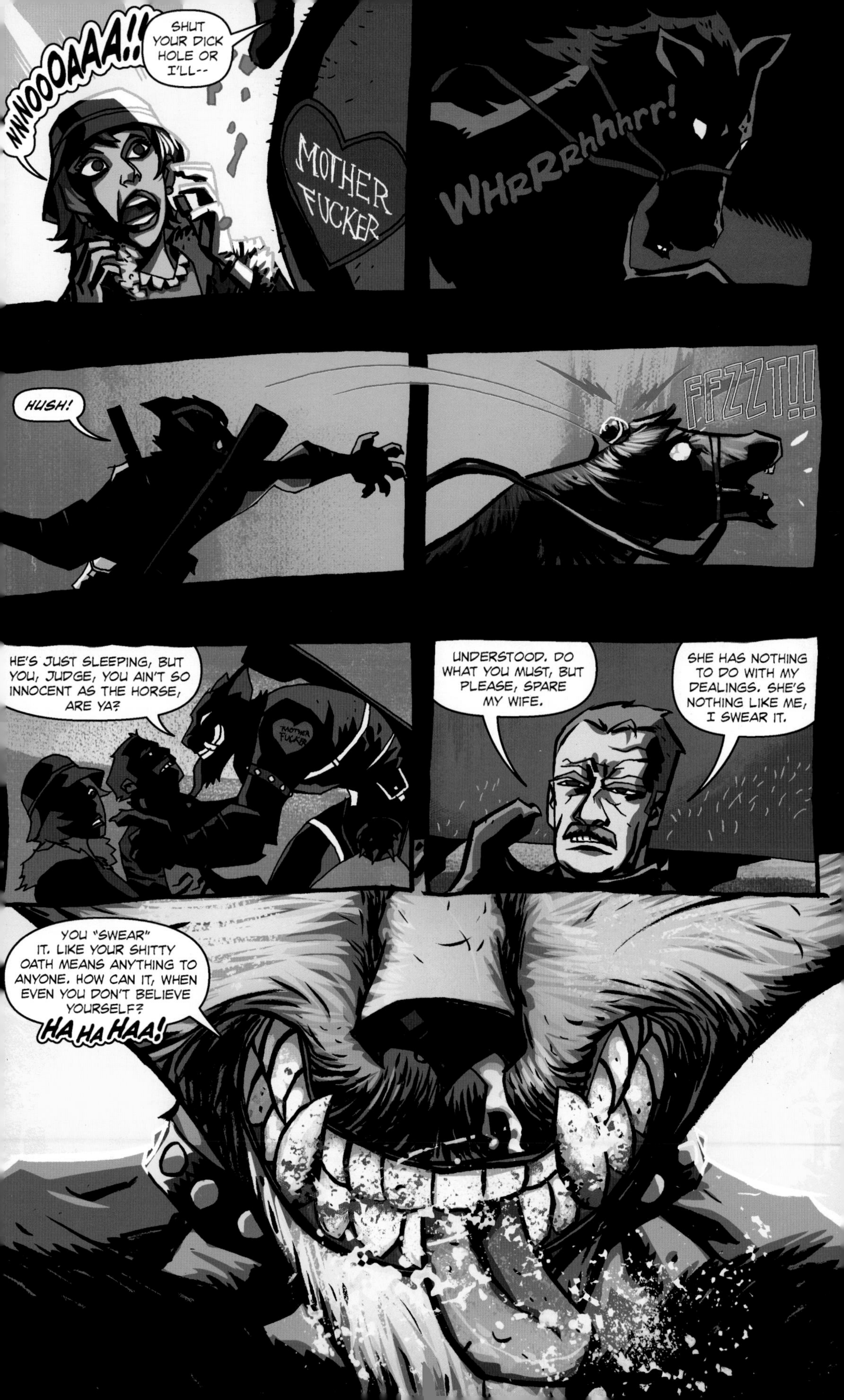
NNNOOOAAA!!
SHUT YOUR DICK HOLE OR I'LL--
MOTHER FUCKER
WHRRRhhhrr!
HUSH!
FFZZZT!!
HE'S JUST SLEEPING, BUT YOU, JUDGE, YOU AIN'T SO INNOCENT AS THE HORSE, ARE YA?
UNDERSTOOD. DO WHAT YOU MUST, BUT PLEASE, SPARE MY WIFE.
SHE HAS NOTHING TO DO WITH MY DEALINGS. SHE'S NOTHING LIKE ME, I SWEAR IT.
YOU "SWEAR" IT. LIKE YOUR SHITTY OATH MEANS ANYTHING TO ANYONE. HOW CAN IT, WHEN EVEN YOU DON'T BELIEVE YOURSELF?
HA HA HAA!

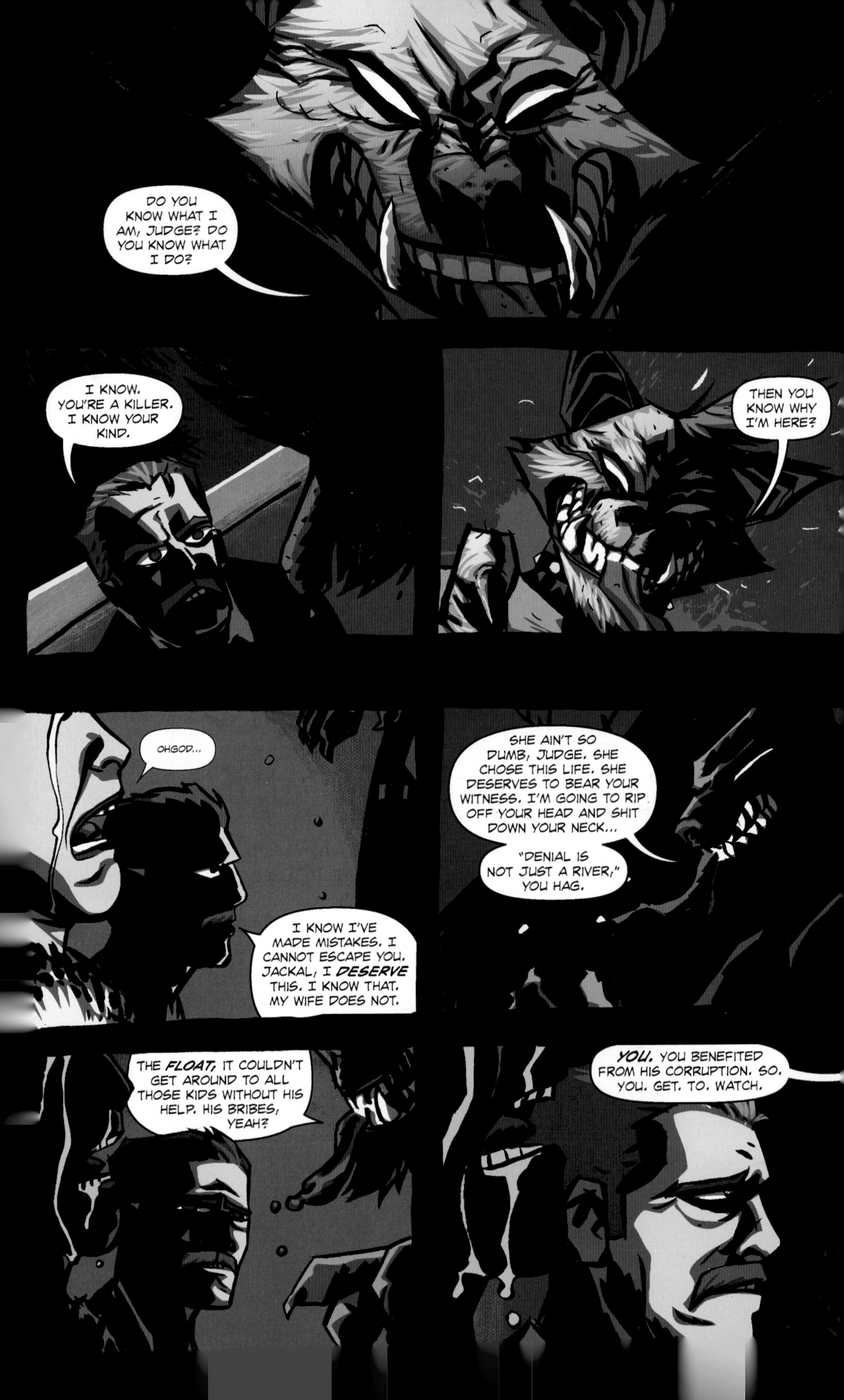
DO YOU KNOW WHAT I AM, JUDGE? DO YOU KNOW WHAT I DO?
I KNOW. YOU'RE A KILLER. I KNOW YOUR KIND.
THEN YOU KNOW WHY I'M HERE?
OHGOD...
I KNOW I'VE MADE MISTAKES. I CANNOT ESCAPE YOU, JACKAL, I *DESERVE* THIS. I KNOW THAT. MY WIFE DOES NOT.
SHE AIN'T SO DUMB, JUDGE. SHE CHOSE THIS LIFE. SHE DESERVES TO BEAR YOUR WITNESS. I'M GOING TO RIP OFF YOUR HEAD AND SHIT DOWN YOUR NECK...
"DENIAL IS NOT JUST A RIVER," YOU HAG.
THE *FLOAT,* IT COULDN'T GET AROUND TO ALL THOSE KIDS WITHOUT HIS HELP. HIS BRIBES, YEAH?
YOU. YOU BENEFITED FROM HIS CORRUPTION. SO. YOU. GET. TO. WATCH.

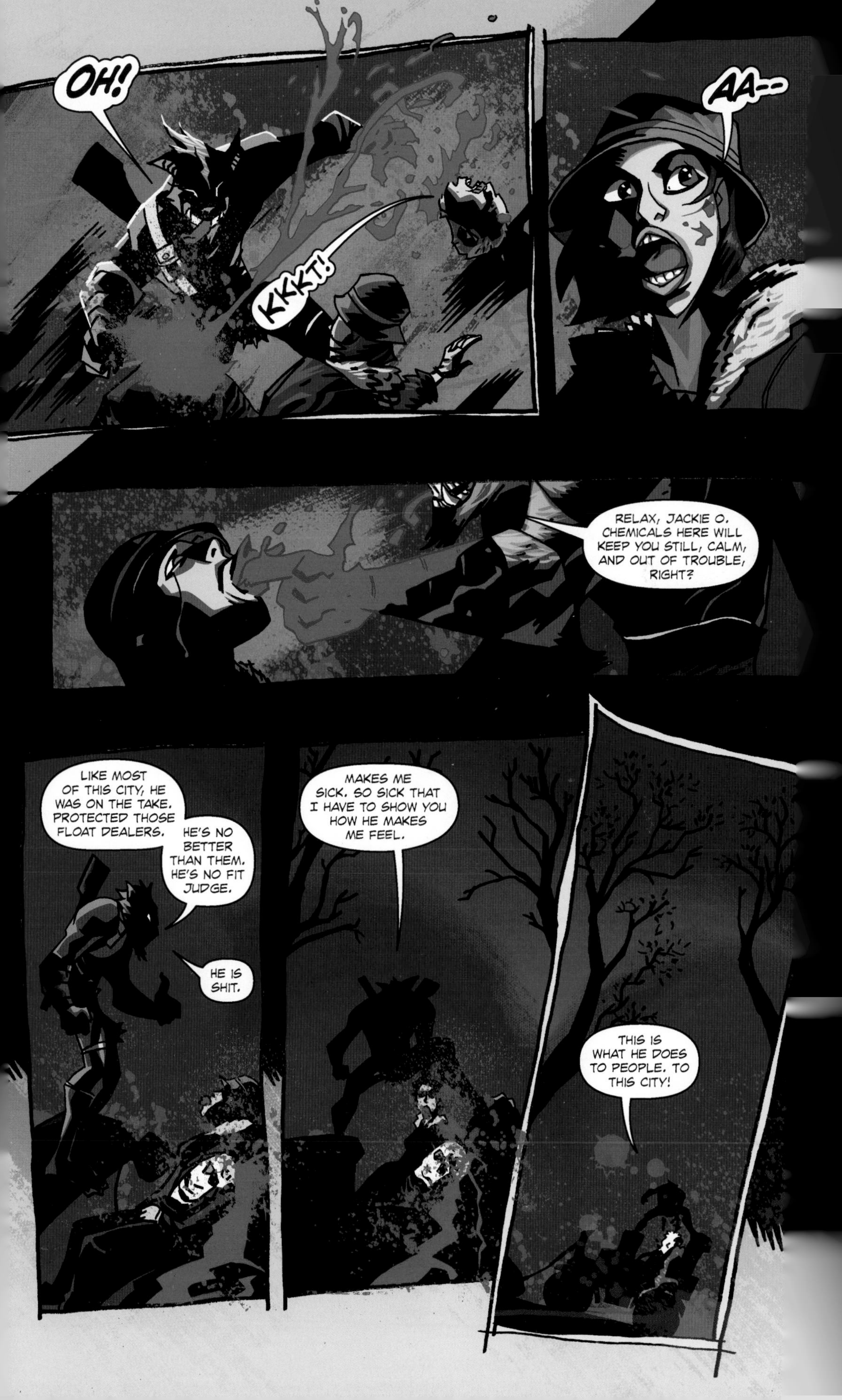
OH!
KKKT!
AA--
RELAX, JACKIE O. CHEMICALS HERE WILL KEEP YOU STILL, CALM, AND OUT OF TROUBLE, RIGHT?
LIKE MOST OF THIS CITY, HE WAS ON THE TAKE. PROTECTED THOSE FLOAT DEALERS.
HE'S NO BETTER THAN THEM. HE'S NO FIT JUDGE.
HE IS SHIT.
MAKES ME SICK. SO SICK THAT I HAVE TO SHOW YOU HOW HE MAKES ME FEEL.
THIS IS WHAT HE DOES TO PEOPLE. TO THIS CITY!

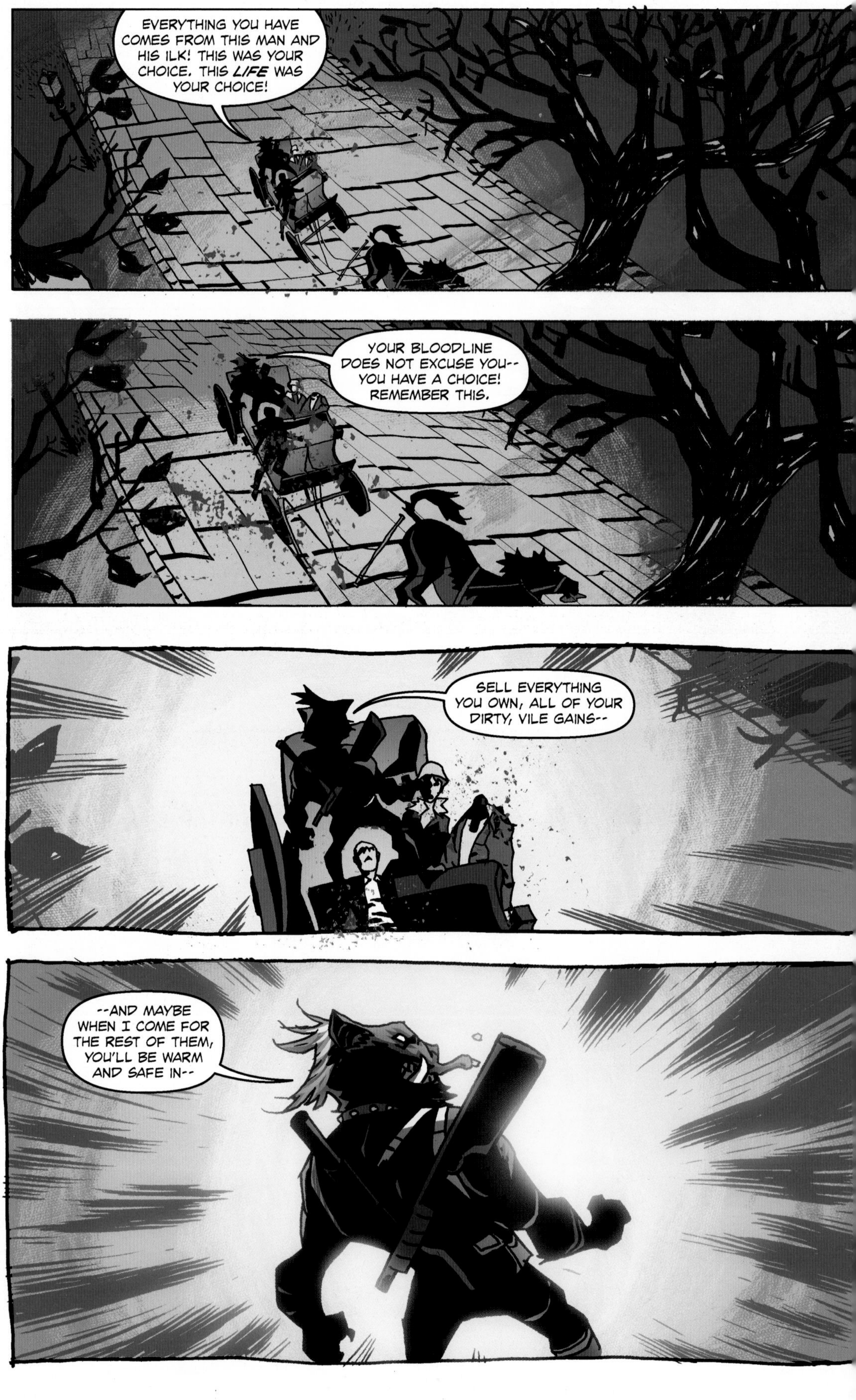
EVERYTHING YOU HAVE COMES FROM THIS MAN AND HIS ILK! THIS WAS YOUR CHOICE. THIS *LIFE* WAS YOUR CHOICE!
YOUR BLOODLINE DOES NOT EXCUSE YOU-- YOU HAVE A CHOICE! REMEMBER THIS.
SELL EVERYTHING YOU OWN, ALL OF YOUR DIRTY, VILE GAINS--
--AND MAYBE WHEN I COME FOR THE REST OF THEM, YOU'LL BE WARM AND SAFE IN--

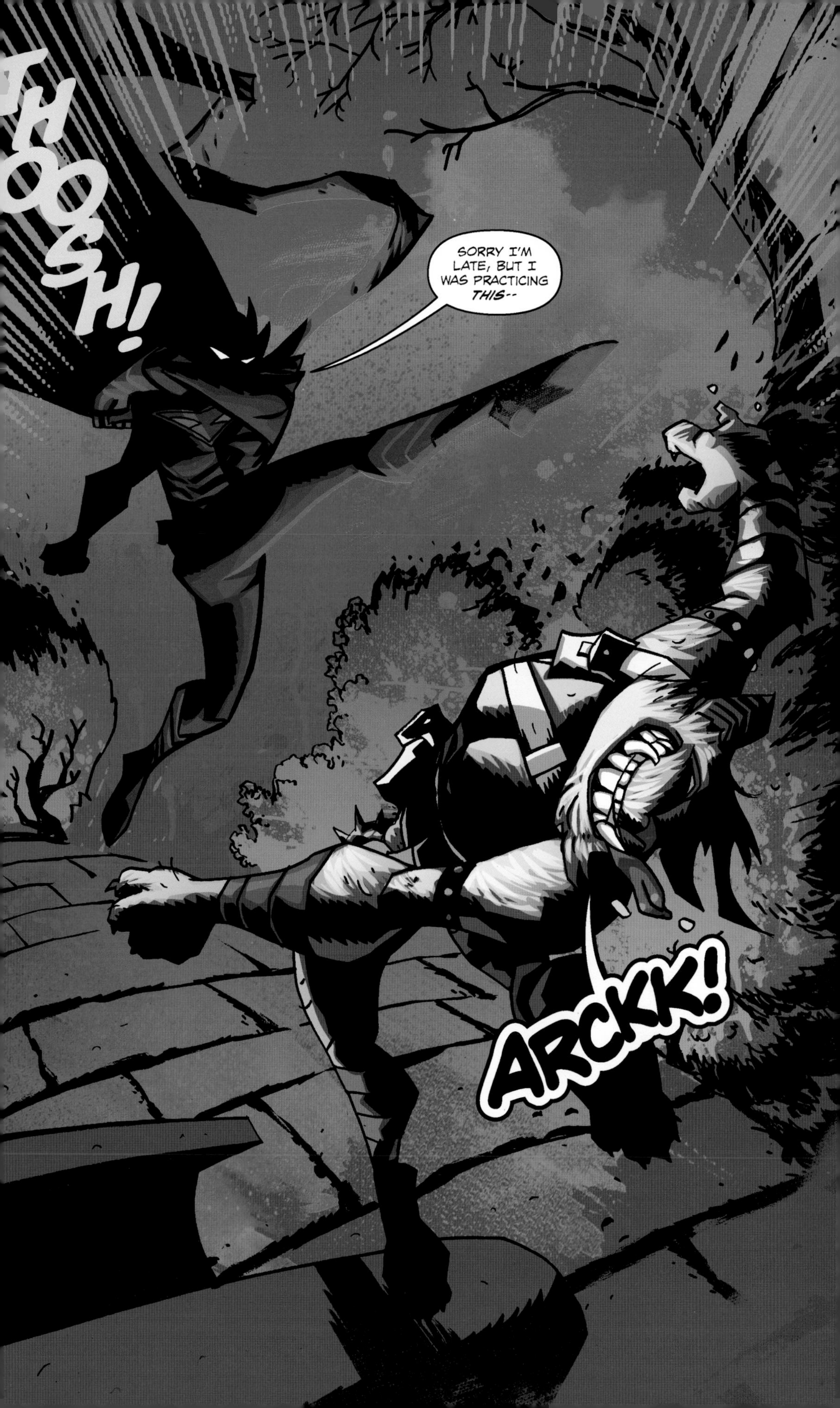
THOOSH!
SORRY I'M LATE, BUT I WAS PRACTICING THIS--
ARCKK!

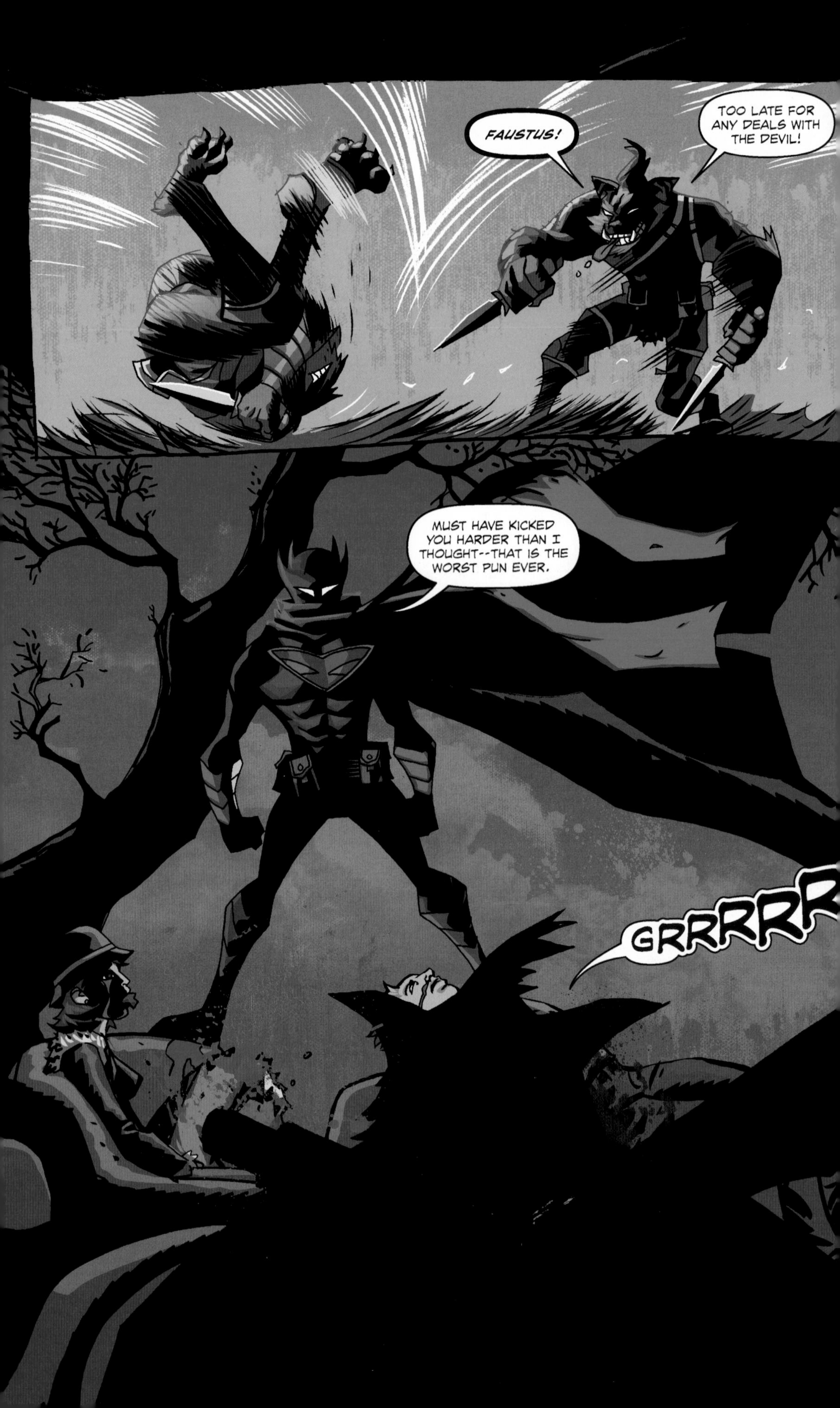

FAUSTUS!
TOO LATE FOR ANY DEALS WITH THE DEVIL!
MUST HAVE KICKED YOU HARDER THAN I THOUGHT--THAT IS THE WORST PUN EVER.
GRRRRR

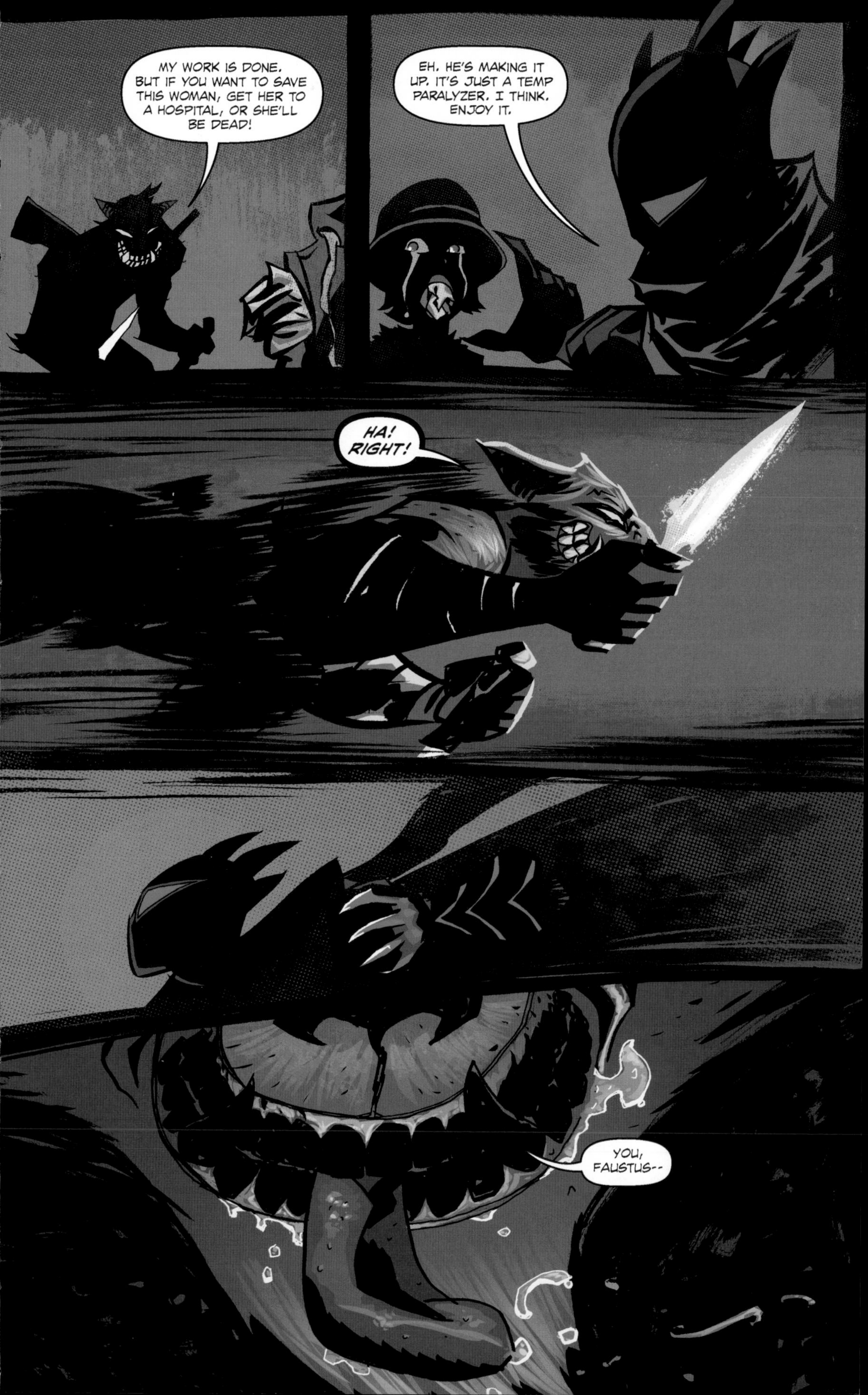
MY WORK IS DONE. BUT IF YOU WANT TO SAVE THIS WOMAN, GET HER TO A HOSPITAL, OR SHE'LL BE DEAD!
EH. HE'S MAKING IT UP. IT'S JUST A TEMP PARALYZER. I THINK. ENJOY IT.
HA! RIGHT!
YOU, FAUSTUS--

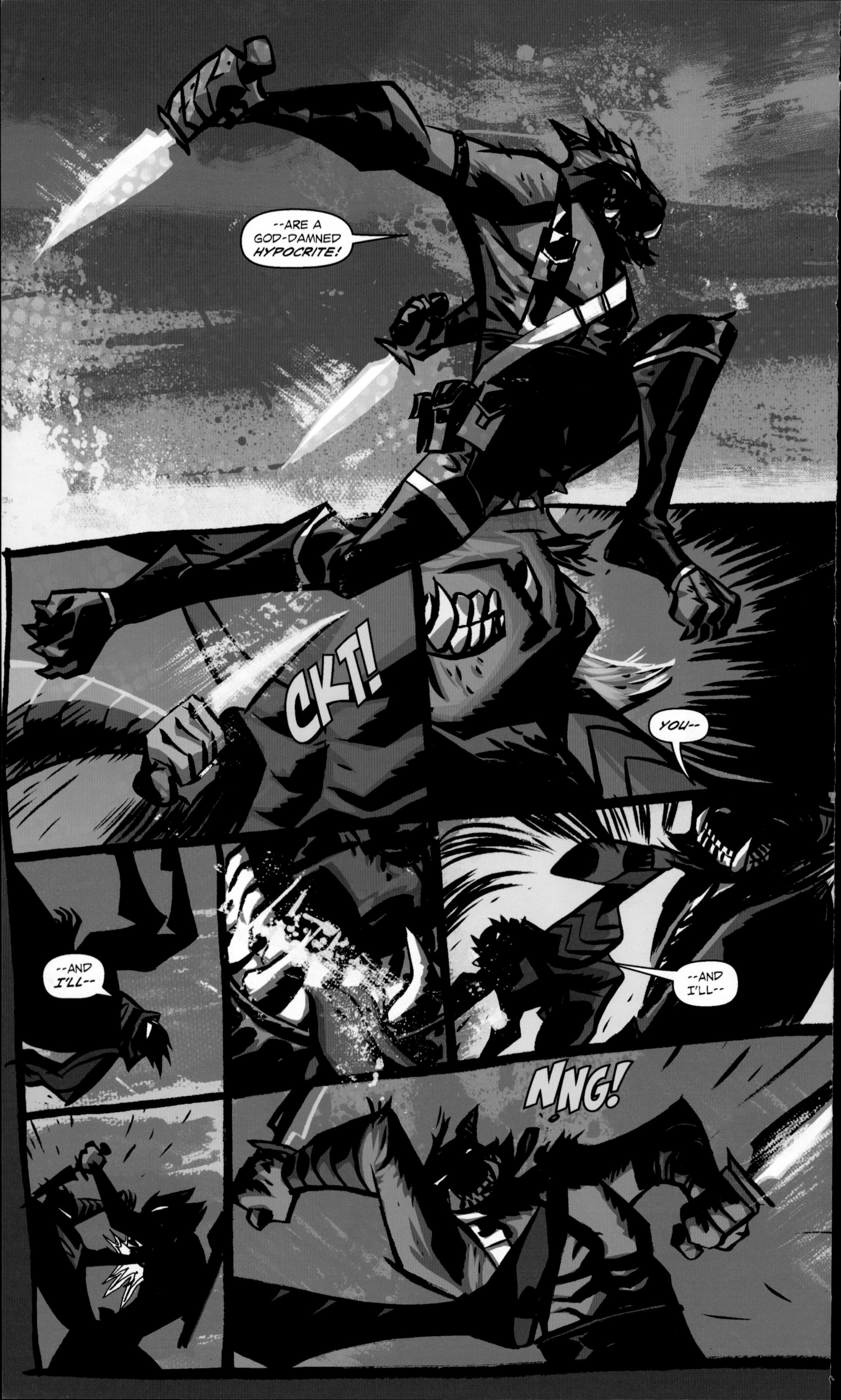
--ARE A GOD-DAMNED *HYPOCRITE!*
CKT!
YOU--
--AND I'LL--
--AND I'LL--
NNG!

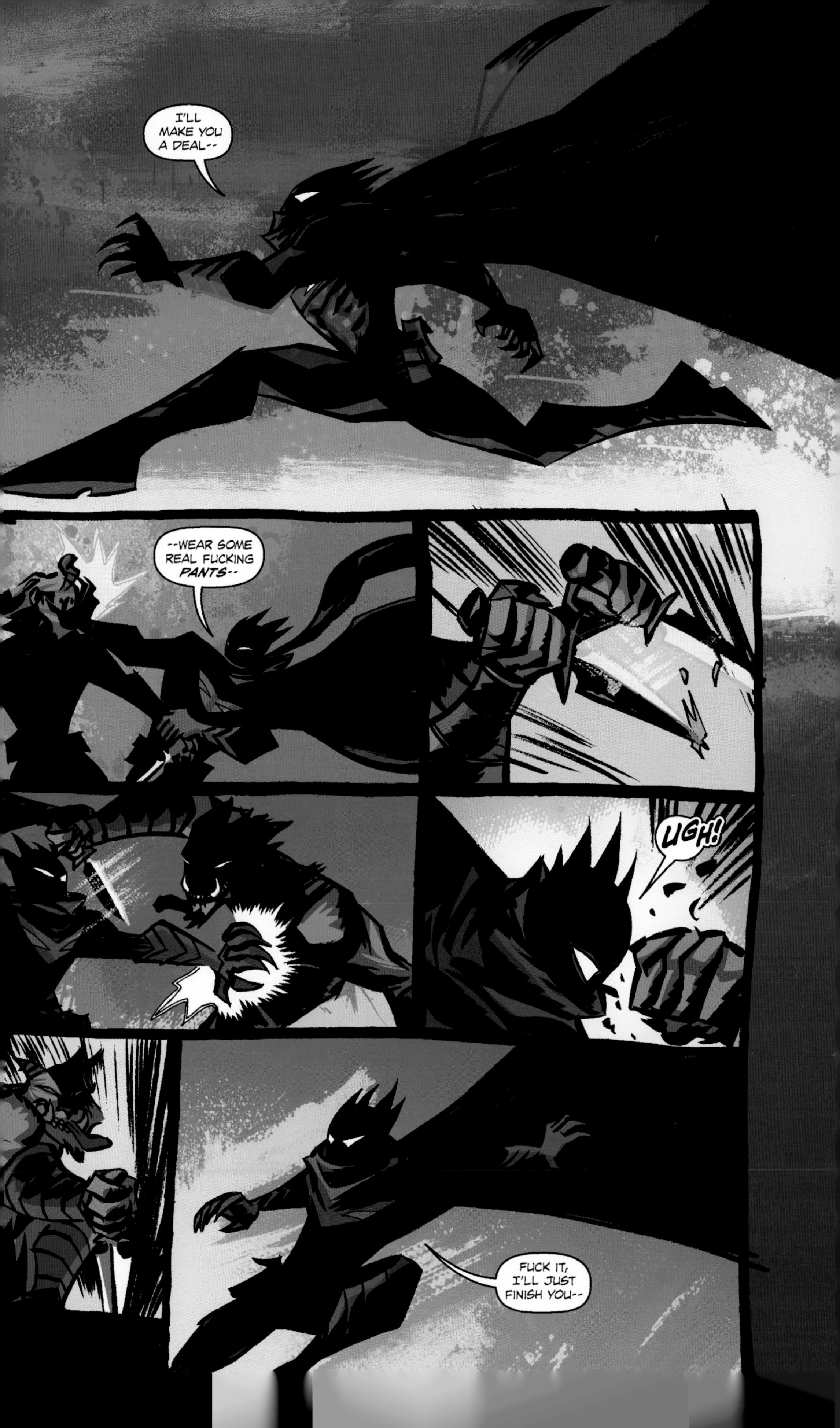
I'LL MAKE YOU A DEAL--
--WEAR SOME REAL FUCKING *PANTS*--
UGH!
FUCK IT, I'LL JUST FINISH YOU--

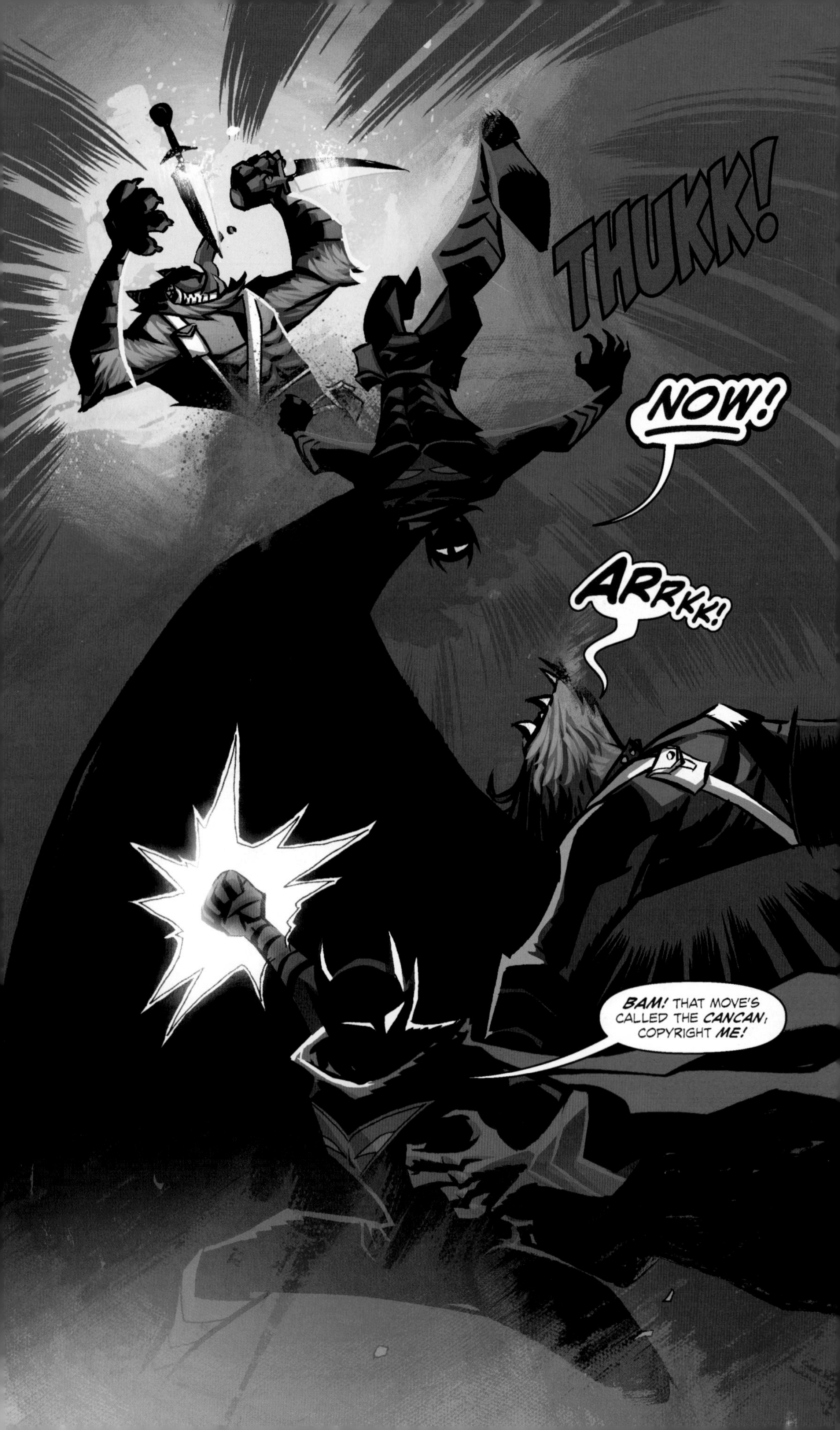
THUKK!
NOW!
ARRKK!
BAM! THAT MOVE'S CALLED THE CANCAN, COPYRIGHT ME!

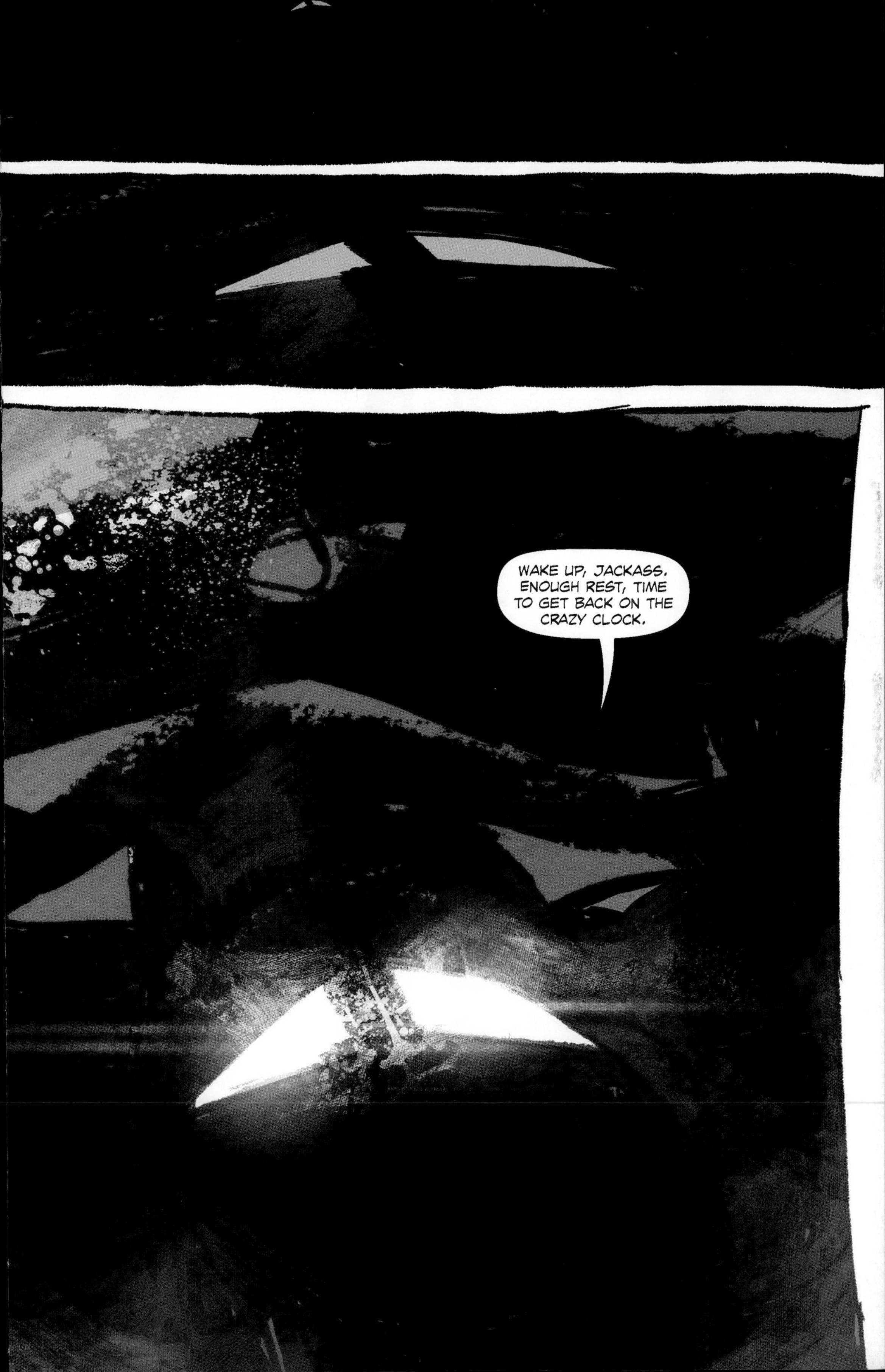
WAKE UP, JACKASS. ENOUGH REST, TIME TO GET BACK ON THE CRAZY CLOCK.

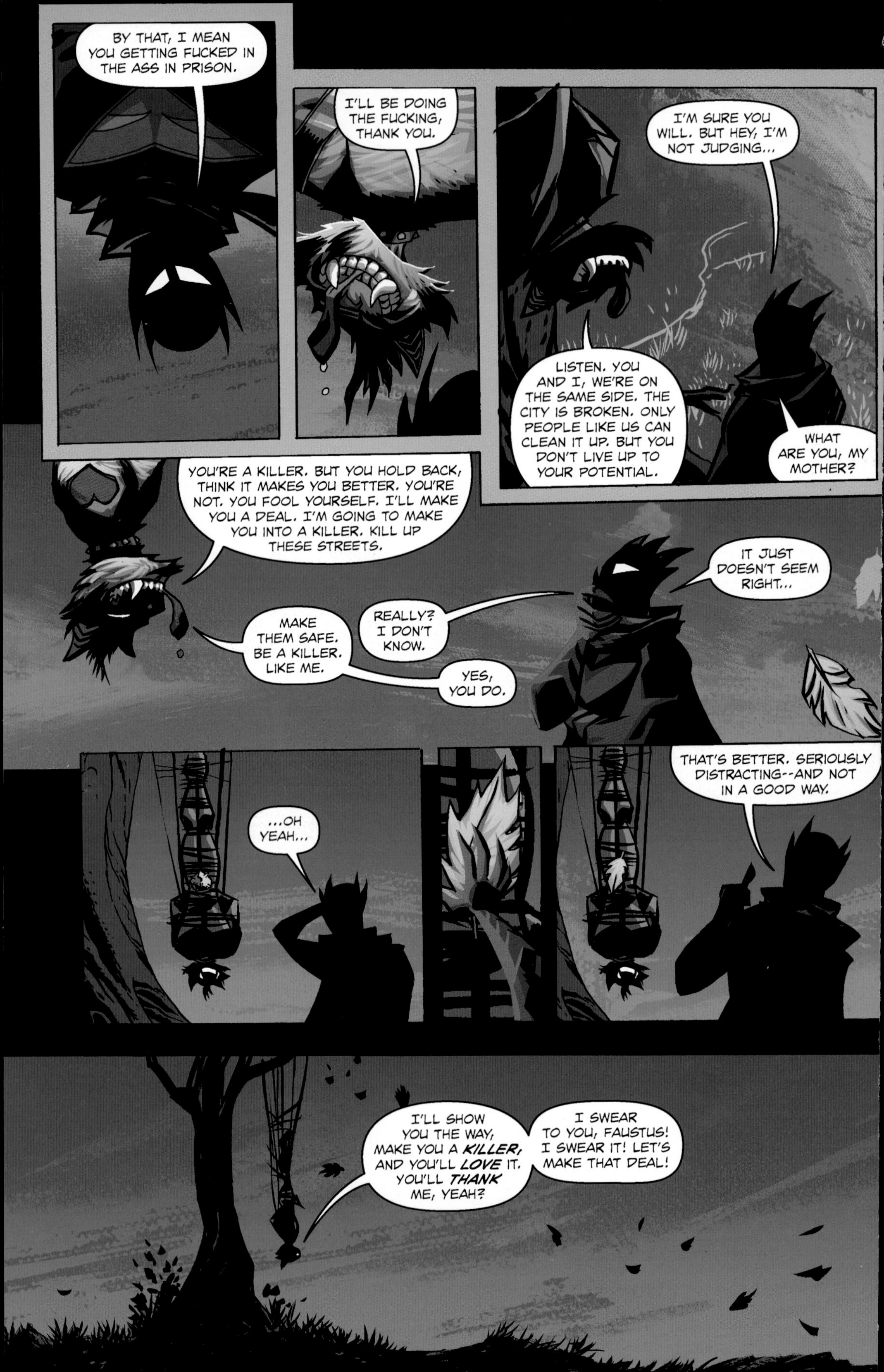
BY THAT, I MEAN YOU GETTING FUCKED IN THE ASS IN PRISON.
I'LL BE DOING THE FUCKING, THANK YOU.
I'M SURE YOU WILL. BUT HEY, I'M NOT JUDGING...
LISTEN. YOU AND I, WE'RE ON THE SAME SIDE. THE CITY IS BROKEN. ONLY PEOPLE LIKE US CAN CLEAN IT UP. BUT YOU DON'T LIVE UP TO YOUR POTENTIAL.
WHAT ARE YOU, MY MOTHER?
YOU'RE A KILLER. BUT YOU HOLD BACK, THINK IT MAKES YOU BETTER. YOU'RE NOT. YOU FOOL YOURSELF. I'LL MAKE YOU A DEAL. I'M GOING TO MAKE YOU INTO A KILLER. KILL UP THESE STREETS.
IT JUST DOESN'T SEEM RIGHT...
MAKE THEM SAFE. BE A KILLER. LIKE ME.
REALLY? I DON'T KNOW.
YES, YOU DO.
...OH YEAH...
THAT'S BETTER. SERIOUSLY DISTRACTING--AND NOT IN A GOOD WAY.
I'LL SHOW YOU THE WAY, MAKE YOU A ***KILLER,*** AND YOU'LL ***LOVE*** IT. YOU'LL ***THANK*** ME, YEAH?
I SWEAR TO YOU, FAUSTUS! I SWEAR IT! LET'S MAKE THAT DEAL!

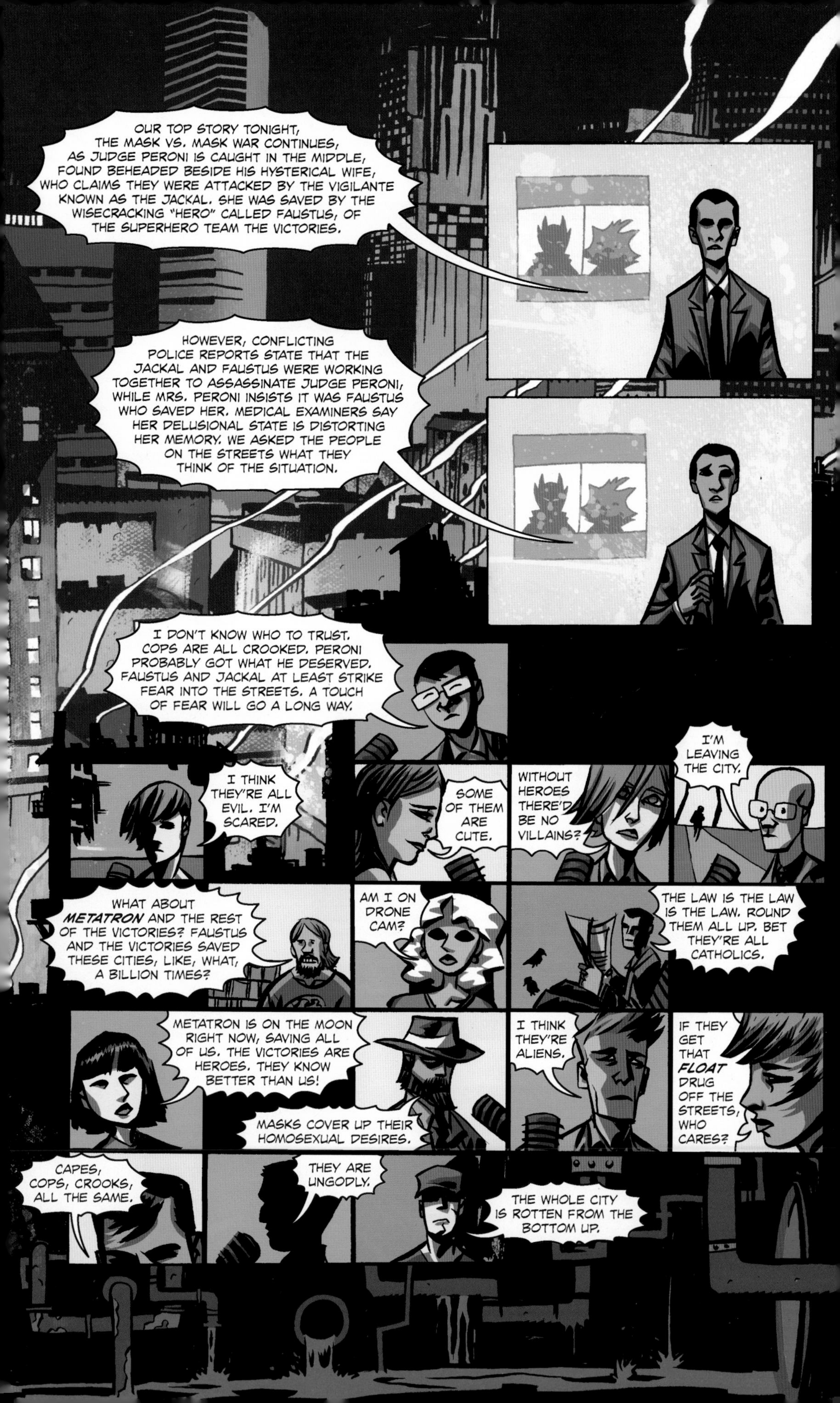
OUR TOP STORY TONIGHT, THE MASK VS. MASK WAR CONTINUES, AS JUDGE PERONI IS CAUGHT IN THE MIDDLE, FOUND BEHEADED BESIDE HIS HYSTERICAL WIFE, WHO CLAIMS THEY WERE ATTACKED BY THE VIGILANTE KNOWN AS THE JACKAL. SHE WAS SAVED BY THE WISECRACKING "HERO" CALLED FAUSTUS, OF THE SUPERHERO TEAM THE VICTORIES.
HOWEVER, CONFLICTING POLICE REPORTS STATE THAT THE JACKAL AND FAUSTUS WERE WORKING TOGETHER TO ASSASSINATE JUDGE PERONI, WHILE MRS. PERONI INSISTS IT WAS FAUSTUS WHO SAVED HER. MEDICAL EXAMINERS SAY HER DELUSIONAL STATE IS DISTORTING HER MEMORY. WE ASKED THE PEOPLE ON THE STREETS WHAT THEY THINK OF THE SITUATION.
I DON'T KNOW WHO TO TRUST. COPS ARE ALL CROOKED. PERONI PROBABLY GOT WHAT HE DESERVED. FAUSTUS AND JACKAL AT LEAST STRIKE FEAR INTO THE STREETS. A TOUCH OF FEAR WILL GO A LONG WAY.
I THINK THEY'RE ALL EVIL. I'M SCARED.
SOME OF THEM ARE CUTE.
WITHOUT HEROES THERE'D BE NO VILLAINS?
I'M LEAVING THE CITY.
WHAT ABOUT *METATRON* AND THE REST OF THE VICTORIES? FAUSTUS AND THE VICTORIES SAVED THESE CITIES, LIKE, WHAT, A BILLION TIMES?
AM I ON DRONE CAM?
THE LAW IS THE LAW IS THE LAW. ROUND THEM ALL UP. BET THEY'RE ALL CATHOLICS.
METATRON IS ON THE MOON RIGHT NOW, SAVING ALL OF US. THE VICTORIES ARE HEROES. THEY KNOW BETTER THAN US!
MASKS COVER UP THEIR HOMOSEXUAL DESIRES.
I THINK THEY'RE ALIENS.
IF THEY GET THAT *FLOAT* DRUG OFF THE STREETS, WHO CARES?
CAPES, COPS, CROOKS, ALL THE SAME.
THEY ARE UNGODLY.
THE WHOLE CITY IS ROTTEN FROM THE BOTTOM UP.

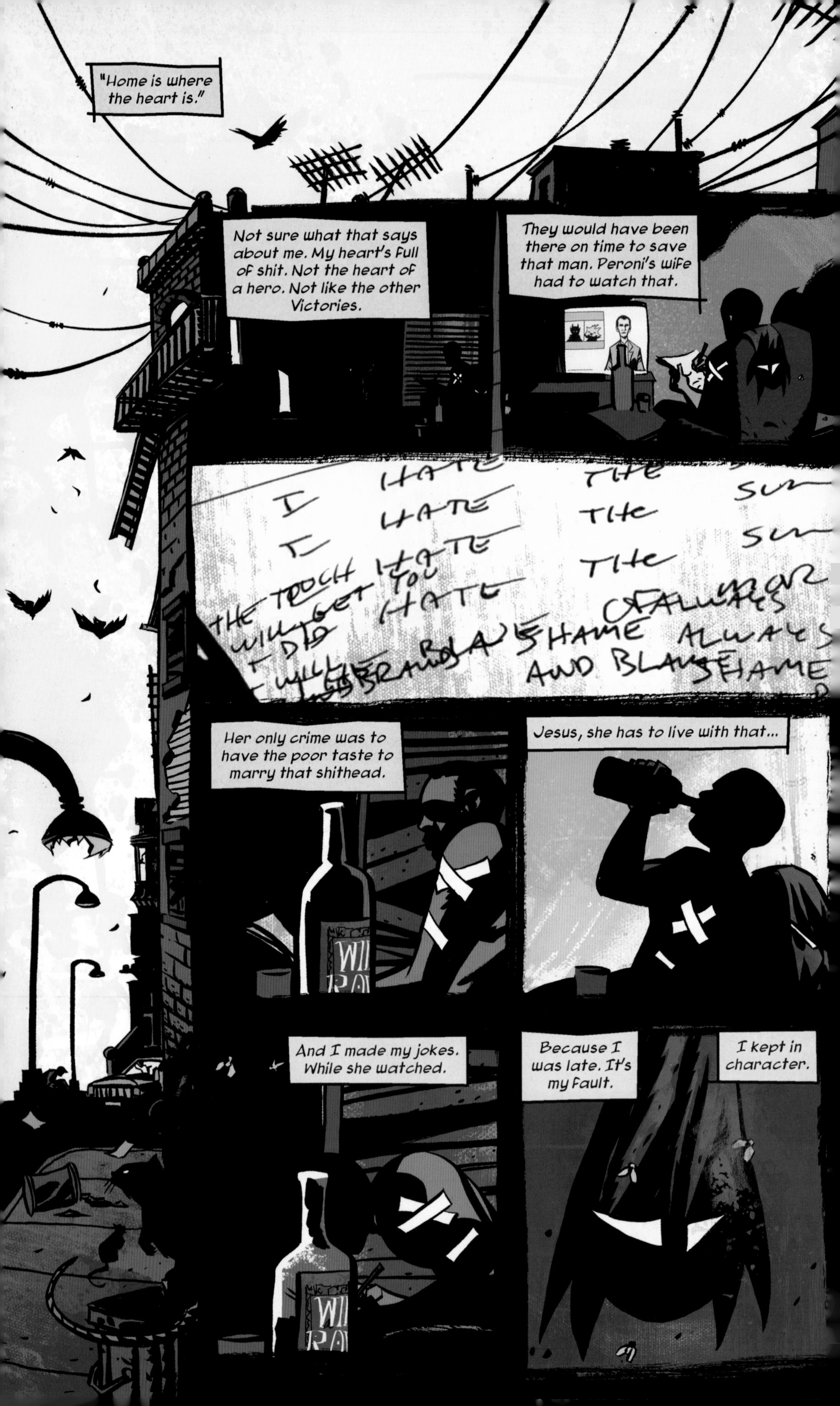
"Home is where the heart is."
Not sure what that says about me. My heart's full of shit. Not the heart of a hero. Not like the other Victories.
They would have been there on time to save that man. Peroni's wife had to watch that.
Her only crime was to have the poor taste to marry that shithead.
Jesus, she has to live with that...
And I made my jokes. While she watched.
Because I was late. It's my fault.
I kept in character.

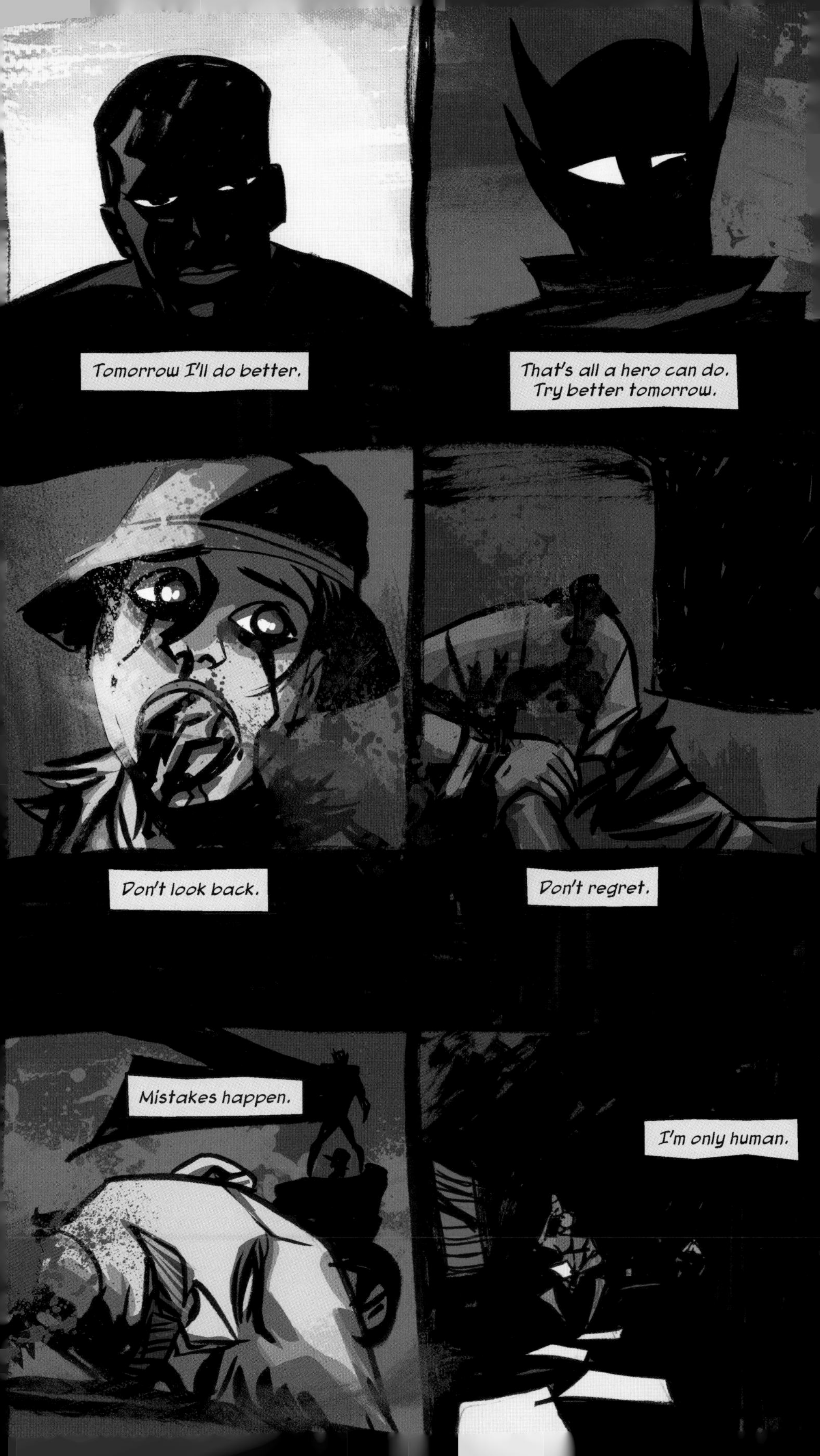
Tomorrow I'll do better.
That's all a hero can do. Try better tomorrow.
Don't look back.
Don't regret.
Mistakes happen.
I'm only human.

WHY AM I LIKE THIS?
WHY AM I LIKE THIS?
WHY AM I LIKE THIS?

WHY AM I LIKE THIS?
WHY AM I LIKE THIS?
WHY AM I LIKE THIS?
WHY I AM I WITH
WHE AM I
WHY AM I
WHY AM I
WHY AM I

MAYBE YOU'RE READY
TO BE A REAL HERO. MAYBE
YOU SHOULD JUST SIT HERE...
SIT HERE AND BE HUMAN
FOR A WHILE.

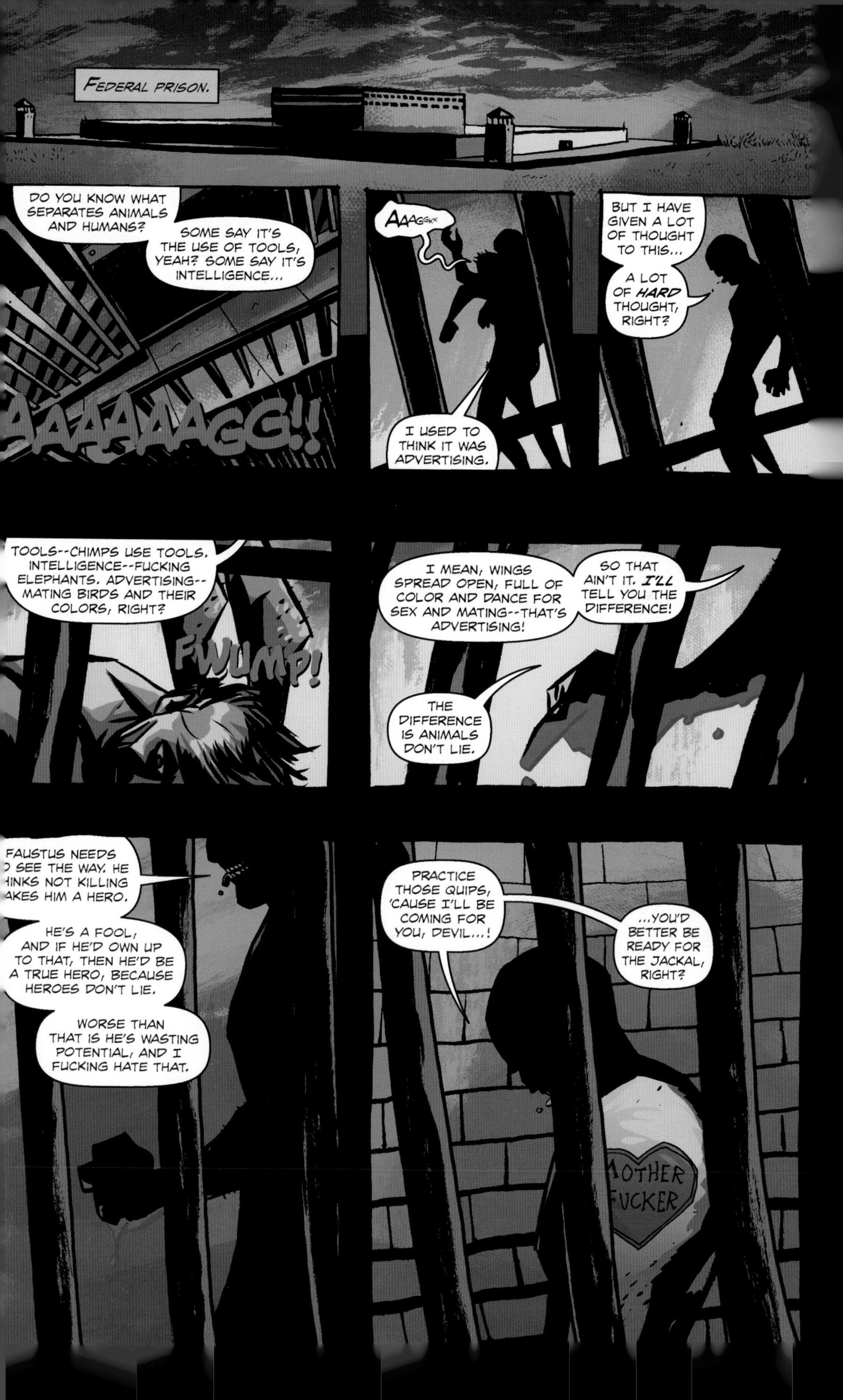
FEDERAL PRISON.
DO YOU KNOW WHAT SEPARATES ANIMALS AND HUMANS?
SOME SAY IT'S THE USE OF TOOLS, YEAH? SOME SAY IT'S INTELLIGENCE...
AAAAAAAGG!!
AAAGGKK
I USED TO THINK IT WAS ADVERTISING.
BUT I HAVE GIVEN A LOT OF THOUGHT TO THIS...
A LOT OF HARD THOUGHT, RIGHT?
TOOLS--CHIMPS USE TOOLS. INTELLIGENCE--FUCKING ELEPHANTS. ADVERTISING--MATING BIRDS AND THEIR COLORS, RIGHT?
FWUMP!
I MEAN, WINGS SPREAD OPEN, FULL OF COLOR AND DANCE FOR SEX AND MATING--THAT'S ADVERTISING!
SO THAT AIN'T IT. I'LL TELL YOU THE DIFFERENCE!
THE DIFFERENCE IS ANIMALS DON'T LIE.
FAUSTUS NEEDS SEE THE WAY. HE INKS NOT KILLING AKES HIM A HERO.
HE'S A FOOL, AND IF HE'D OWN UP TO THAT, THEN HE'D BE A TRUE HERO, BECAUSE HEROES DON'T LIE.
WORSE THAN THAT IS HE'S WASTING POTENTIAL, AND I FUCKING HATE THAT.
PRACTICE THOSE QUIPS, 'CAUSE I'LL BE COMING FOR YOU, DEVIL...!
...YOU'D BETTER BE READY FOR THE JACKAL, RIGHT?
MOTHER FUCKER

CHAPTER TWO

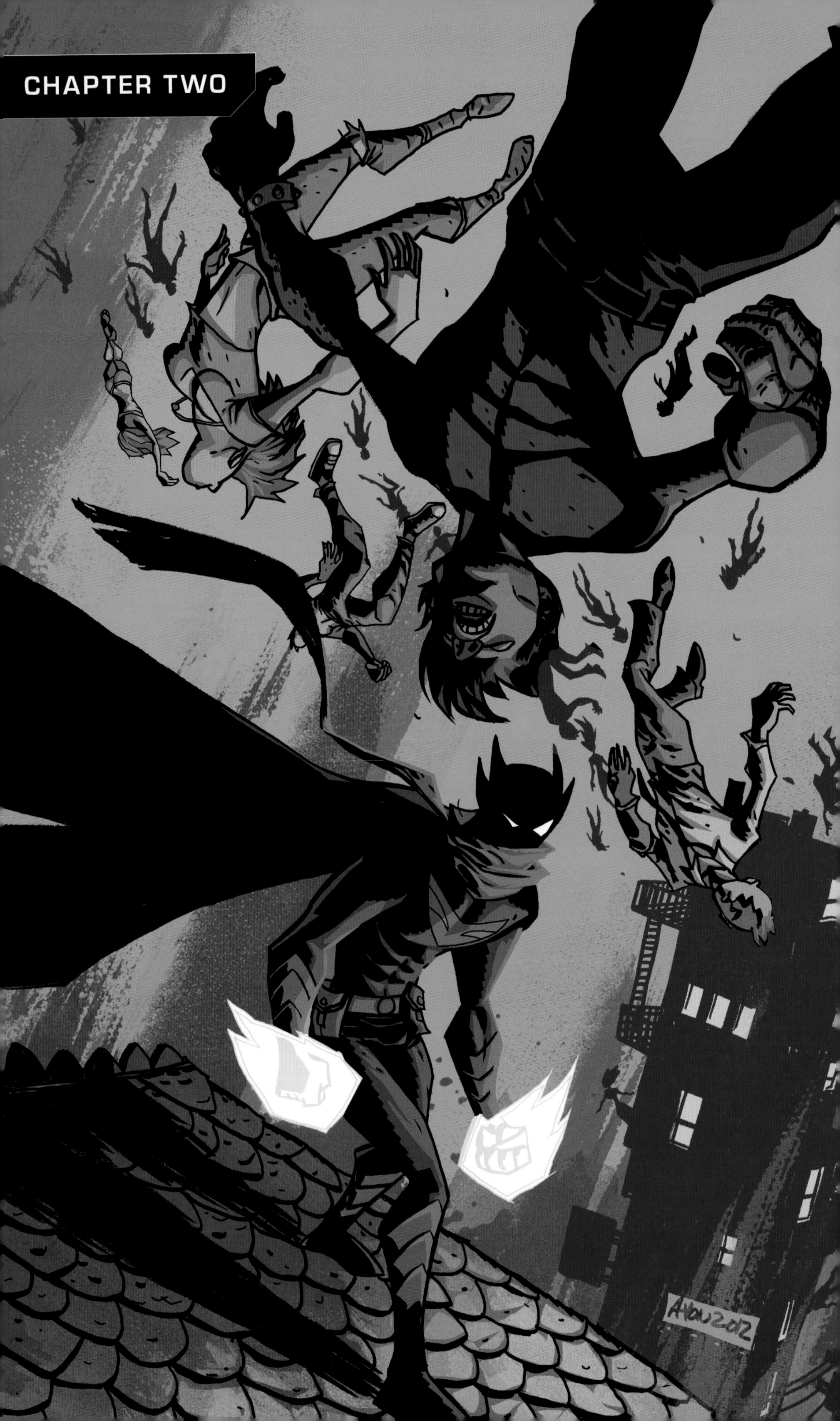

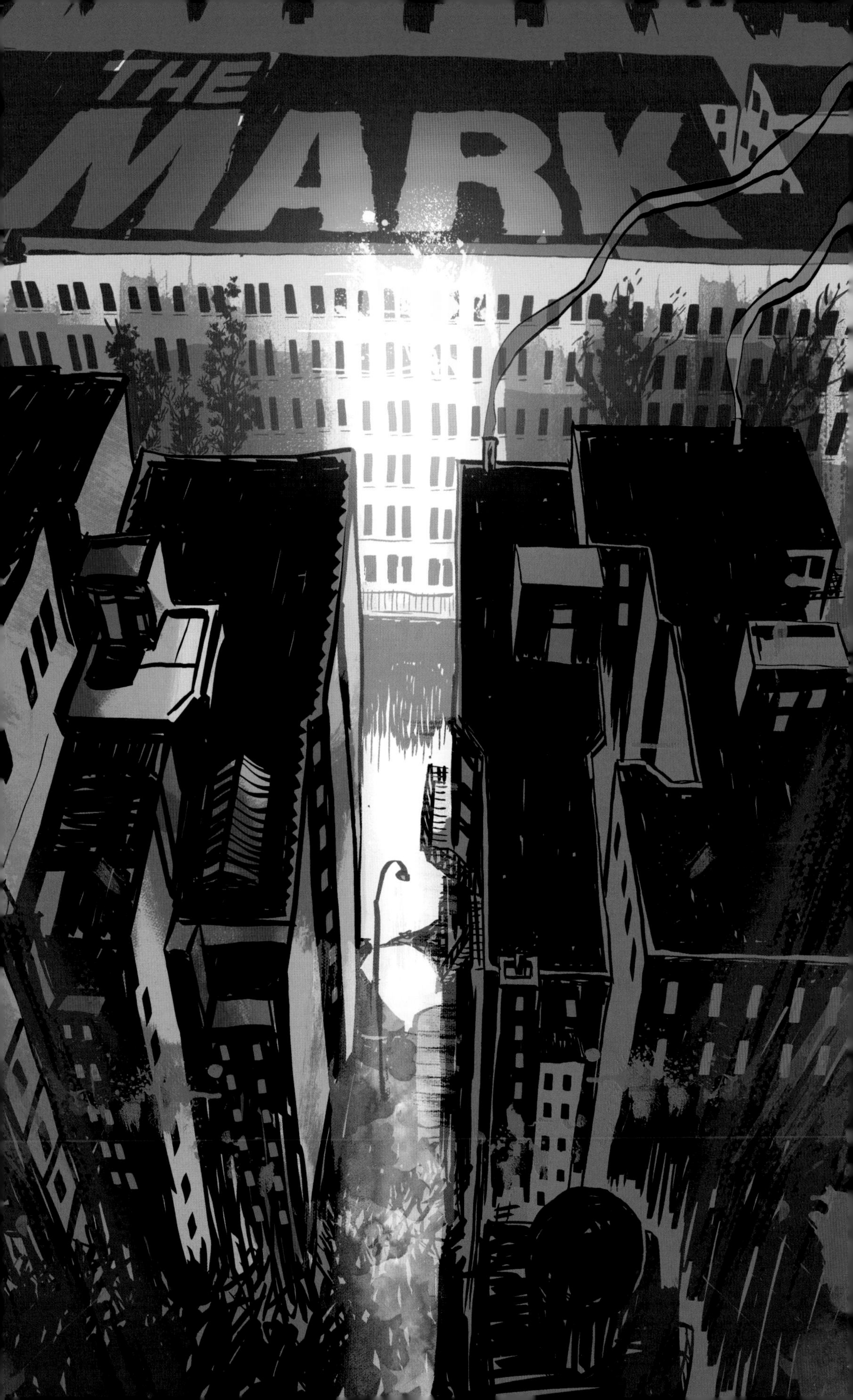
THE
MARK

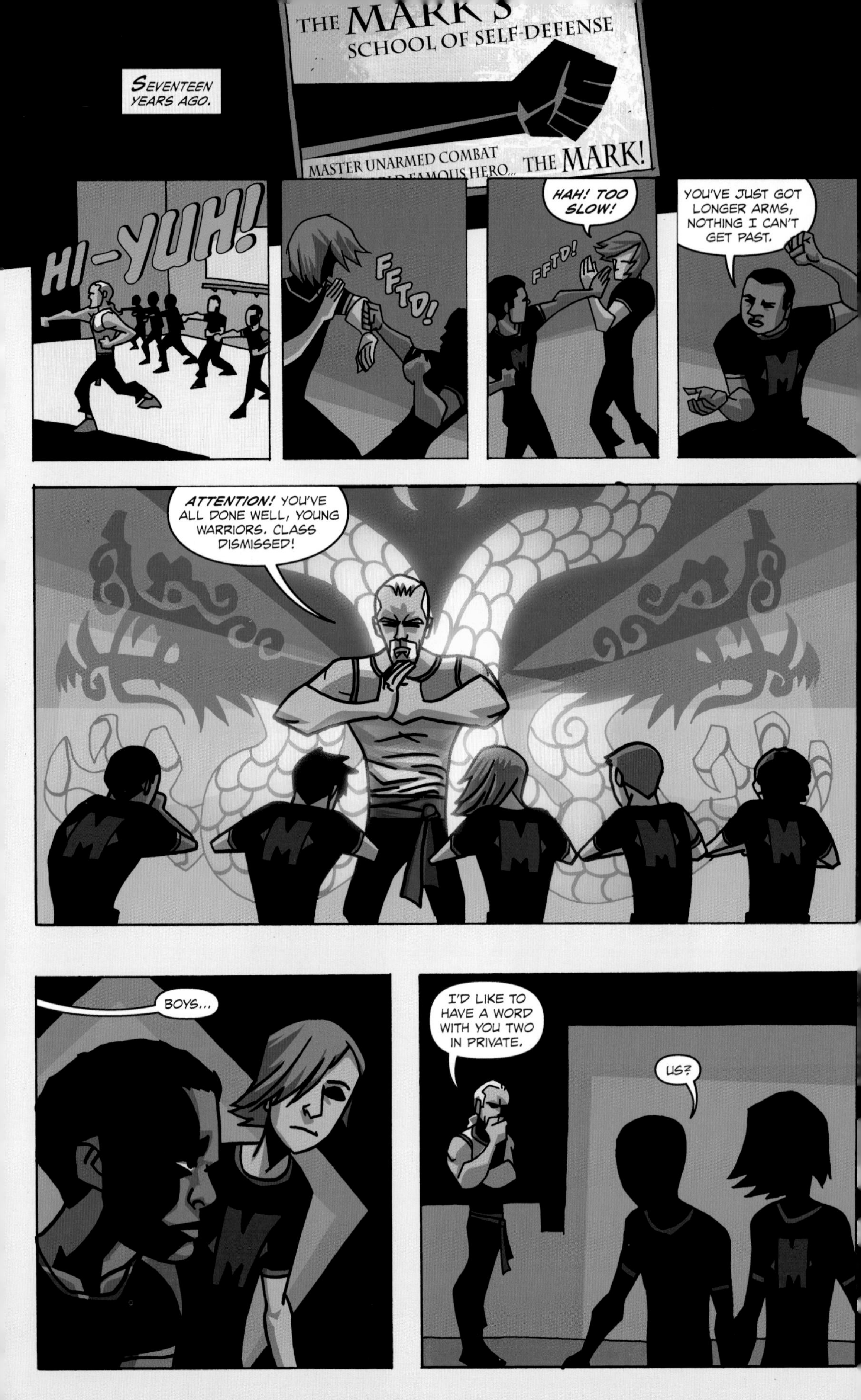
THE MARK'S
SCHOOL OF SELF-DEFENSE
MASTER UNARMED COMBAT
THE MARK!
SEVENTEEN YEARS AGO.
HI-YUH!
FFTD!
FFTD!
HAH! TOO SLOW!
YOU'VE JUST GOT LONGER ARMS, NOTHING I CAN'T GET PAST.
ATTENTION! YOU'VE ALL DONE WELL, YOUNG WARRIORS. CLASS DISMISSED!
BOYS...
I'D LIKE TO HAVE A WORD WITH YOU TWO IN PRIVATE.
US?

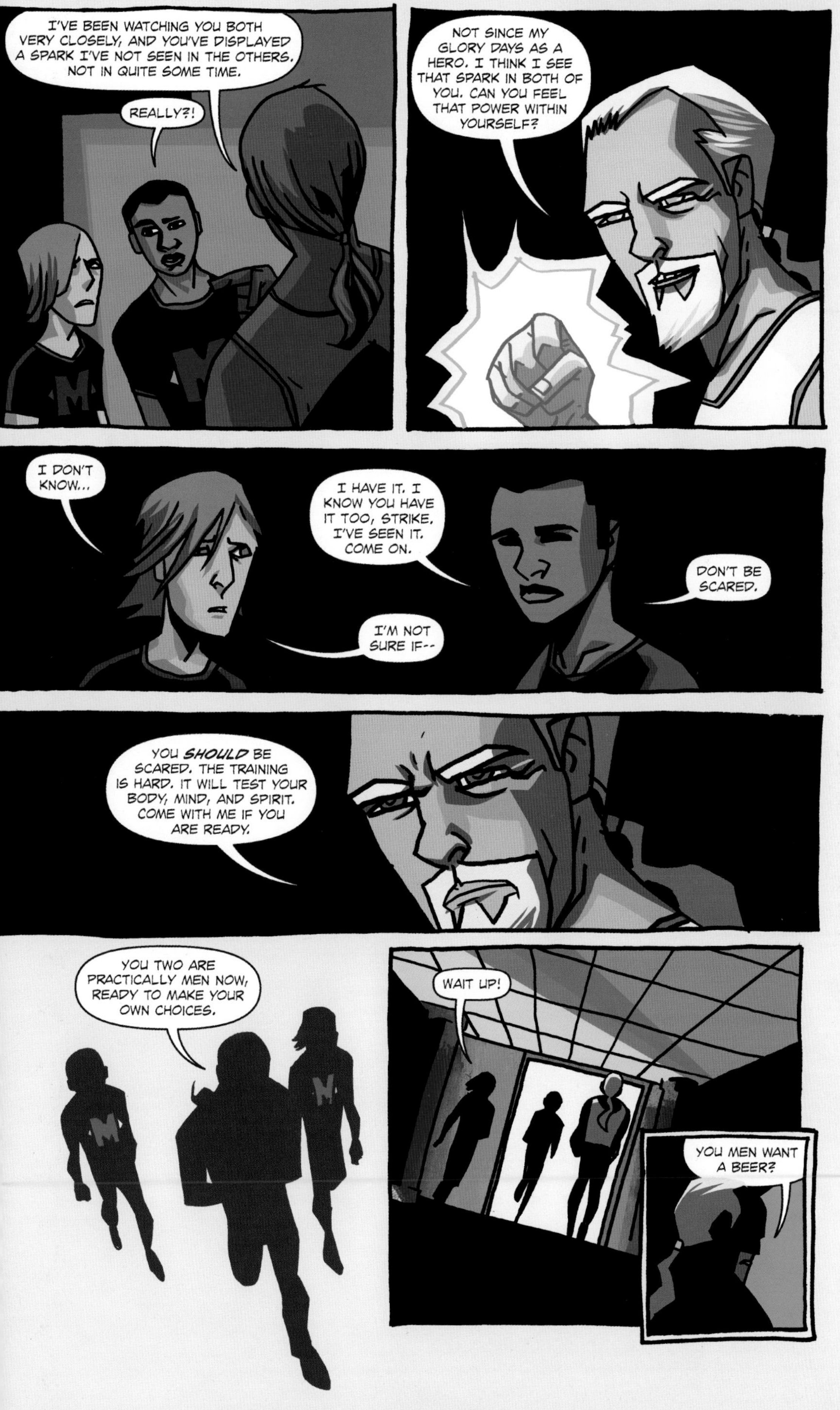
I'VE BEEN WATCHING YOU BOTH VERY CLOSELY, AND YOU'VE DISPLAYED A SPARK I'VE NOT SEEN IN THE OTHERS. NOT IN QUITE SOME TIME.
REALLY?!
NOT SINCE MY GLORY DAYS AS A HERO. I THINK I SEE THAT SPARK IN BOTH OF YOU. CAN YOU FEEL THAT POWER WITHIN YOURSELF?
I DON'T KNOW...
I HAVE IT. I KNOW YOU HAVE IT TOO, STRIKE. I'VE SEEN IT. COME ON.
DON'T BE SCARED.
I'M NOT SURE IF--
YOU ***SHOULD*** BE SCARED. THE TRAINING IS HARD. IT WILL TEST YOUR BODY, MIND, AND SPIRIT. COME WITH ME IF YOU ARE READY.
YOU TWO ARE PRACTICALLY MEN NOW, READY TO MAKE YOUR OWN CHOICES.
WAIT UP!
YOU MEN WANT A BEER?

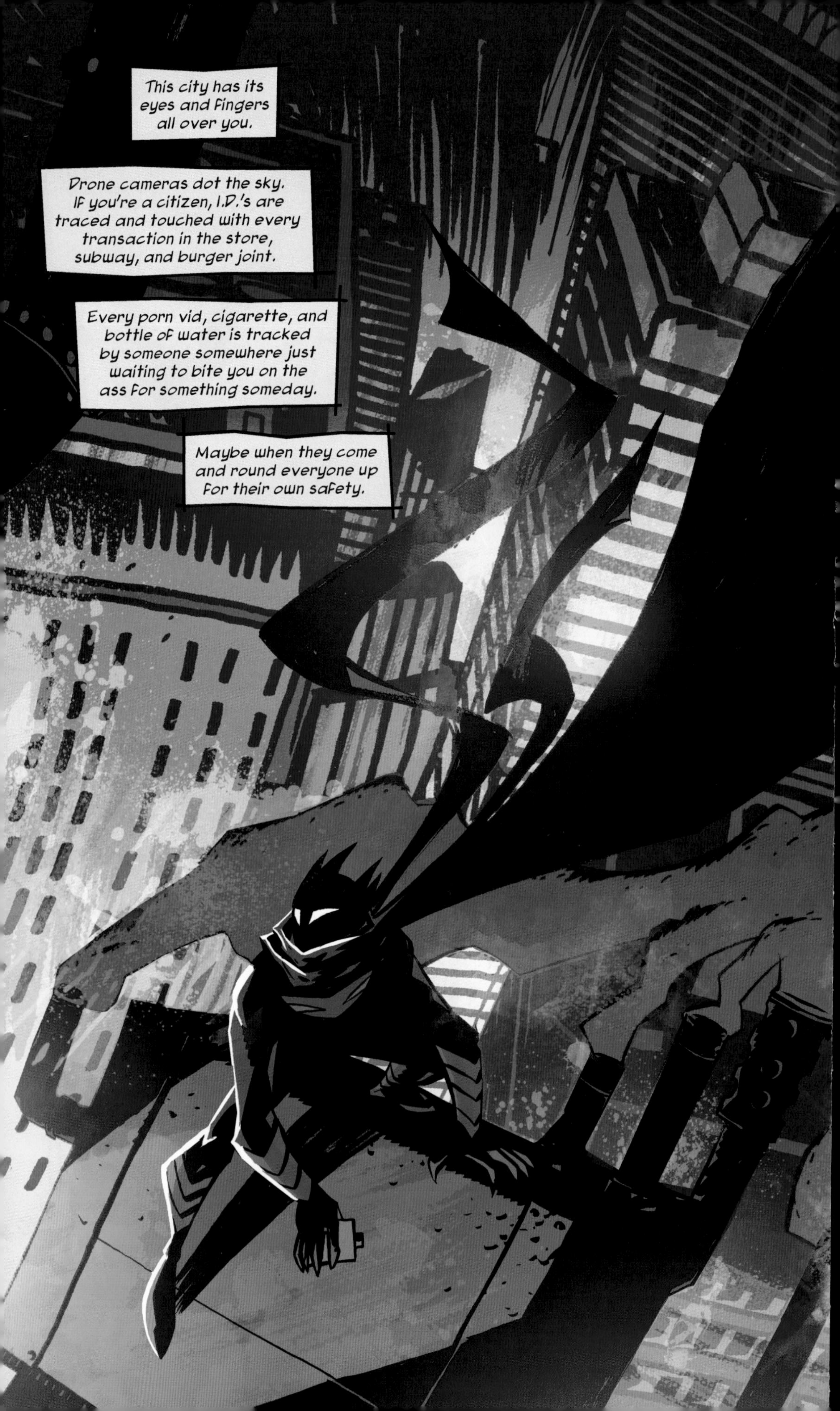
This city has its eyes and fingers all over you.
Drone cameras dot the sky. If you're a citizen, I.D.'s are traced and touched with every transaction in the store, subway, and burger joint.
Every porn vid, cigarette, and bottle of water is tracked by someone somewhere just waiting to bite you on the ass for something someday.
Maybe when they come and round everyone up for their own safety.

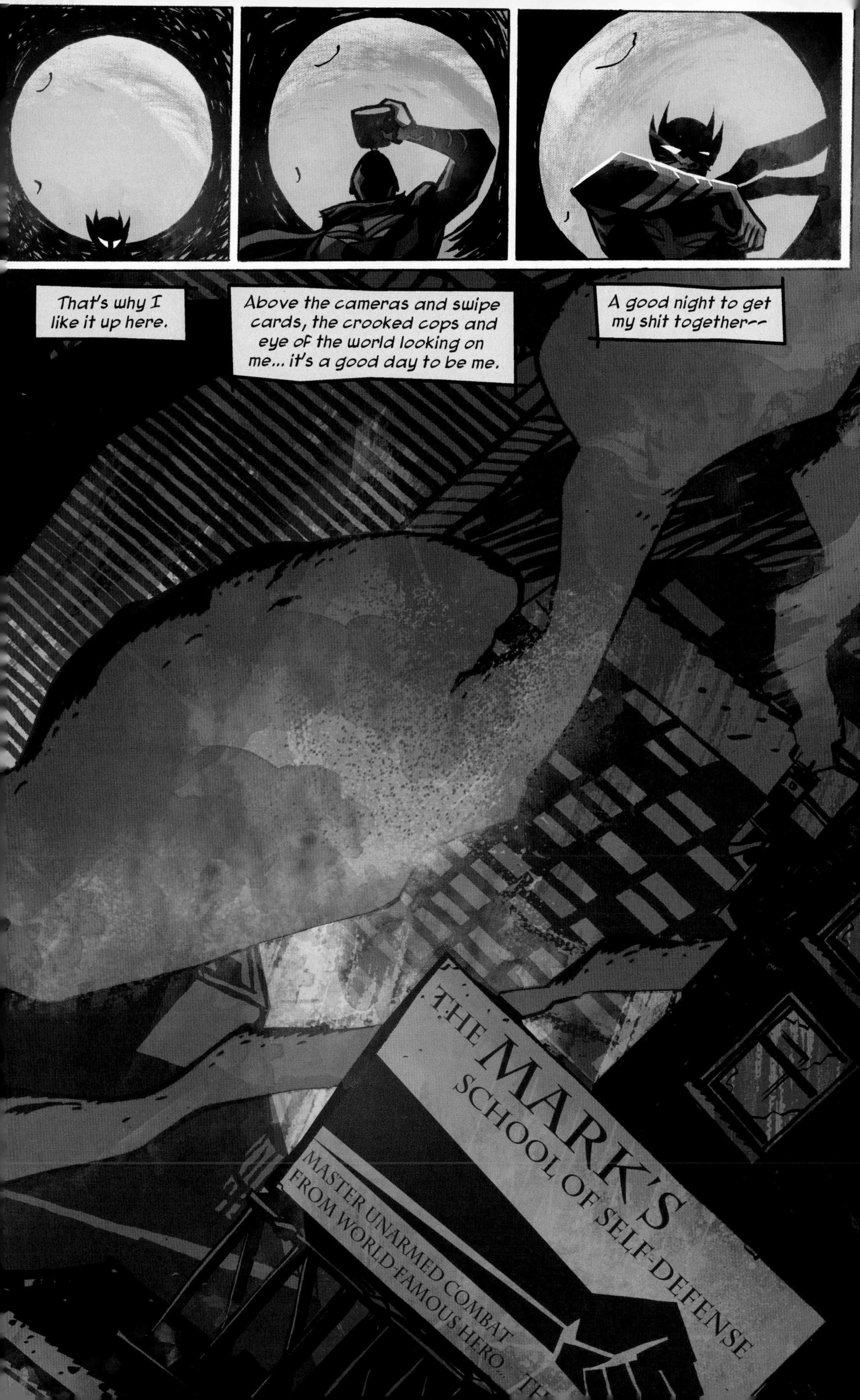

That's why I like it up here.
Above the cameras and swipe cards, the crooked cops and eye of the world looking on me... it's a good day to be me.
A good night to get my shit together--
THE MARK'S
SCHOOL OF SELF-DEFENSE
MASTER UNARMED COMBAT
FROM WORLD-FAMOUS HERO...

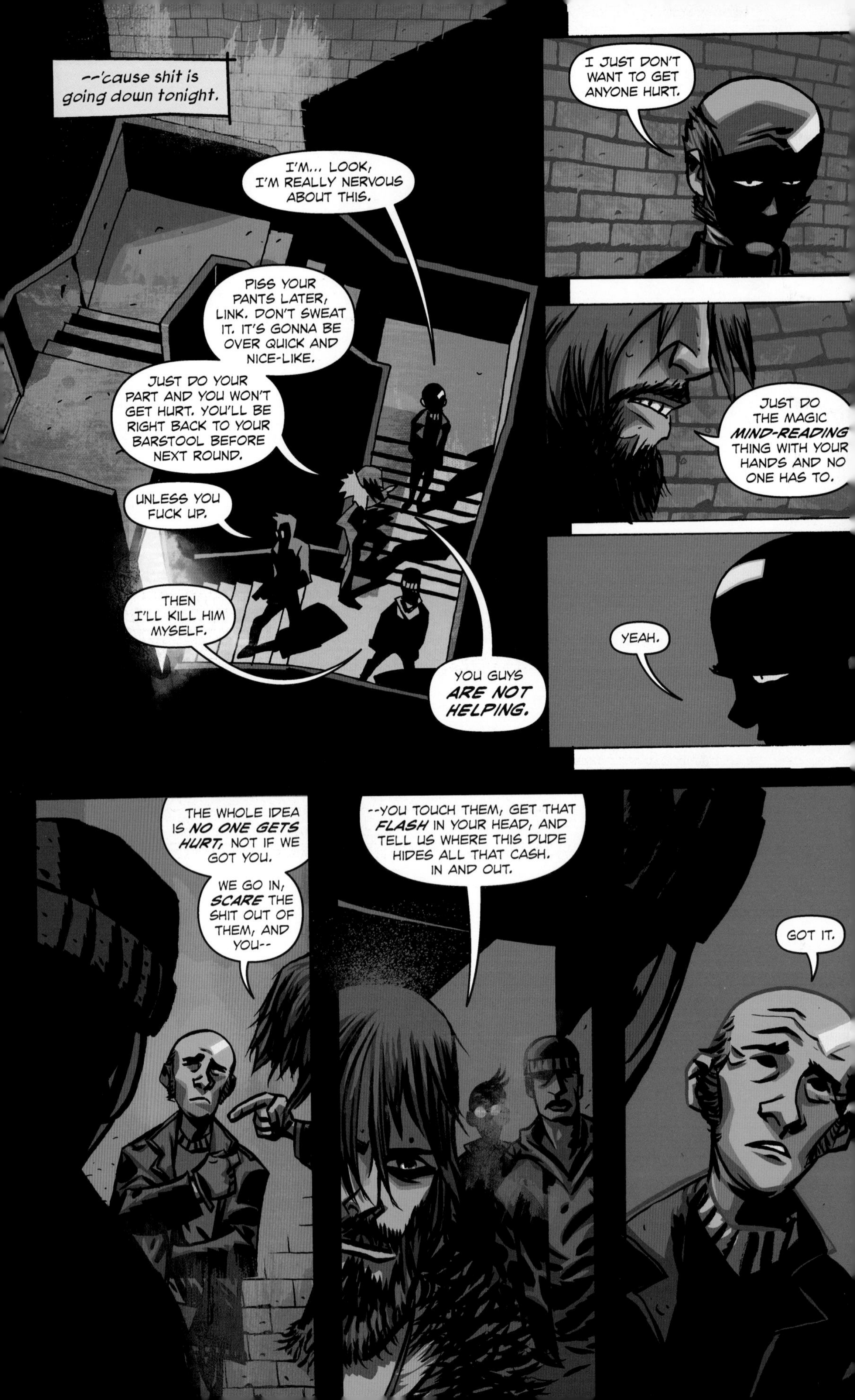
--'cause shit is going down tonight.
I'M... LOOK, I'M REALLY NERVOUS ABOUT THIS.
PISS YOUR PANTS LATER, LINK. DON'T SWEAT IT. IT'S GONNA BE OVER QUICK AND NICE-LIKE.
JUST DO YOUR PART AND YOU WON'T GET HURT. YOU'LL BE RIGHT BACK TO YOUR BARSTOOL BEFORE NEXT ROUND.
UNLESS YOU FUCK UP.
THEN I'LL KILL HIM MYSELF.
YOU GUYS ARE NOT HELPING.
I JUST DON'T WANT TO GET ANYONE HURT.
JUST DO THE MAGIC MIND-READING THING WITH YOUR HANDS AND NO ONE HAS TO.
YEAH.
THE WHOLE IDEA IS NO ONE GETS HURT, NOT IF WE GOT YOU.
WE GO IN, SCARE THE SHIT OUT OF THEM, AND YOU--
--YOU TOUCH THEM, GET THAT FLASH IN YOUR HEAD, AND TELL US WHERE THIS DUDE HIDES ALL THAT CASH. IN AND OUT.
GOT IT.

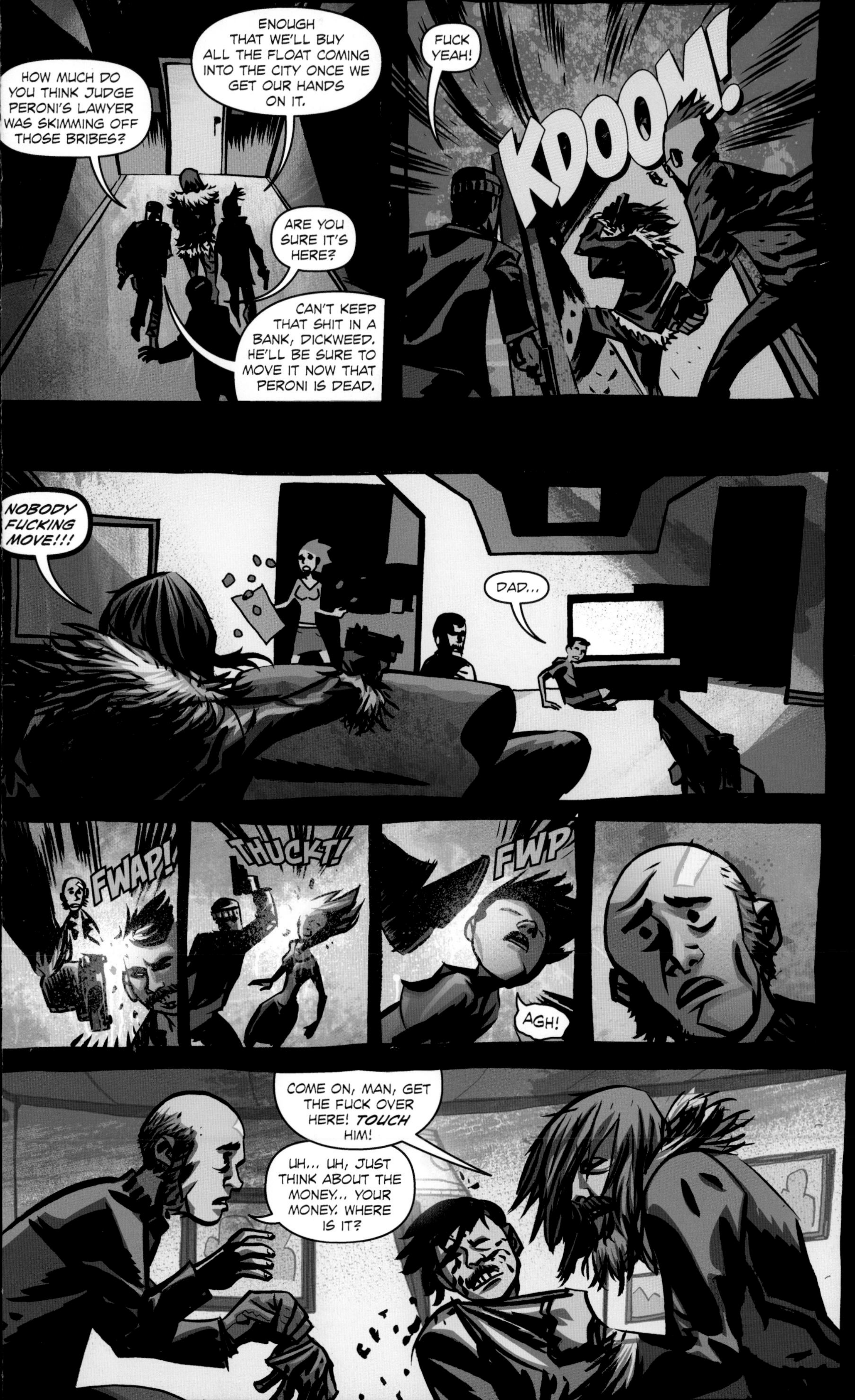
HOW MUCH DO YOU THINK JUDGE PERONI'S LAWYER WAS SKIMMING OFF THOSE BRIBES?
ENOUGH THAT WE'LL BUY ALL THE FLOAT COMING INTO THE CITY ONCE WE GET OUR HANDS ON IT.
ARE YOU SURE IT'S HERE?
CAN'T KEEP THAT SHIT IN A BANK, DICKWEED. HE'LL BE SURE TO MOVE IT NOW THAT PERONI IS DEAD.
FUCK YEAH!
KDOOM!
NOBODY FUCKING MOVE!!!
DAD...
FWAP!
THUCKT!
FWP
AGH!
COME ON, MAN, GET THE FUCK OVER HERE! TOUCH HIM!
UH... UH, JUST THINK ABOUT THE MONEY... YOUR MONEY. WHERE IS IT?

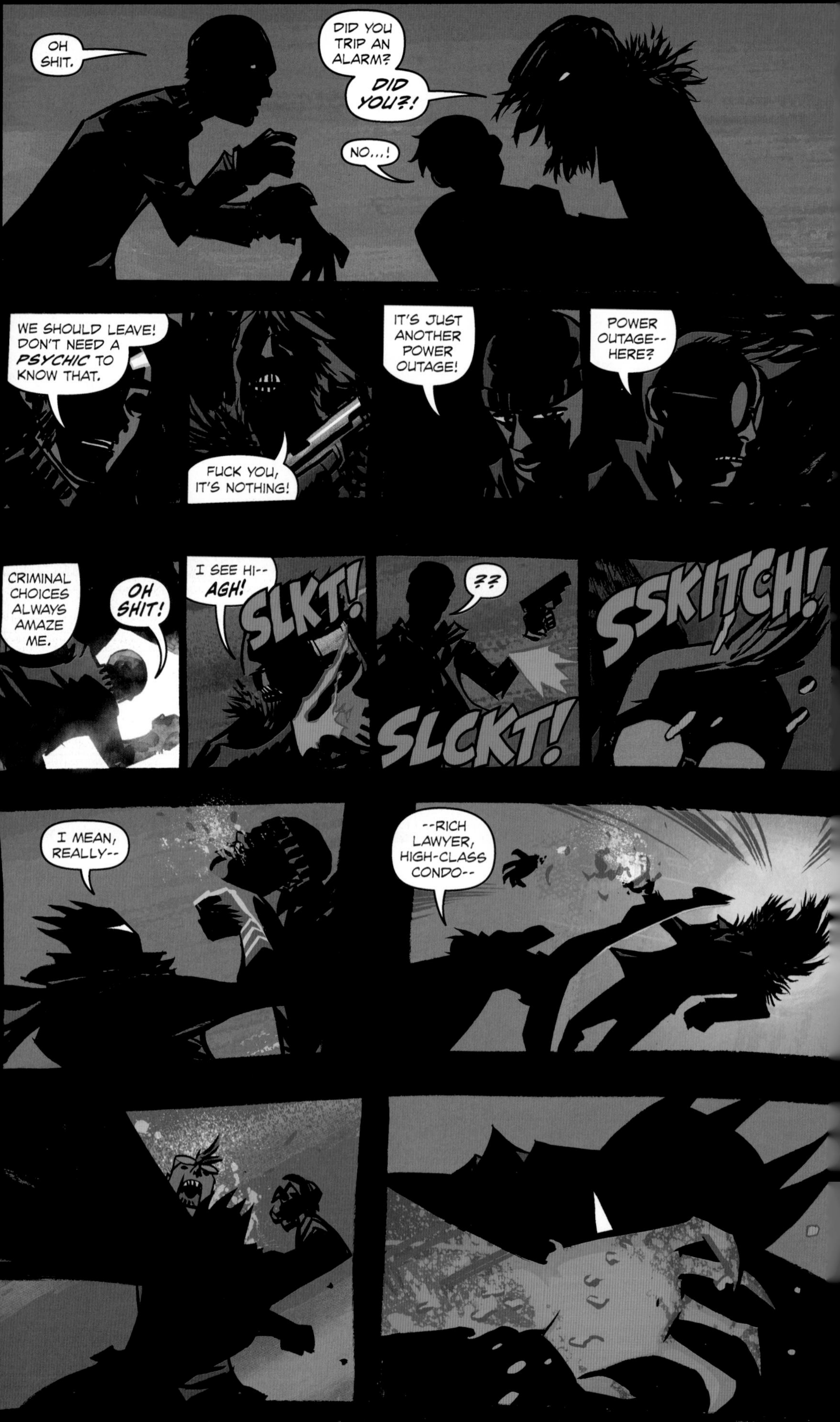
OH SHIT.
DID YOU TRIP AN ALARM? DID YOU?!
NO...!
WE SHOULD LEAVE! DON'T NEED A PSYCHIC TO KNOW THAT.
FUCK YOU, IT'S NOTHING!
IT'S JUST ANOTHER POWER OUTAGE!
POWER OUTAGE-- HERE?
CRIMINAL CHOICES ALWAYS AMAZE ME.
OH SHIT!
I SEE HI-- AGH!
SLKT!
??
SLCKT!
SSKITCH!
I MEAN, REALLY--
--RICH LAWYER, HIGH-CLASS CONDO--

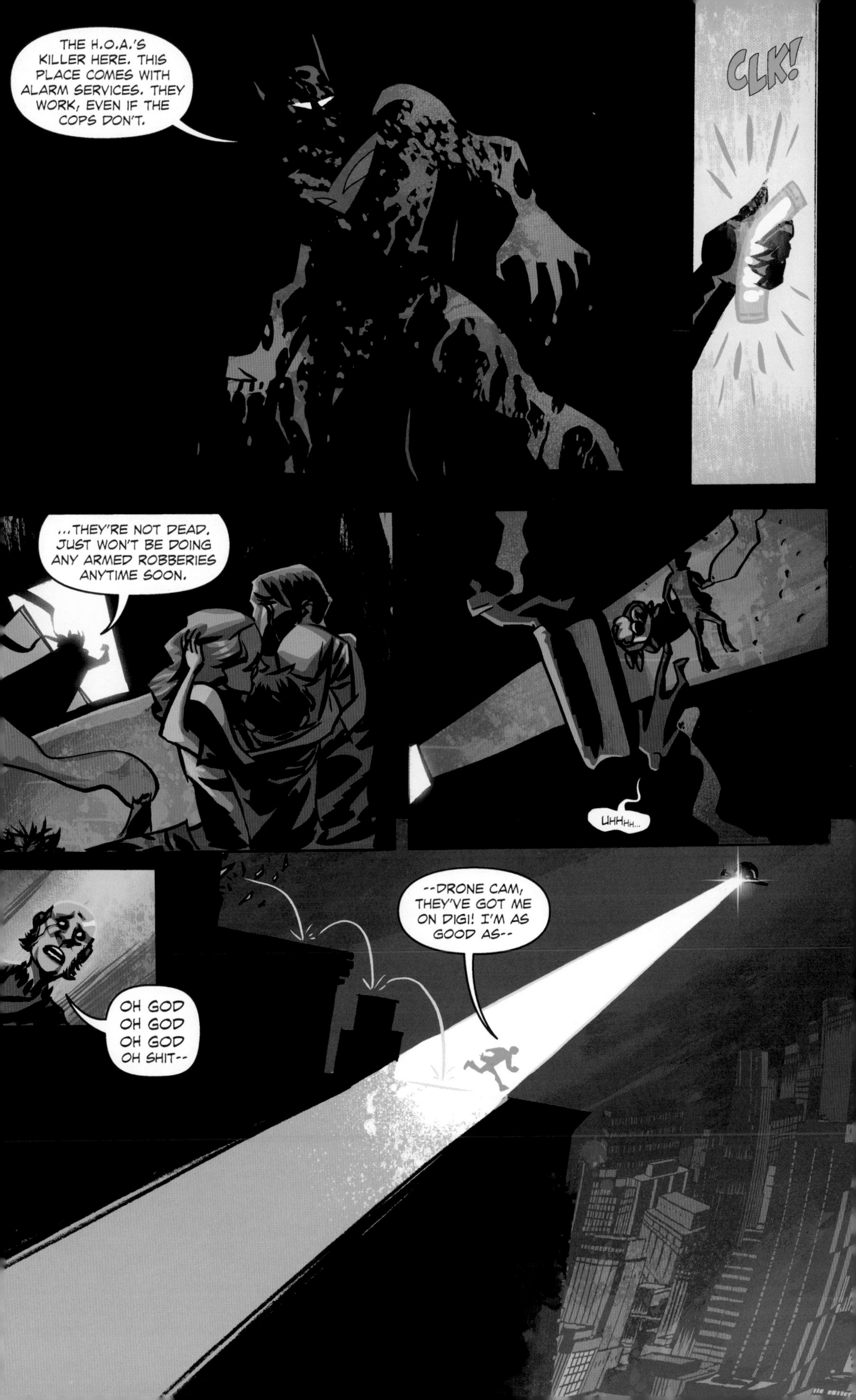
THE H.O.A.'S KILLER HERE. THIS PLACE COMES WITH ALARM SERVICES. THEY WORK, EVEN IF THE COPS DON'T.
CLK!
...THEY'RE NOT DEAD. JUST WON'T BE DOING ANY ARMED ROBBERIES ANYTIME SOON.
UHHHH...
OH GOD OH GOD OH GOD OH SHIT--
--DRONE CAM, THEY'VE GOT ME ON DIGI! I'M AS GOOD AS--

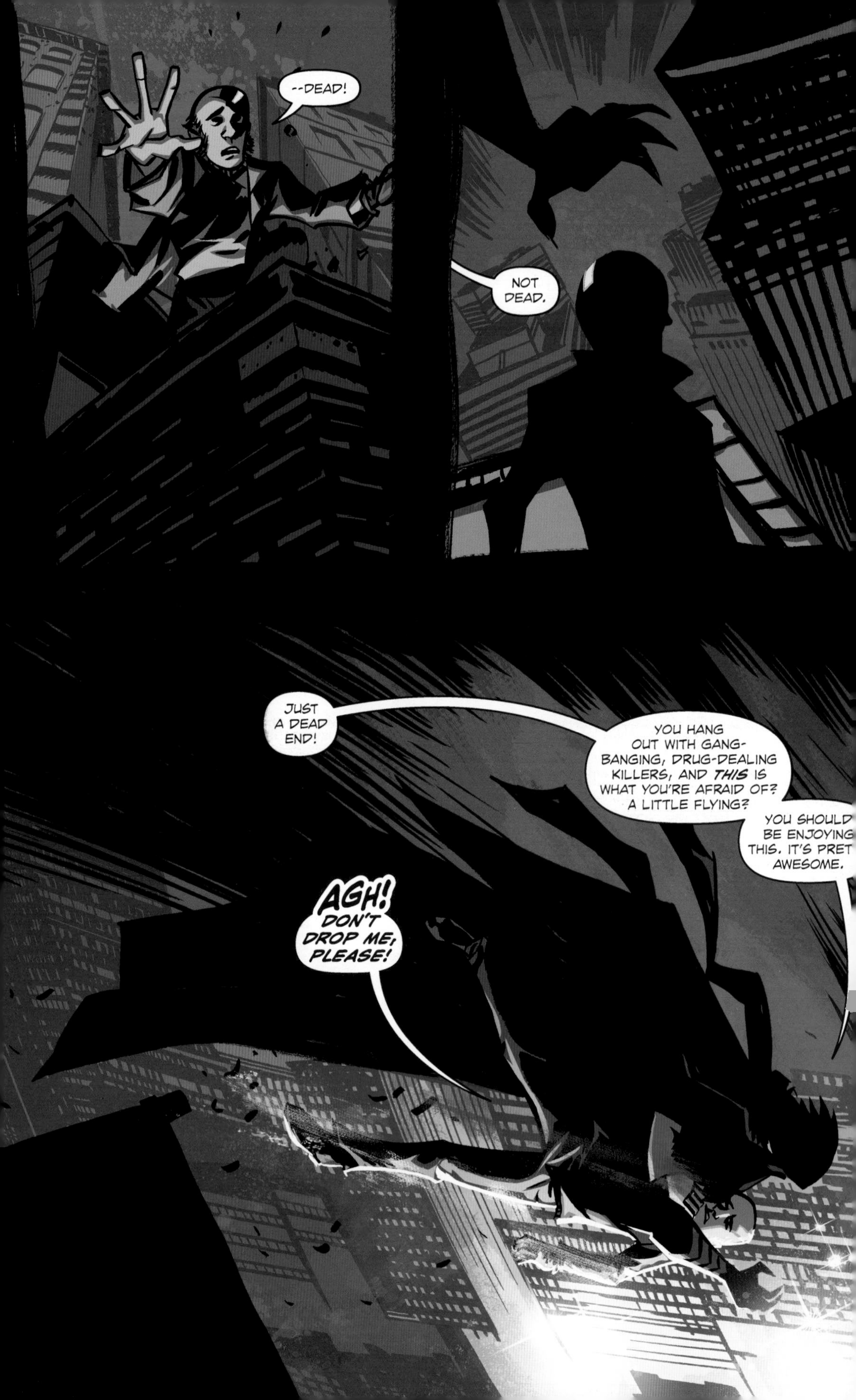
--DEAD!
NOT DEAD.
JUST A DEAD END!
YOU HANG OUT WITH GANG-BANGING, DRUG-DEALING KILLERS, AND *THIS* IS WHAT YOU'RE AFRAID OF? A LITTLE FLYING?
YOU SHOULD BE ENJOYING THIS. IT'S PRET
AWESOME.
AGH! DON'T DROP ME, PLEASE!

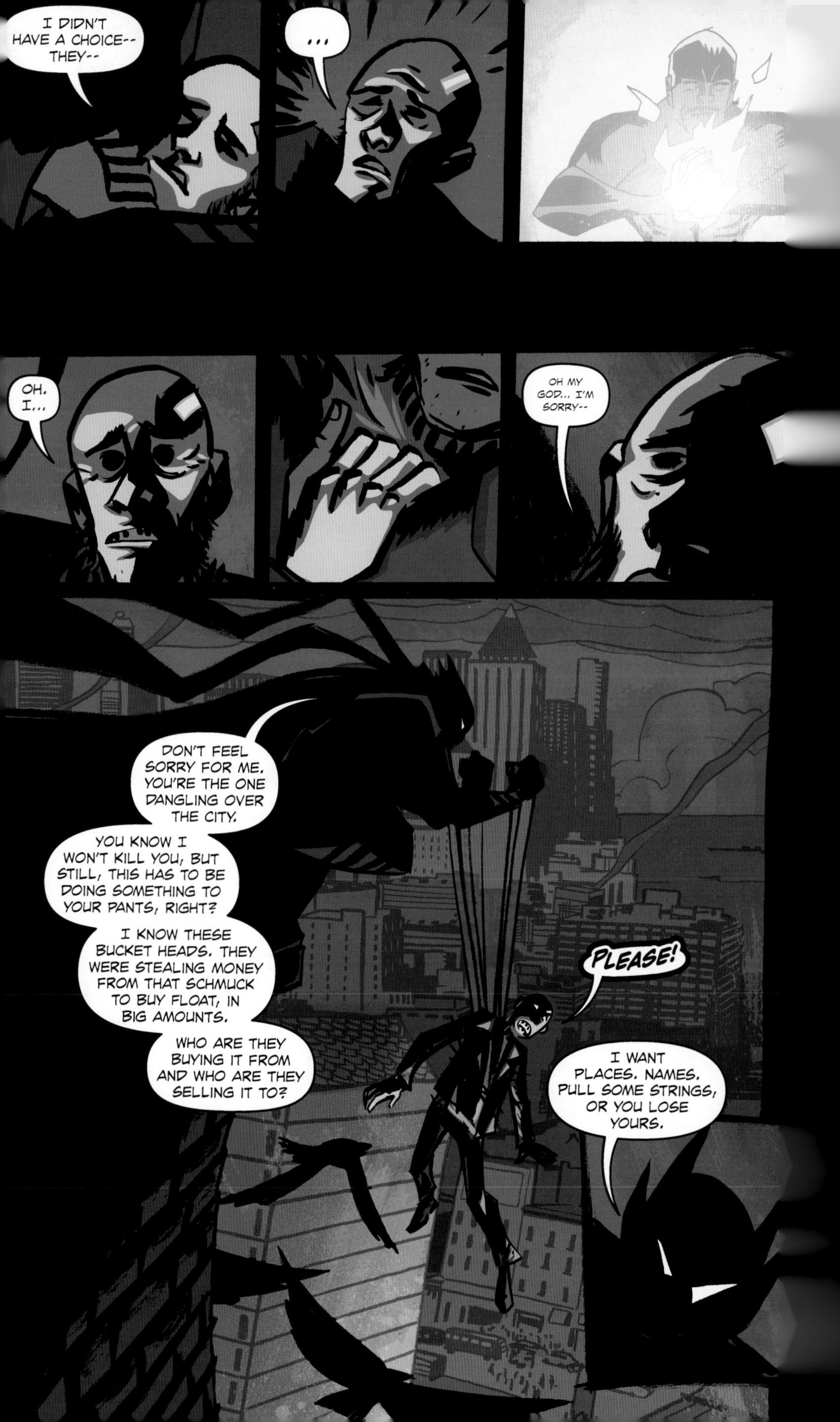
I DIDN'T HAVE A CHOICE-- THEY--
...
OH. I...
OH MY GOD... I'M SORRY--
DON'T FEEL SORRY FOR ME. YOU'RE THE ONE DANGLING OVER THE CITY.
YOU KNOW I WON'T KILL YOU, BUT STILL, THIS HAS TO BE DOING SOMETHING TO YOUR PANTS, RIGHT?
I KNOW THESE BUCKET HEADS. THEY WERE STEALING MONEY FROM THAT SCHMUCK TO BUY FLOAT, IN BIG AMOUNTS.
WHO ARE THEY BUYING IT FROM AND WHO ARE THEY SELLING IT TO?
PLEASE!
I WANT PLACES. NAMES. PULL SOME STRINGS, OR YOU LOSE YOURS.

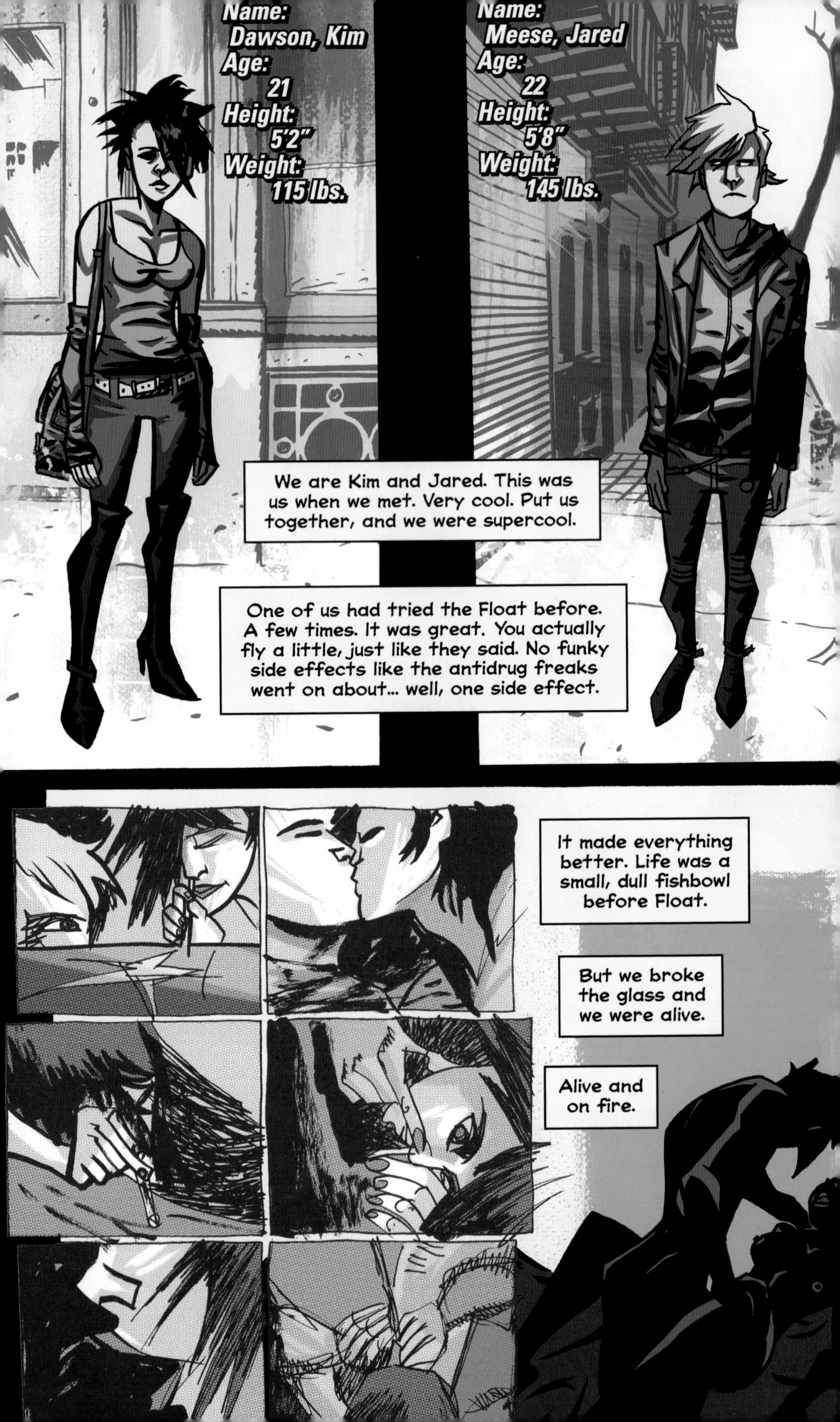

Name:
Dawson, Kim
Age:
21
Height:
5'2"
Weight:
115 lbs.
Name:
Meese, Jared
Age:
22
Height:
5'8"
Weight:
145 lbs.
We are Kim and Jared. This was us when we met. Very cool. Put us together, and we were supercool.
One of us had tried the Float before. A few times. It was great. You actually fly a little, just like they said. No funky side effects like the antidrug freaks went on about... well, one side effect.
It made everything better. Life was a small, dull fishbowl before Float.
But we broke the glass and we were alive.
Alive and on fire.

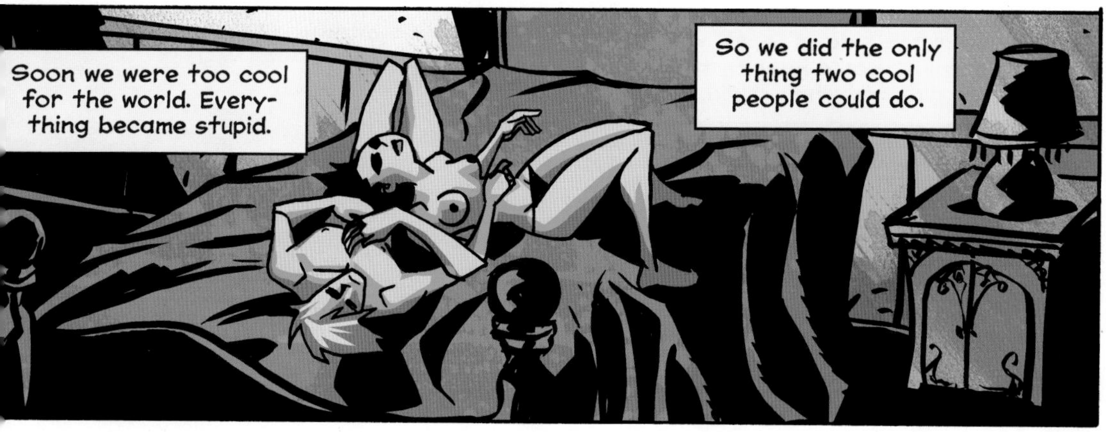
Soon we were too cool for the world. Every-thing became stupid.
So we did the only thing two cool people could do.

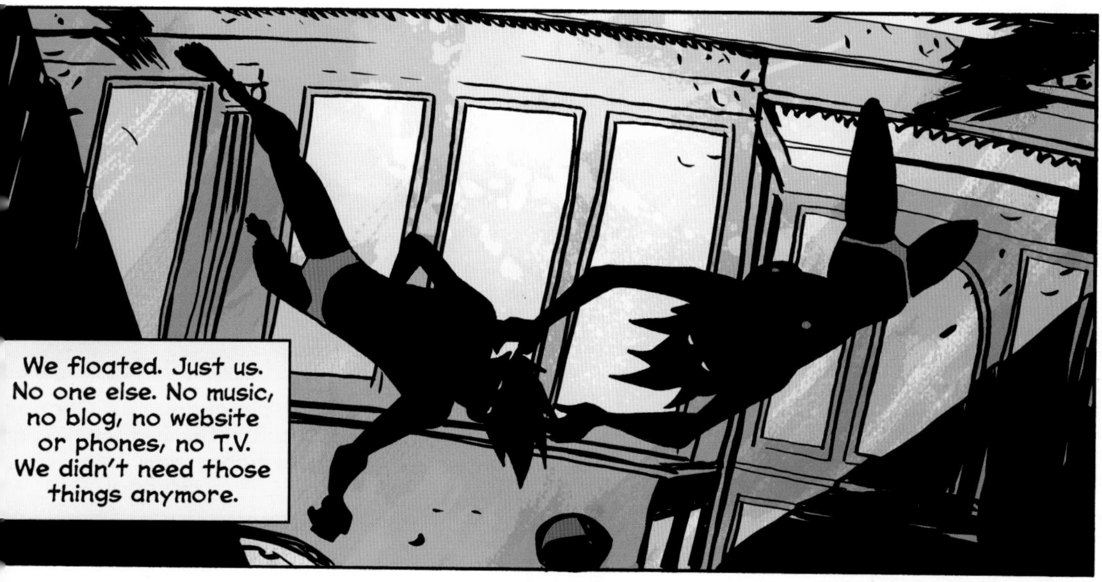
We floated. Just us. No one else. No music, no blog, no website or phones, no T.V. We didn't need those things anymore.

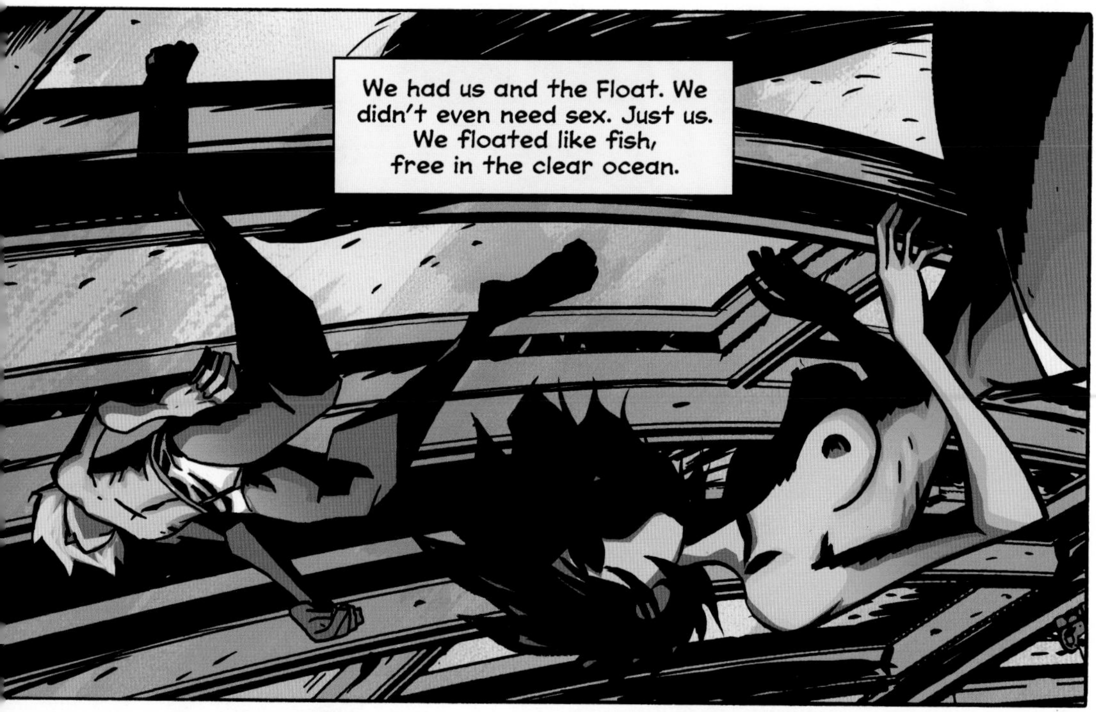
We had us and the Float. We didn't even need sex. Just us. We floated like fish, free in the clear ocean.

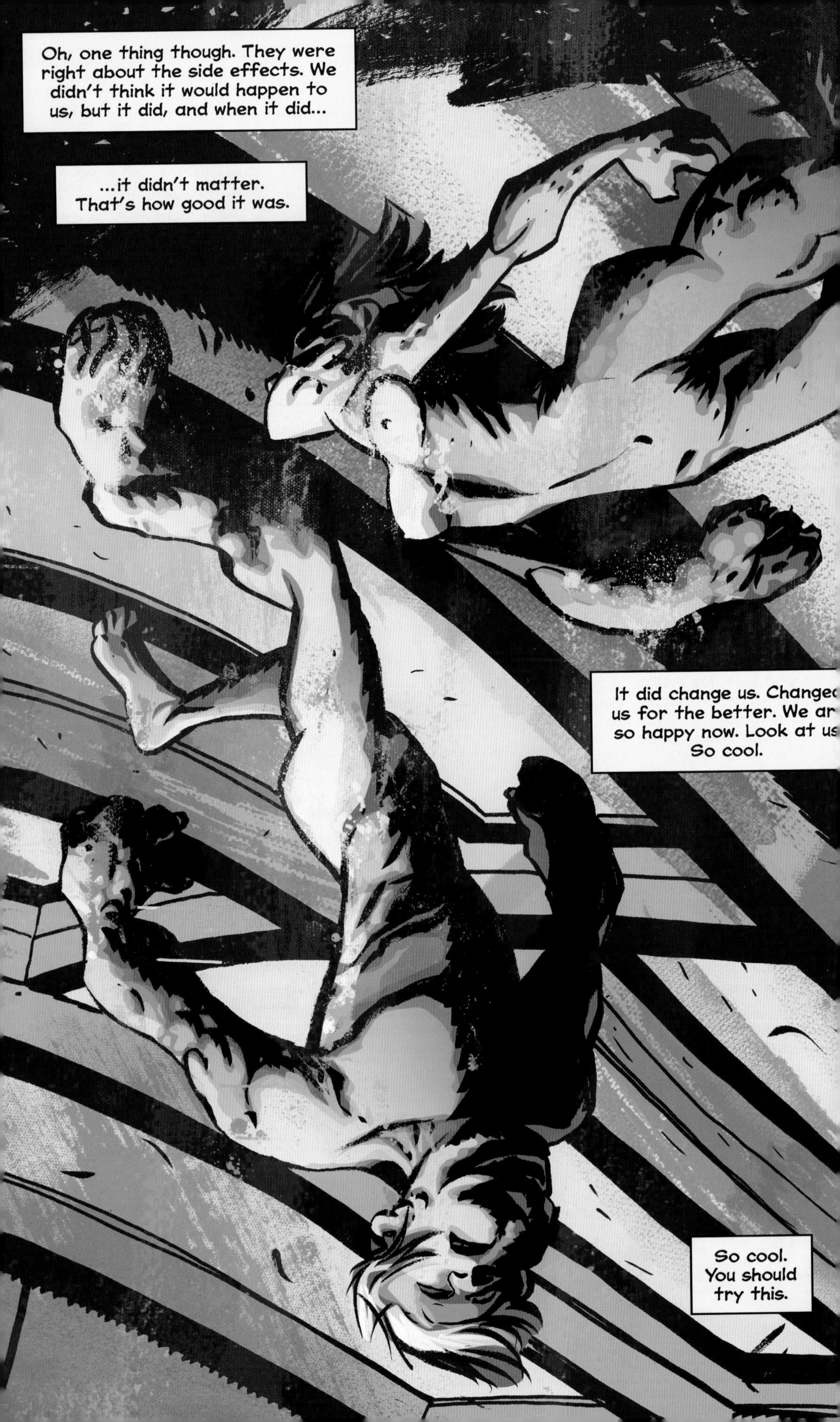
Oh, one thing though. They were right about the side effects. We didn't think it would happen to us, but it did, and when it did...
...it didn't matter. That's how good it was.
It did change us. Changed us for the better. We are so happy now. Look at us. So cool.
So cool. You should try this.

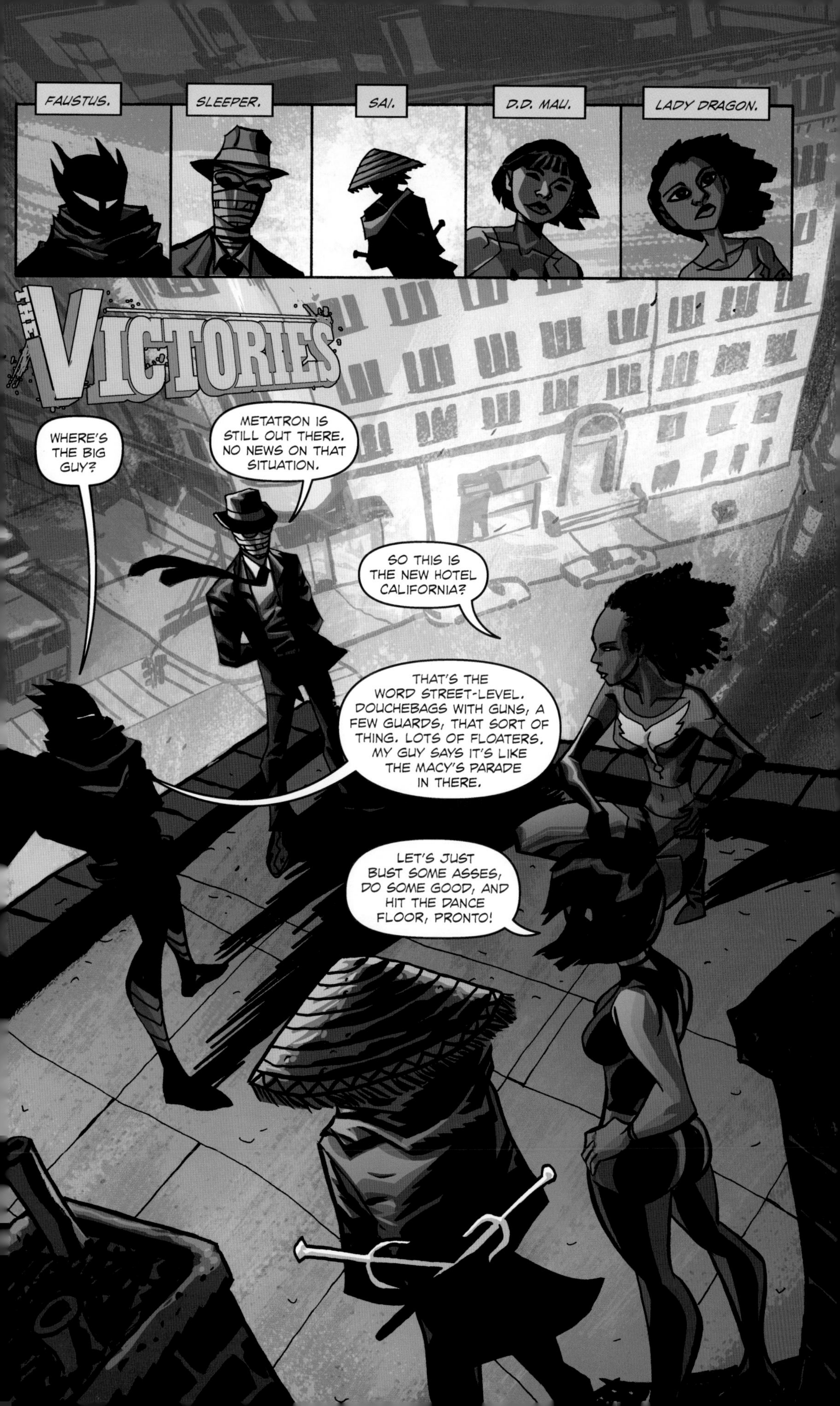
FAUSTUS.
SLEEPER.
SAI.
D.D. MAU.
LADY DRAGON.
THE VICTORIES
WHERE'S THE BIG GUY?
METATRON IS STILL OUT THERE. NO NEWS ON THAT SITUATION.
SO THIS IS THE NEW HOTEL CALIFORNIA?
THAT'S THE WORD STREET-LEVEL. DOUCHEBAGS WITH GUNS, A FEW GUARDS, THAT SORT OF THING. LOTS OF FLOATERS. MY GUY SAYS IT'S LIKE THE MACY'S PARADE IN THERE.
LET'S JUST BUST SOME ASSES, DO SOME GOOD, AND HIT THE DANCE FLOOR, PRONTO!

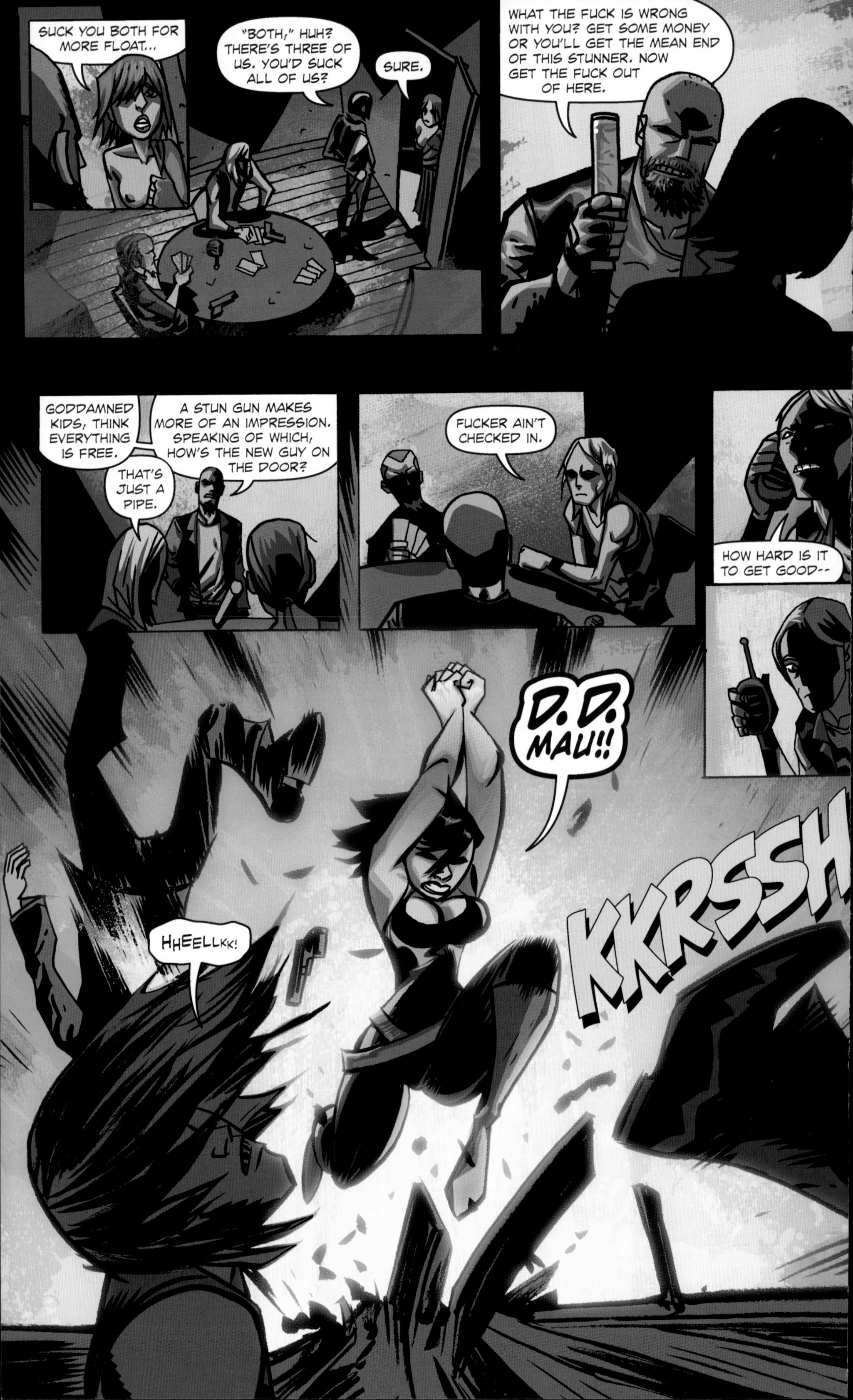
SUCK YOU BOTH FOR MORE FLOAT...
"BOTH," HUH? THERE'S THREE OF US. YOU'D SUCK ALL OF US?
SURE.
WHAT THE FUCK IS WRONG WITH YOU? GET SOME MONEY OR YOU'LL GET THE MEAN END OF THIS STUNNER. NOW GET THE FUCK OUT OF HERE.
GODDAMNED KIDS, THINK EVERYTHING IS FREE.
THAT'S JUST A PIPE.
A STUN GUN MAKES MORE OF AN IMPRESSION. SPEAKING OF WHICH, HOW'S THE NEW GUY ON THE DOOR?
FUCKER AIN'T CHECKED IN.
HOW HARD IS IT TO GET GOOD--
D.D. MAU!!
HHEELLKK!
KKRSSH

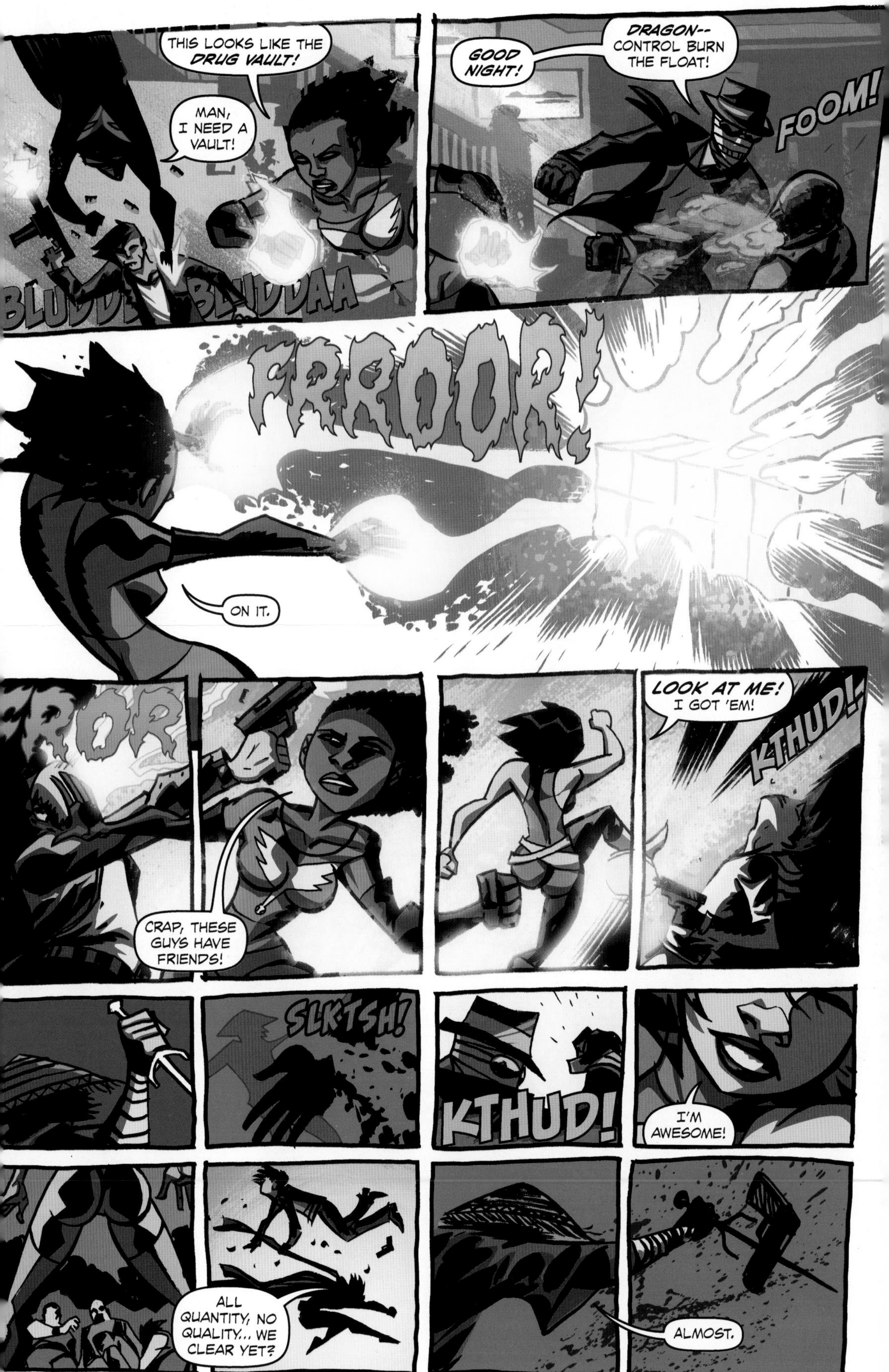

THIS LOOKS LIKE THE DRUG VAULT!
MAN, I NEED A VAULT!
BLUDDDA BLUDDAA
DRAGON-- CONTROL BURN THE FLOAT!
GOOD NIGHT!
FOOM!
FRROOR!
ON IT.
ROR
CRAP, THESE GUYS HAVE FRIENDS!
LOOK AT ME! I GOT 'EM!
KTHUD!
SLKTSH!
KTHUD!
I'M AWESOME!
ALL QUANTITY, NO QUALITY... WE CLEAR YET?
ALMOST.

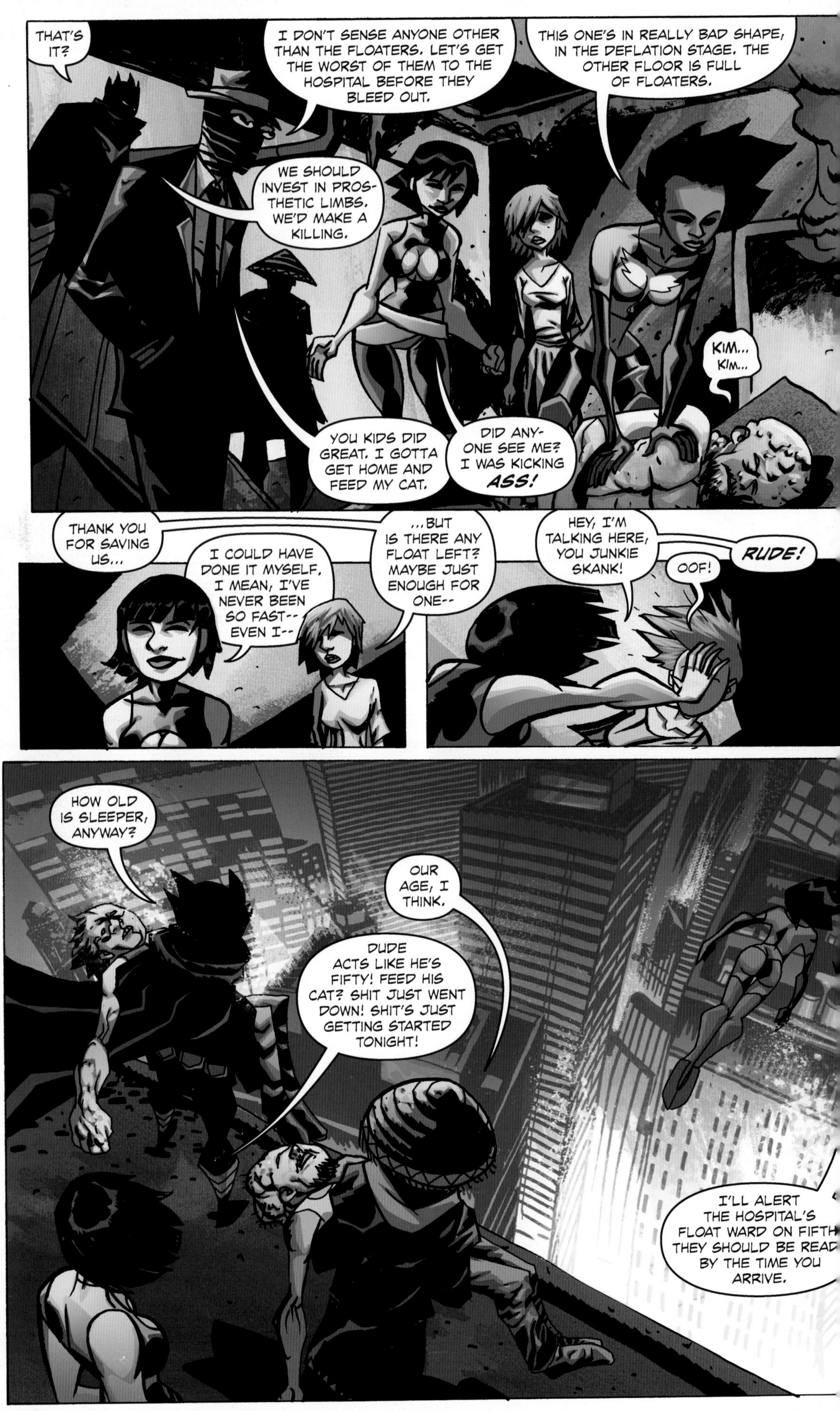
THAT'S IT?
I DON'T SENSE ANYONE OTHER THAN THE FLOATERS. LET'S GET THE WORST OF THEM TO THE HOSPITAL BEFORE THEY BLEED OUT.
THIS ONE'S IN REALLY BAD SHAPE, IN THE DEFLATION STAGE. THE OTHER FLOOR IS FULL OF FLOATERS.
WE SHOULD INVEST IN PROSTHETIC LIMBS. WE'D MAKE A KILLING.
KIM... KIM...
YOU KIDS DID GREAT. I GOTTA GET HOME AND FEED MY CAT.
DID ANYONE SEE ME? I WAS KICKING ASS!
THANK YOU FOR SAVING US...
I COULD HAVE DONE IT MYSELF. I MEAN, I'VE NEVER BEEN SO FAST-- EVEN I--
...BUT IS THERE ANY FLOAT LEFT? MAYBE JUST ENOUGH FOR ONE--
HEY, I'M TALKING HERE, YOU JUNKIE SKANK!
RUDE!
OOF!
HOW OLD IS SLEEPER, ANYWAY?
OUR AGE, I THINK.
DUDE ACTS LIKE HE'S FIFTY! FEED HIS CAT? SHIT JUST WENT DOWN! SHIT'S JUST GETTING STARTED TONIGHT!
I'LL ALERT THE HOSPITAL'S FLOAT WARD ON FIFTH THEY SHOULD BE READ BY THE TIME YOU ARRIVE.

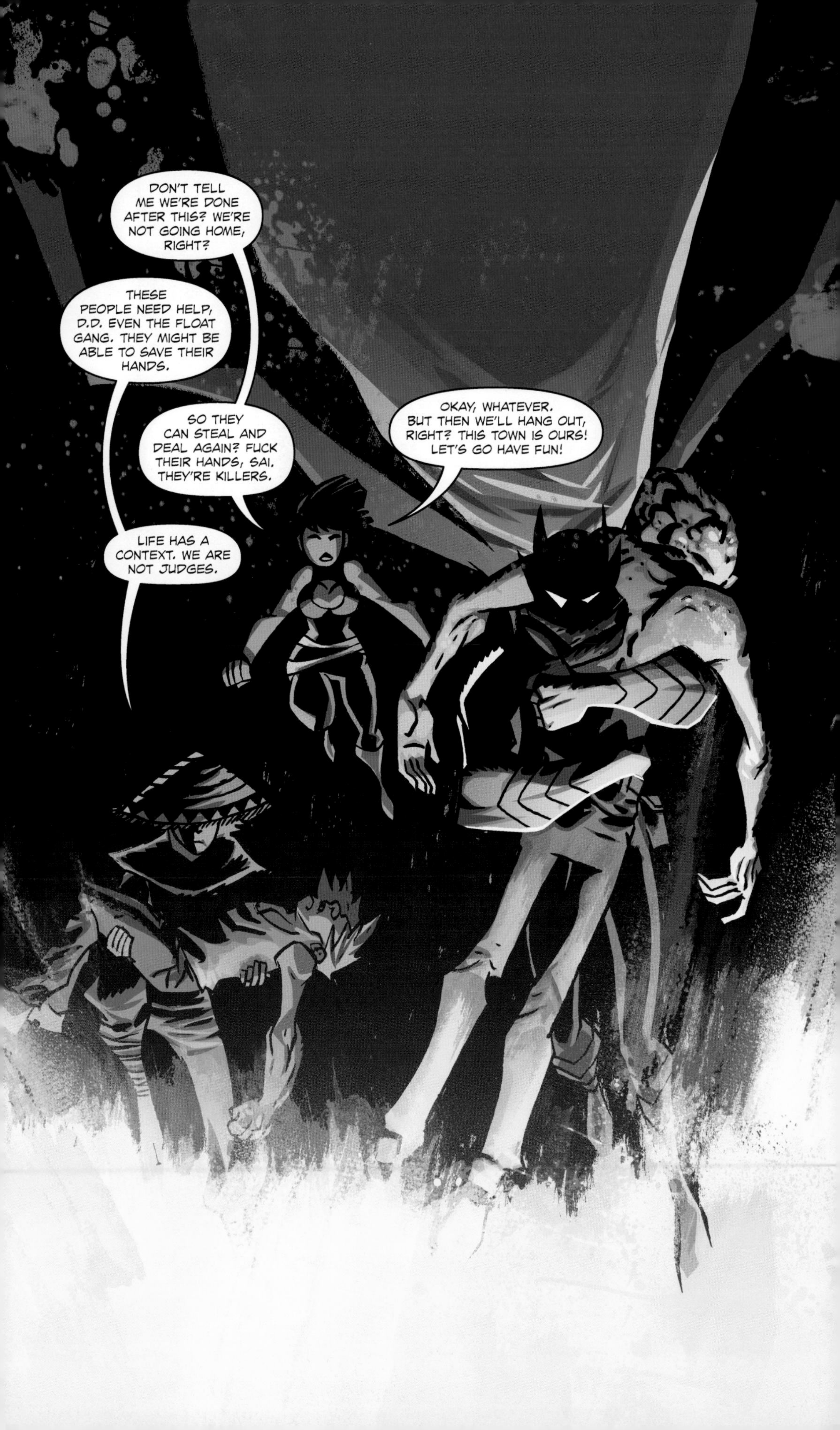
DON'T TELL ME WE'RE DONE AFTER THIS? WE'RE NOT GOING HOME, RIGHT?
THESE PEOPLE NEED HELP, D.D. EVEN THE FLOAT GANG. THEY MIGHT BE ABLE TO SAVE THEIR HANDS.
SO THEY CAN STEAL AND DEAL AGAIN? FUCK THEIR HANDS, SAI. THEY'RE KILLERS.
LIFE HAS A CONTEXT. WE ARE NOT JUDGES.
OKAY, WHATEVER. BUT THEN WE'LL HANG OUT, RIGHT? THIS TOWN IS OURS! LET'S GO HAVE FUN!

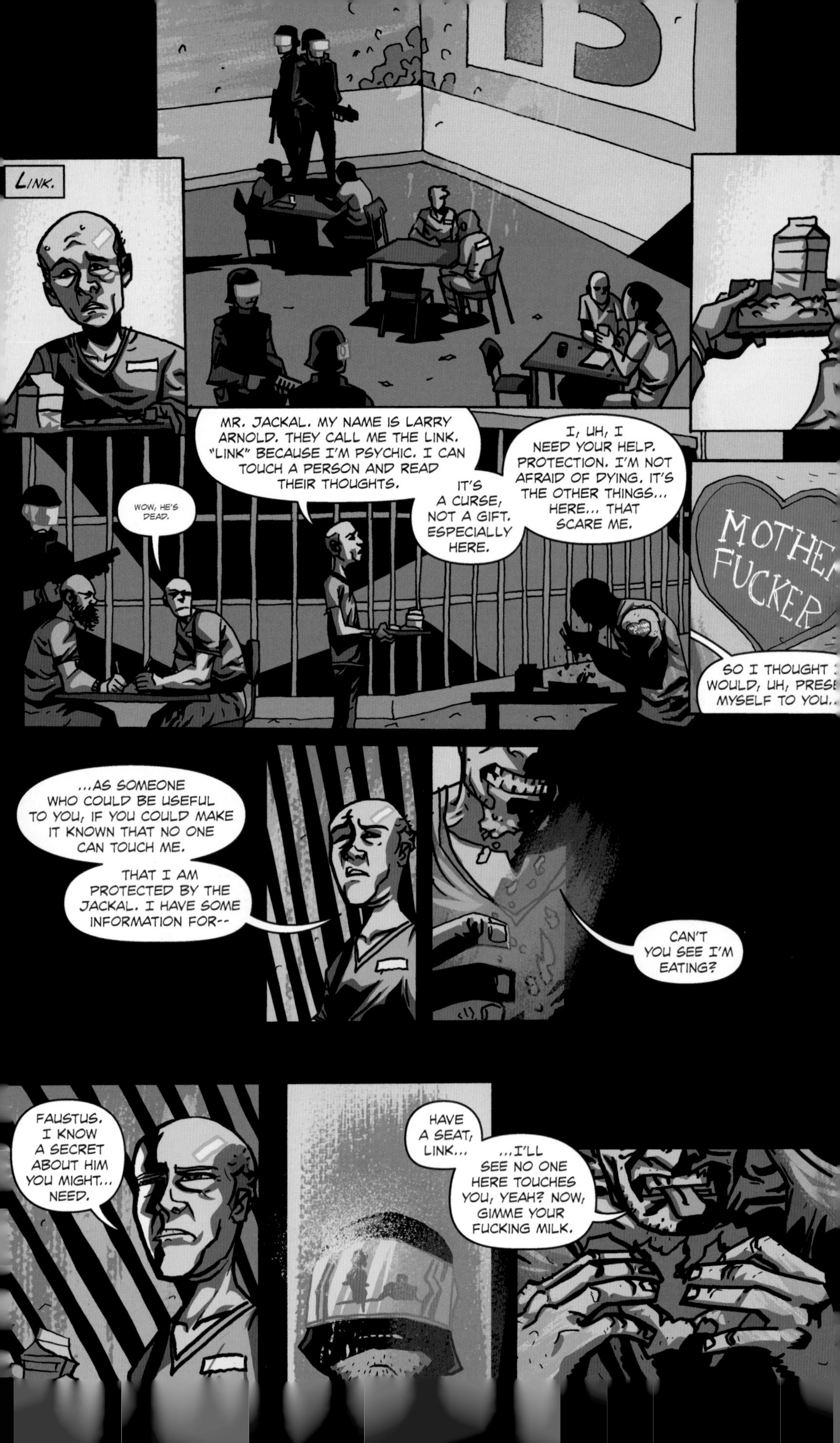
LINK.
WOW, HE'S DEAD.
MR. JACKAL. MY NAME IS LARRY ARNOLD. THEY CALL ME THE LINK. "LINK" BECAUSE I'M PSYCHIC. I CAN TOUCH A PERSON AND READ THEIR THOUGHTS.
IT'S A CURSE, NOT A GIFT. ESPECIALLY HERE.
I, UH, I NEED YOUR HELP. PROTECTION. I'M NOT AFRAID OF DYING. IT'S THE OTHER THINGS... HERE... THAT SCARE ME.
MOTHE
FUCKER
SO I THOUGHT I WOULD, UH, PRESE MYSELF TO YOU...
...AS SOMEONE WHO COULD BE USEFUL TO YOU, IF YOU COULD MAKE IT KNOWN THAT NO ONE CAN TOUCH ME.
THAT I AM PROTECTED BY THE JACKAL. I HAVE SOME INFORMATION FOR--
CAN'T YOU SEE I'M EATING?
FAUSTUS. I KNOW A SECRET ABOUT HIM YOU MIGHT... NEED.
HAVE A SEAT, LINK...
...I'LL SEE NO ONE HERE TOUCHES YOU, YEAH? NOW, GIMME YOUR FUCKING MILK.

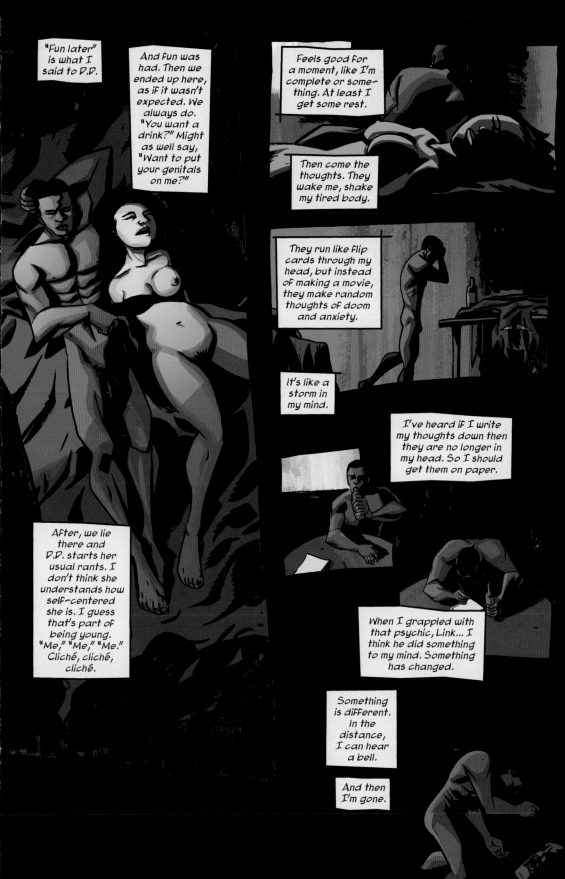

"Fun later" is what I said to D.D.

And Fun was had. Then we ended up here, as if it wasn't expected. We always do. "You want a drink?" Might as well say, "Want to put your genitals on me?"

Feels good for a moment, like I'm complete or something. At least I get some rest.

Then come the thoughts. They wake me, shake my tired body.

They run like flip cards through my head, but instead of making a movie, they make random thoughts of doom and anxiety.

It's like a storm in my mind.

I've heard if I write my thoughts down then they are no longer in my head. So I should get them on paper.

After, we lie there and D.D. starts her usual rants. I don't think she understands how self-centered she is. I guess that's part of being young. "Me," "Me," "Me." Cliché, cliché, cliché.

When I grappled with that psychic, Link... I think he did something to my mind. Something has changed.

Something is different. In the distance, I can hear a bell.

And then I'm gone.

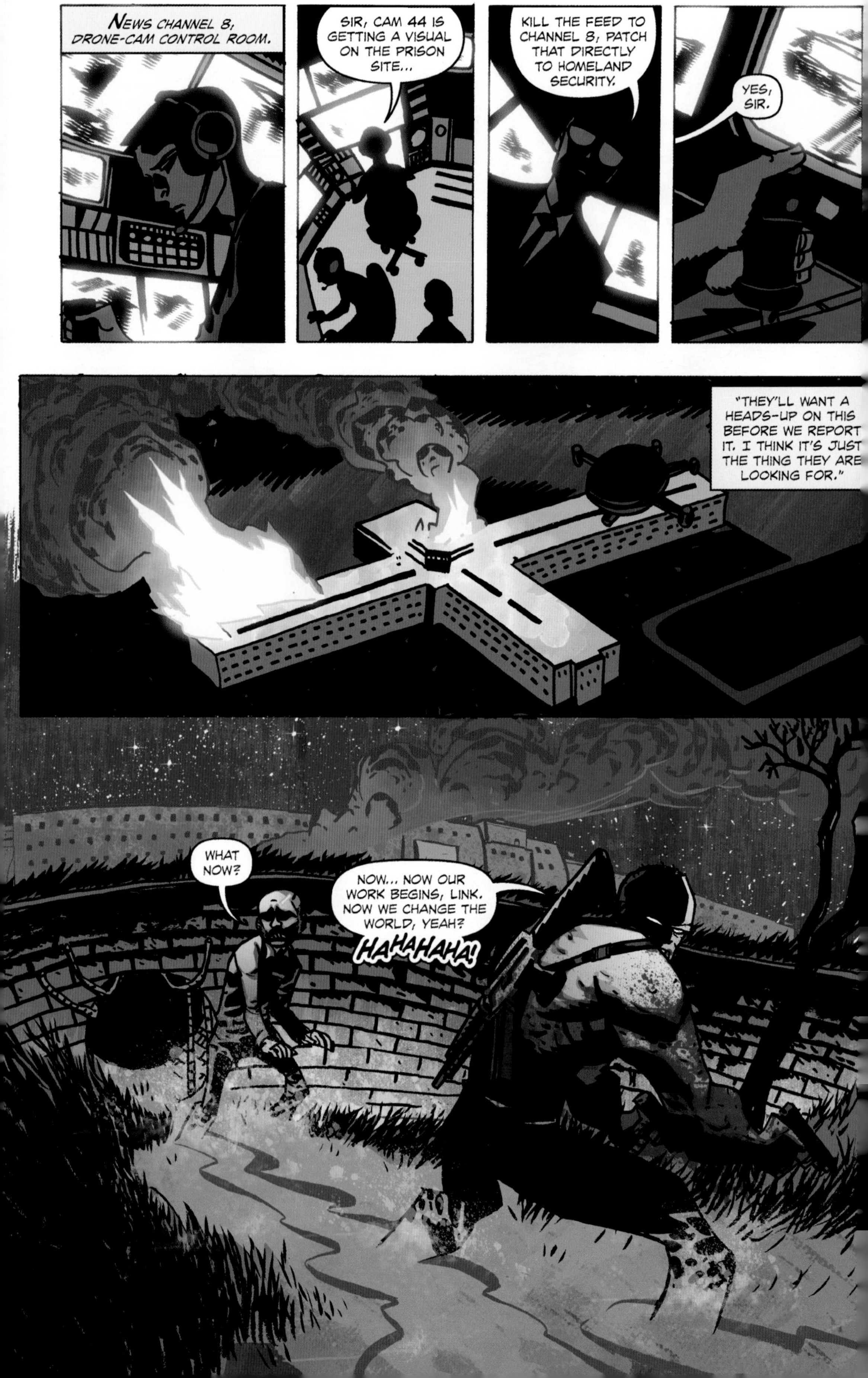

NEWS CHANNEL 8, DRONE-CAM CONTROL ROOM.
SIR, CAM 44 IS GETTING A VISUAL ON THE PRISON SITE...
KILL THE FEED TO CHANNEL 8, PATCH THAT DIRECTLY TO HOMELAND SECURITY.
YES, SIR.
"THEY'LL WANT A HEADS-UP ON THIS BEFORE WE REPORT IT. I THINK IT'S JUST THE THING THEY ARE LOOKING FOR."
WHAT NOW?
NOW... NOW OUR WORK BEGINS, LINK. NOW WE CHANGE THE WORLD, YEAH?
HAHAHAHA!

CHAPTER THREE

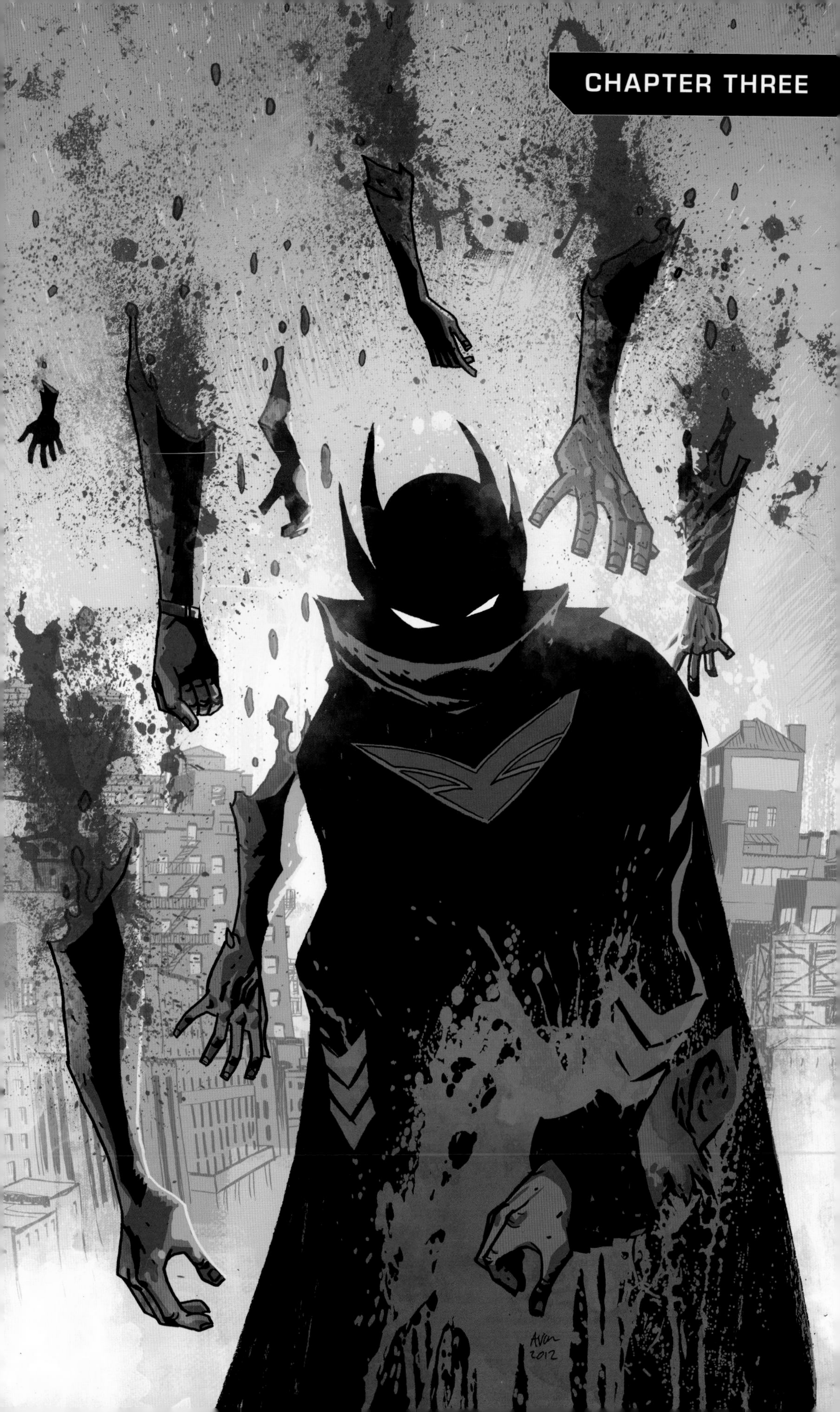

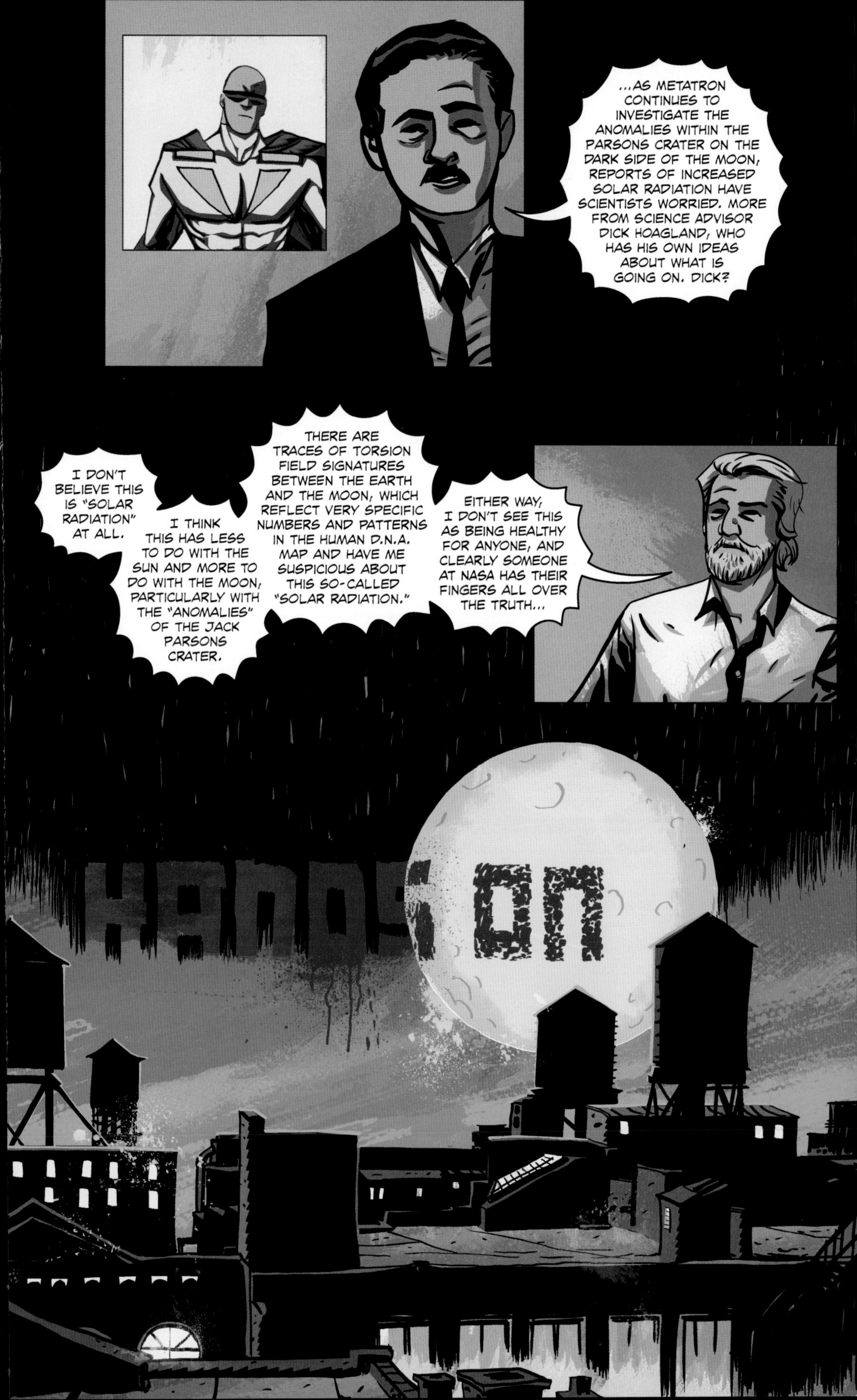
...AS METATRON CONTINUES TO INVESTIGATE THE ANOMALIES WITHIN THE PARSONS CRATER ON THE DARK SIDE OF THE MOON, REPORTS OF INCREASED SOLAR RADIATION HAVE SCIENTISTS WORRIED. MORE FROM SCIENCE ADVISOR DICK HOAGLAND, WHO HAS HIS OWN IDEAS ABOUT WHAT IS GOING ON. DICK?
I DON'T BELIEVE THIS IS "SOLAR RADIATION" AT ALL.
I THINK THIS HAS LESS TO DO WITH THE SUN AND MORE TO DO WITH THE MOON, PARTICULARLY WITH THE "ANOMALIES" OF THE JACK PARSONS CRATER.
THERE ARE TRACES OF TORSION FIELD SIGNATURES BETWEEN THE EARTH AND THE MOON, WHICH REFLECT VERY SPECIFIC NUMBERS AND PATTERNS IN THE HUMAN D.N.A. MAP AND HAVE ME SUSPICIOUS ABOUT THIS SO-CALLED "SOLAR RADIATION."
EITHER WAY, I DON'T SEE THIS AS BEING HEALTHY FOR ANYONE, AND CLEARLY SOMEONE AT NASA HAS THEIR FINGERS ALL OVER THE TRUTH...
HANDS ON

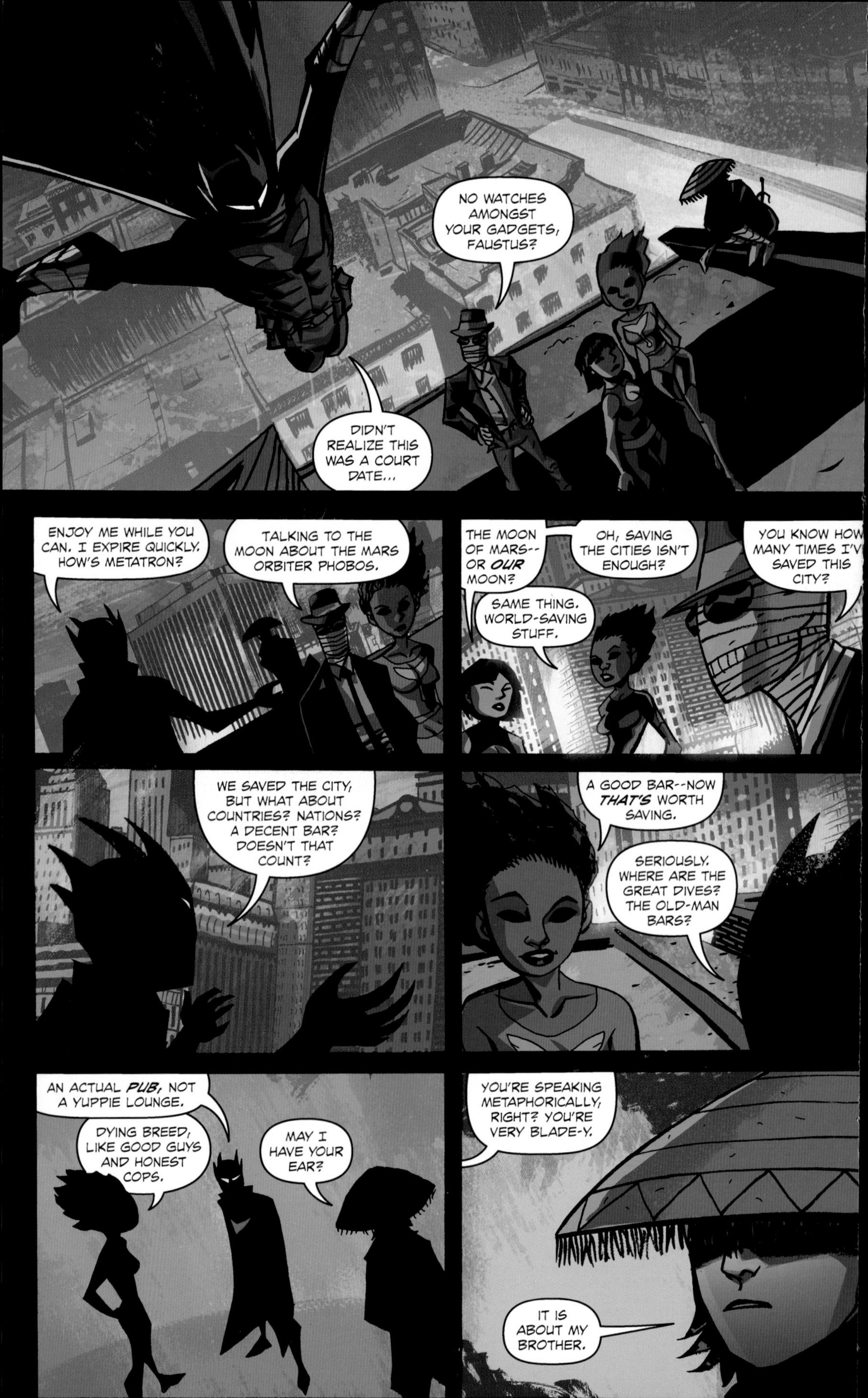
NO WATCHES AMONGST YOUR GADGETS, FAUSTUS?
DIDN'T REALIZE THIS WAS A COURT DATE...
ENJOY ME WHILE YOU CAN. I EXPIRE QUICKLY. HOW'S METATRON?
TALKING TO THE MOON ABOUT THE MARS ORBITER PHOBOS.
THE MOON OF MARS-- OR *OUR* MOON?
OH, SAVING THE CITIES ISN'T ENOUGH?
SAME THING. WORLD-SAVING STUFF.
YOU KNOW HOW MANY TIMES I'VE SAVED THIS CITY?
WE SAVED THE CITY, BUT WHAT ABOUT COUNTRIES? NATIONS? A DECENT BAR? DOESN'T THAT COUNT?
A GOOD BAR--NOW *THAT'S* WORTH SAVING.
SERIOUSLY. WHERE ARE THE GREAT DIVES? THE OLD-MAN BARS?
AN ACTUAL *PUB*, NOT A YUPPIE LOUNGE.
DYING BREED, LIKE GOOD GUYS AND HONEST COPS.
MAY I HAVE YOUR EAR?
YOU'RE SPEAKING METAPHORICALLY, RIGHT? YOU'RE VERY BLADE-Y.
IT IS ABOUT MY BROTHER.

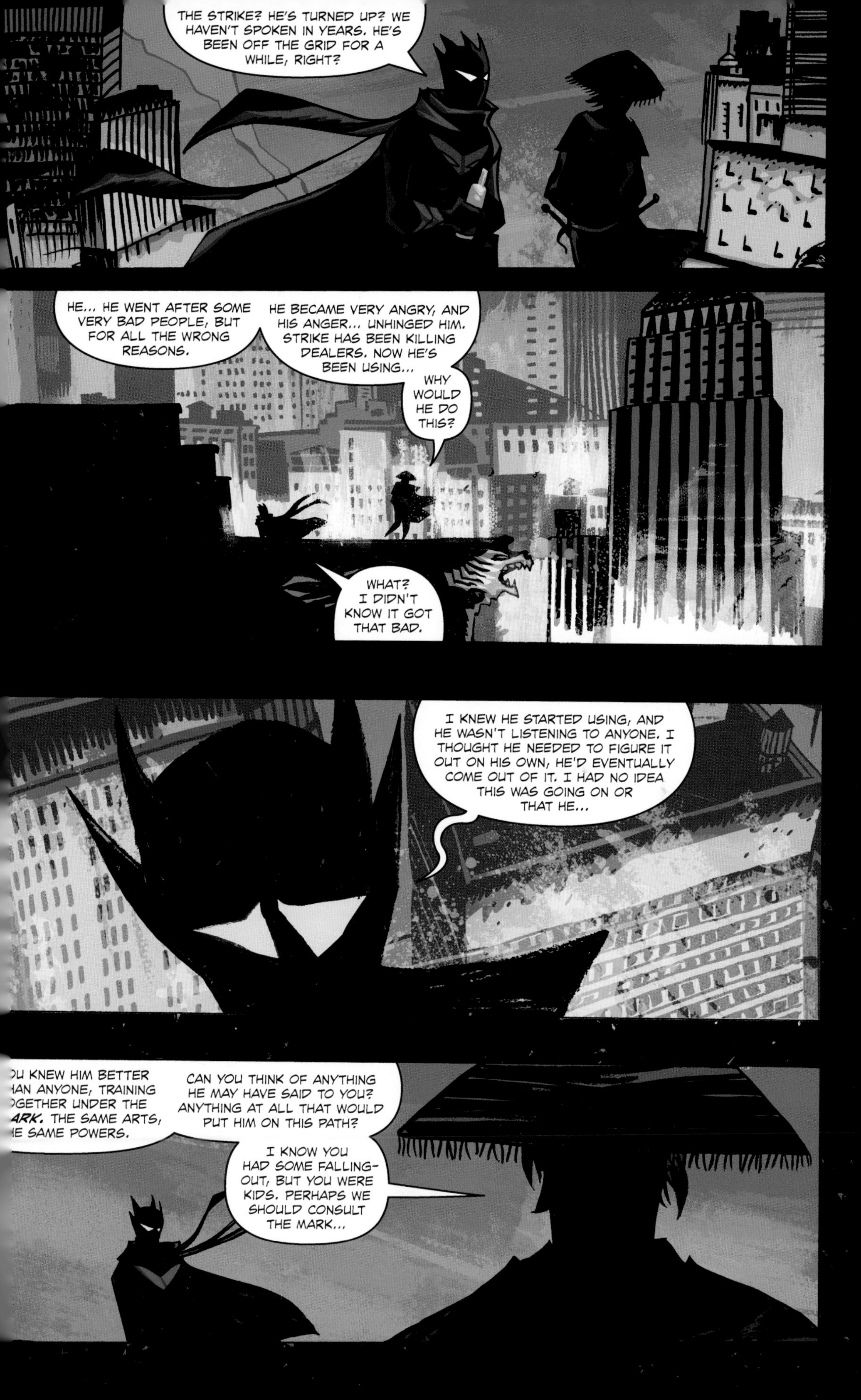
THE STRIKE? HE'S TURNED UP? WE HAVEN'T SPOKEN IN YEARS. HE'S BEEN OFF THE GRID FOR A WHILE, RIGHT?
HE... HE WENT AFTER SOME VERY BAD PEOPLE, BUT FOR ALL THE WRONG REASONS.
HE BECAME VERY ANGRY, AND HIS ANGER... UNHINGED HIM. STRIKE HAS BEEN KILLING DEALERS. NOW HE'S BEEN USING...
WHY WOULD HE DO THIS?
WHAT? I DIDN'T KNOW IT GOT THAT BAD.
I KNEW HE STARTED USING, AND HE WASN'T LISTENING TO ANYONE. I THOUGHT HE NEEDED TO FIGURE IT OUT ON HIS OWN, HE'D EVENTUALLY COME OUT OF IT. I HAD NO IDEA THIS WAS GOING ON OR THAT HE...
CAN YOU THINK OF ANYTHING HE MAY HAVE SAID TO YOU? ANYTHING AT ALL THAT WOULD PUT HIM ON THIS PATH?
I KNOW YOU HAD SOME FALLING-OUT, BUT YOU WERE KIDS. PERHAPS WE SHOULD CONSULT THE MARK...

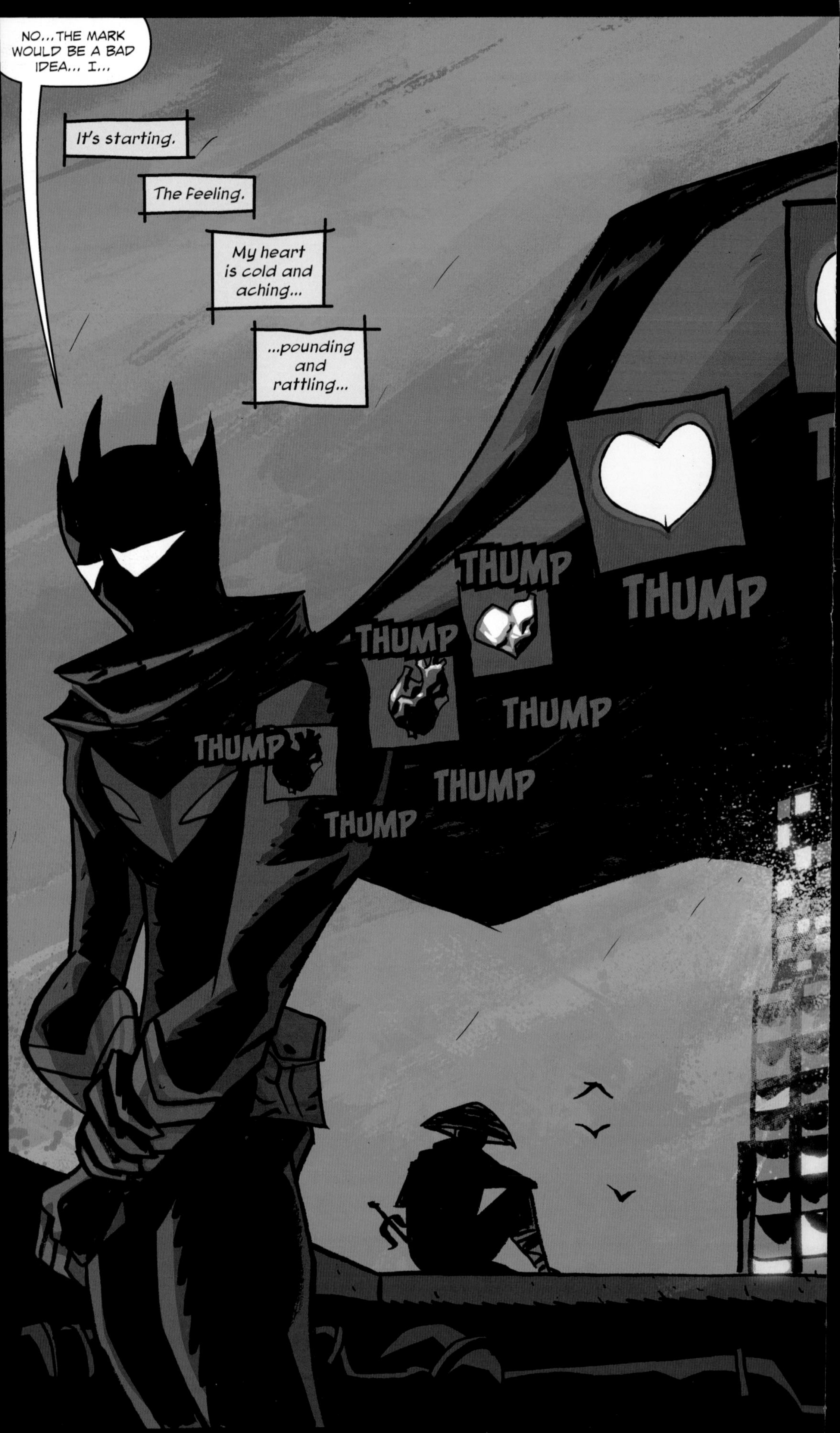
NO... THE MARK WOULD BE A BAD IDEA... I...
It's starting.
The feeling.
My heart is cold and aching...
...pounding and rattling...
THUMP
THUMP
THUMP
THUMP
THUMP
THUMP
THUMP

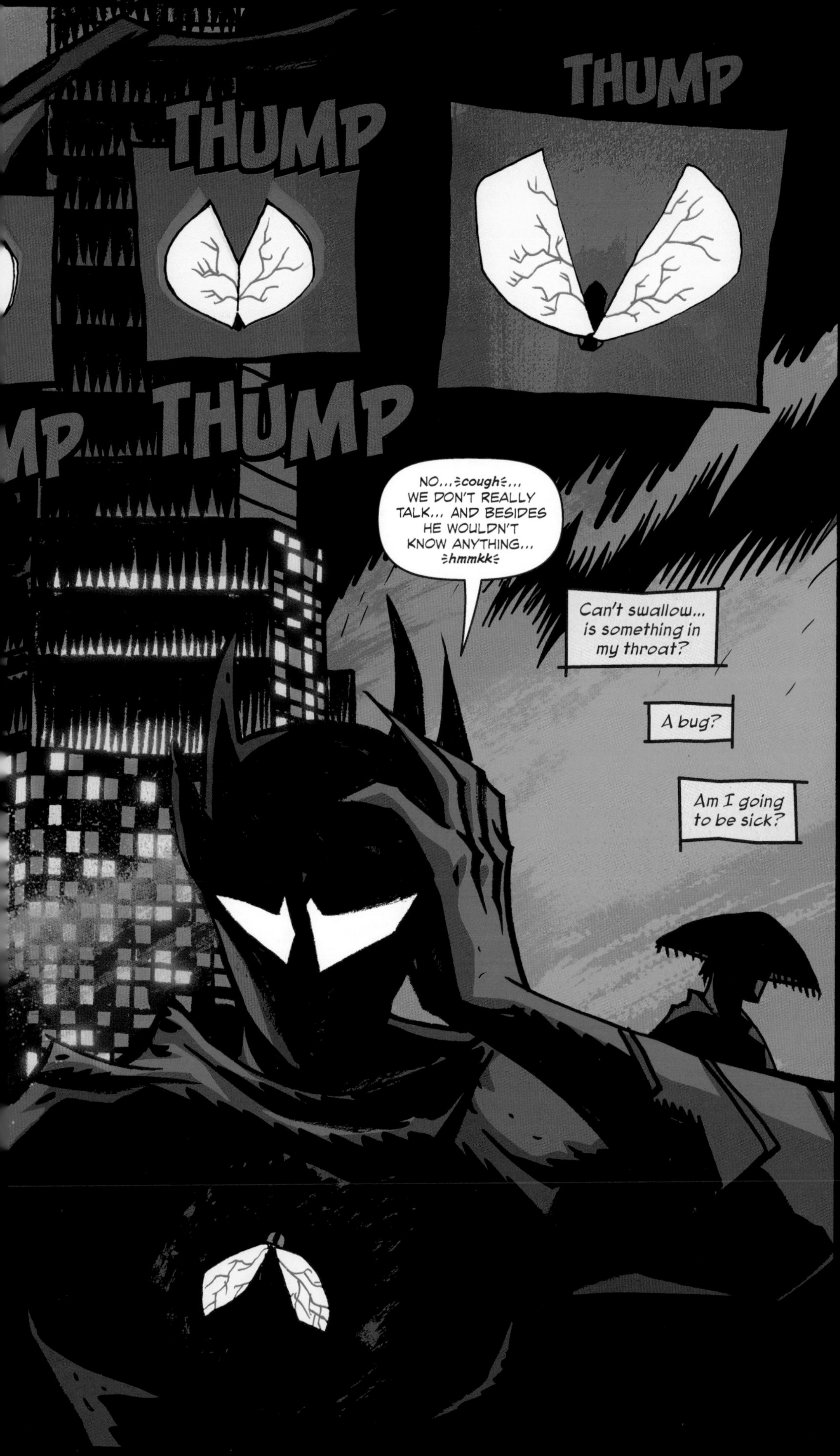
THUMP
THUMP
THUMP
MP
NO... ≷cough≷... WE DON'T REALLY TALK... AND BESIDES HE WOULDN'T KNOW ANYTHING... ≷hmmkk≷
Can't swallow... is something in my throat?
A bug?
Am I going to be sick?

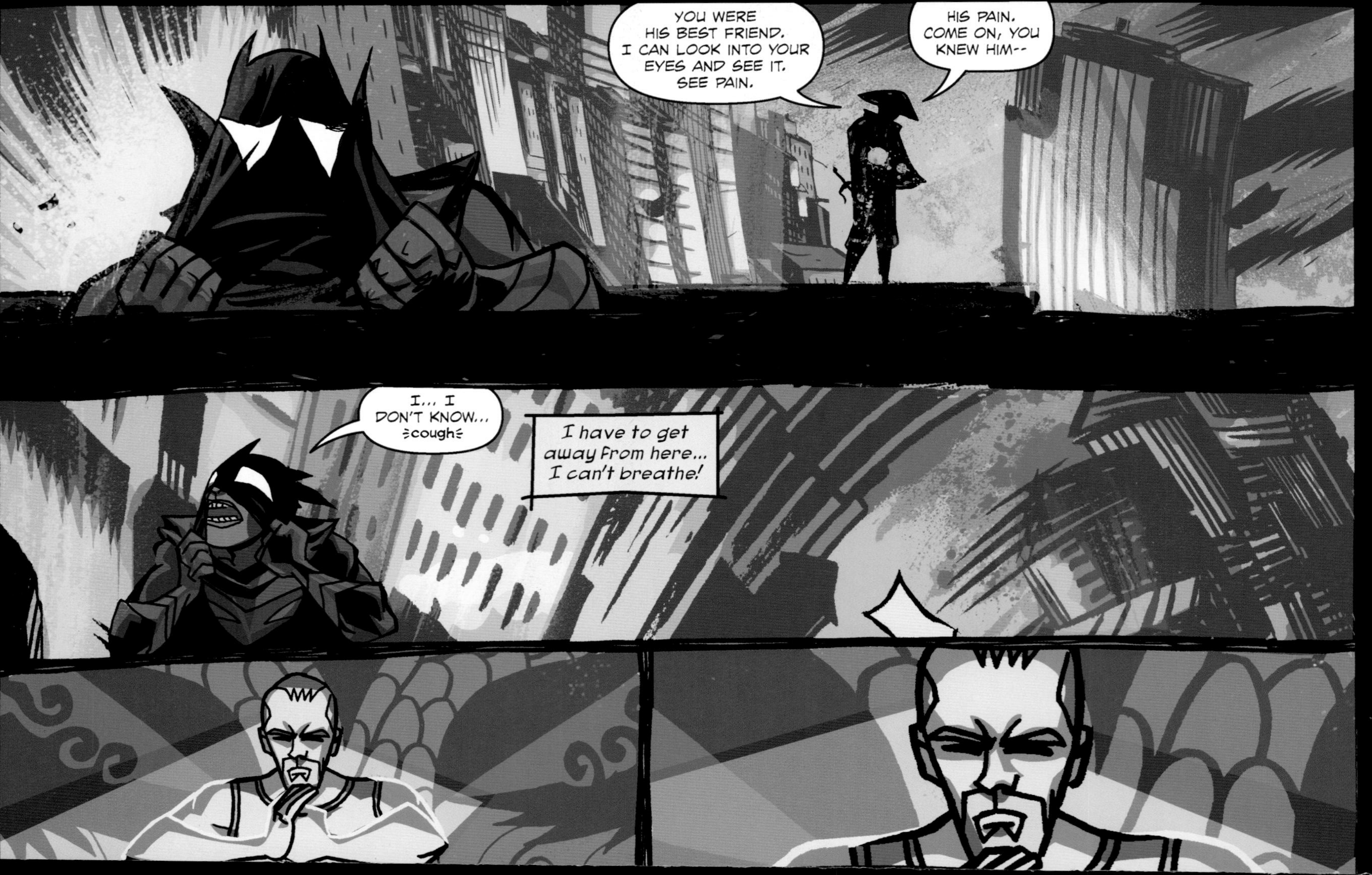
YOU WERE HIS BEST FRIEND. I CAN LOOK INTO YOUR EYES AND SEE IT. SEE PAIN.
HIS PAIN. COME ON, YOU KNEW HIM--
I... I DON'T KNOW... ≈cough≈
I have to get away from here... I can't breathe!

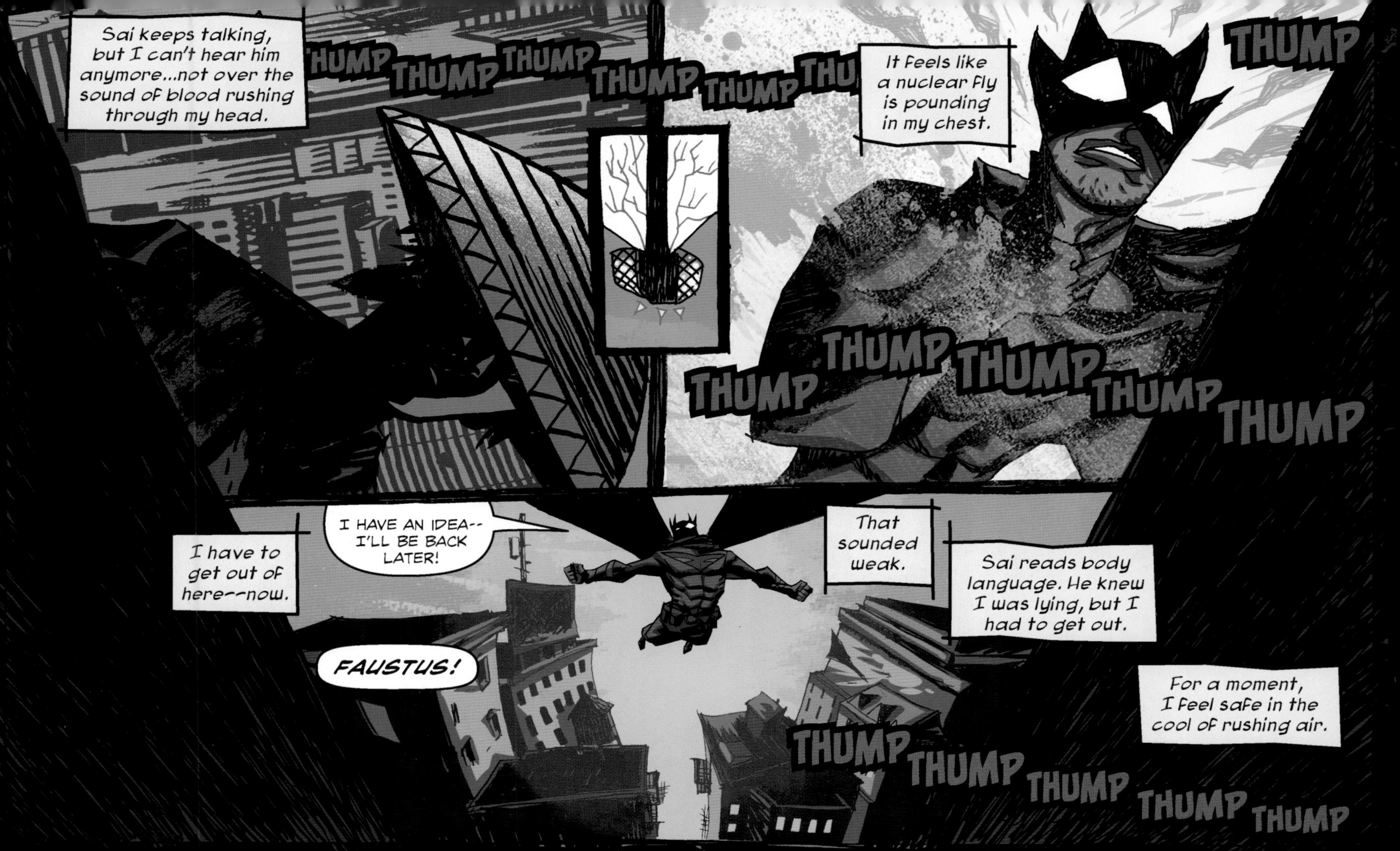
Sai keeps talking, but I can't hear him anymore...not over the sound of blood rushing through my head.
HUMP THUMP THUMP THUMP THUMP THU
It feels like a nuclear fly is pounding in my chest.
THUMP
THUMP THUMP THUMP THUMP THUMP
I have to get out of here--now.
I HAVE AN IDEA-- I'LL BE BACK LATER!
FAUSTUS!
That sounded weak.
Sai reads body language. He knew I was lying, but I had to get out.
For a moment, I feel safe in the cool of rushing air.
THUMP THUMP THUMP THUMP THUMP

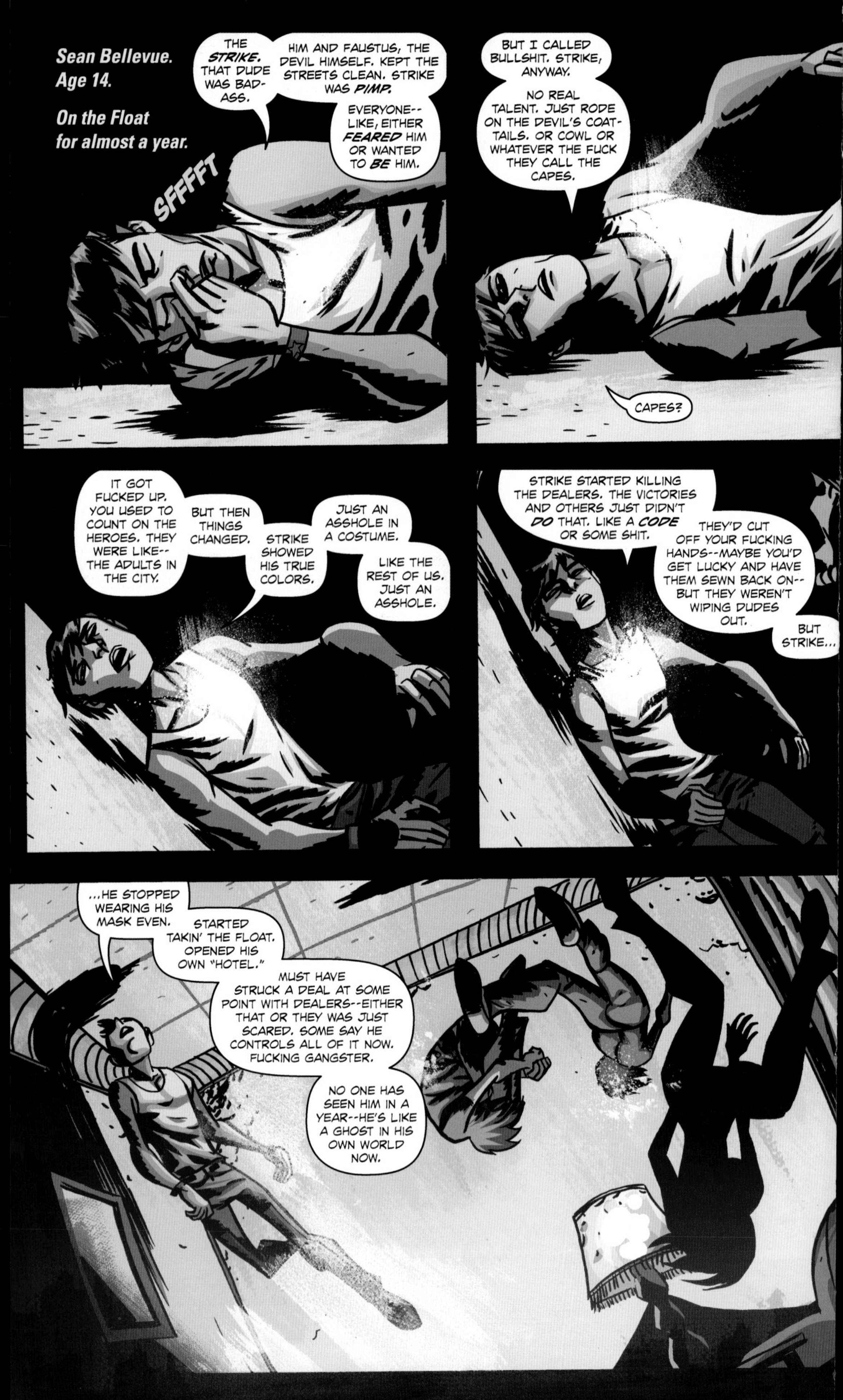

Sean Bellevue.
Age 14.
On the Float for almost a year.
THE STRIKE. THAT DUDE WAS BAD-ASS.
HIM AND FAUSTUS, THE DEVIL HIMSELF. KEPT THE STREETS CLEAN. STRIKE WAS PIMP.
EVERYONE--LIKE, EITHER FEARED HIM OR WANTED TO BE HIM.
SFFFFT
BUT I CALLED BULLSHIT. STRIKE, ANYWAY.
NO REAL TALENT. JUST RODE ON THE DEVIL'S COAT-TAILS. OR COWL OR WHATEVER THE FUCK THEY CALL THE CAPES.
CAPES?
IT GOT FUCKED UP. YOU USED TO COUNT ON THE HEROES. THEY WERE LIKE--THE ADULTS IN THE CITY.
BUT THEN THINGS CHANGED.
STRIKE SHOWED HIS TRUE COLORS.
JUST AN ASSHOLE IN A COSTUME.
LIKE THE REST OF US. JUST AN ASSHOLE.
STRIKE STARTED KILLING THE DEALERS. THE VICTORIES AND OTHERS JUST DIDN'T DO THAT. LIKE A CODE OR SOME SHIT.
THEY'D CUT OFF YOUR FUCKING HANDS--MAYBE YOU'D GET LUCKY AND HAVE THEM SEWN BACK ON--BUT THEY WEREN'T WIPING DUDES OUT.
BUT STRIKE...
...HE STOPPED WEARING HIS MASK EVEN.
STARTED TAKIN' THE FLOAT. OPENED HIS OWN "HOTEL."
MUST HAVE STRUCK A DEAL AT SOME POINT WITH DEALERS--EITHER THAT OR THEY WAS JUST SCARED. SOME SAY HE CONTROLS ALL OF IT NOW. FUCKING GANGSTER.
NO ONE HAS SEEN HIM IN A YEAR--HE'S LIKE A GHOST IN HIS OWN WORLD NOW.

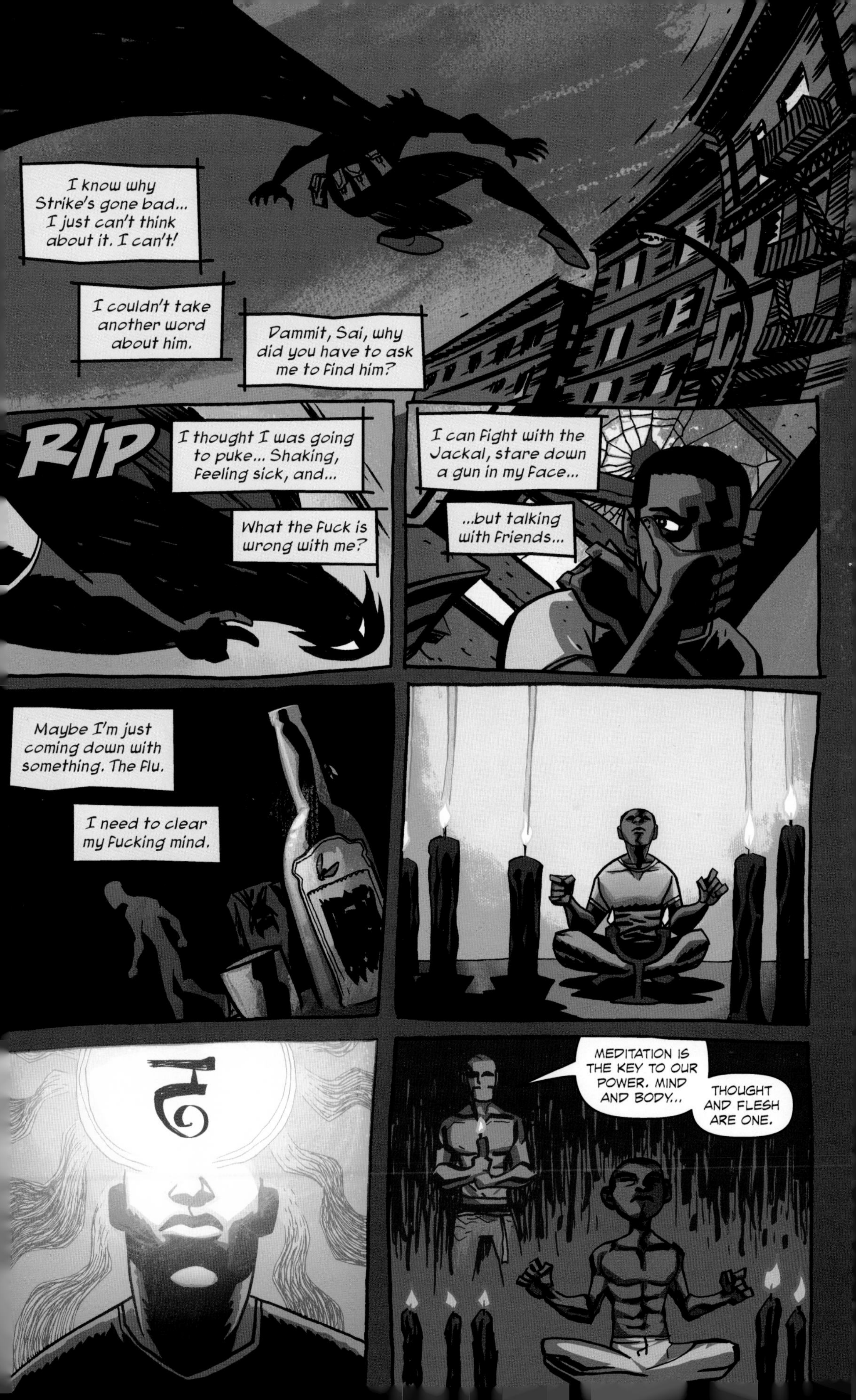
I know why Strike's gone bad... I just can't think about it. I can't!
I couldn't take another word about him.
Dammit, Sai, why did you have to ask me to find him?
RIP
I thought I was going to puke... Shaking, feeling sick, and...
What the fuck is wrong with me?
I can fight with the Jackal, stare down a gun in my face...
...but talking with friends...
Maybe I'm just coming down with something. The flu.
I need to clear my fucking mind.
MEDITATION IS THE KEY TO OUR POWER. MIND AND BODY...
THOUGHT AND FLESH ARE ONE.

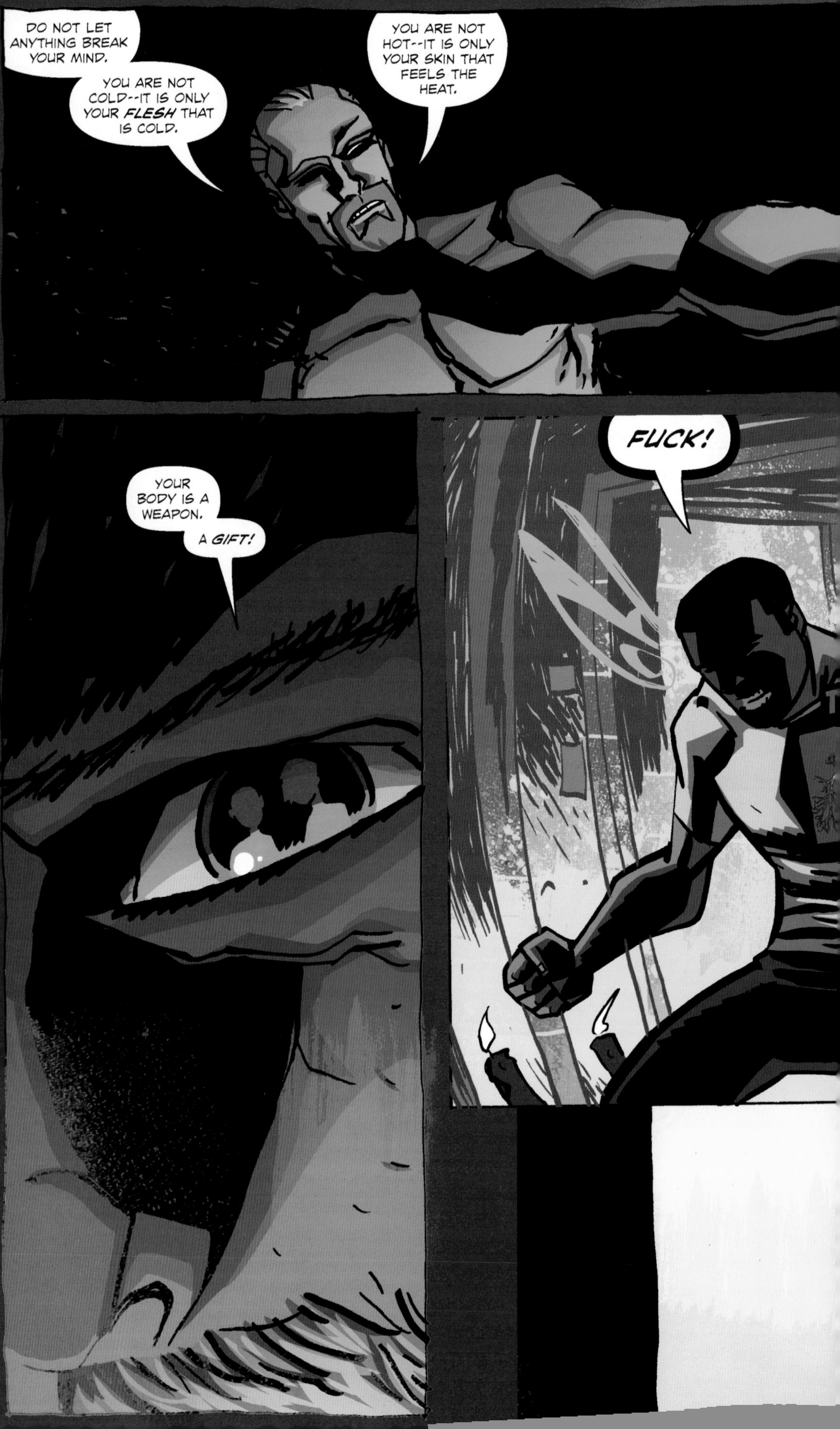
DO NOT LET ANYTHING BREAK YOUR MIND.
YOU ARE NOT COLD--IT IS ONLY YOUR FLESH THAT IS COLD.
YOU ARE NOT HOT--IT IS ONLY YOUR SKIN THAT FEELS THE HEAT.
YOUR BODY IS A WEAPON.
A GIFT!
FUCK!

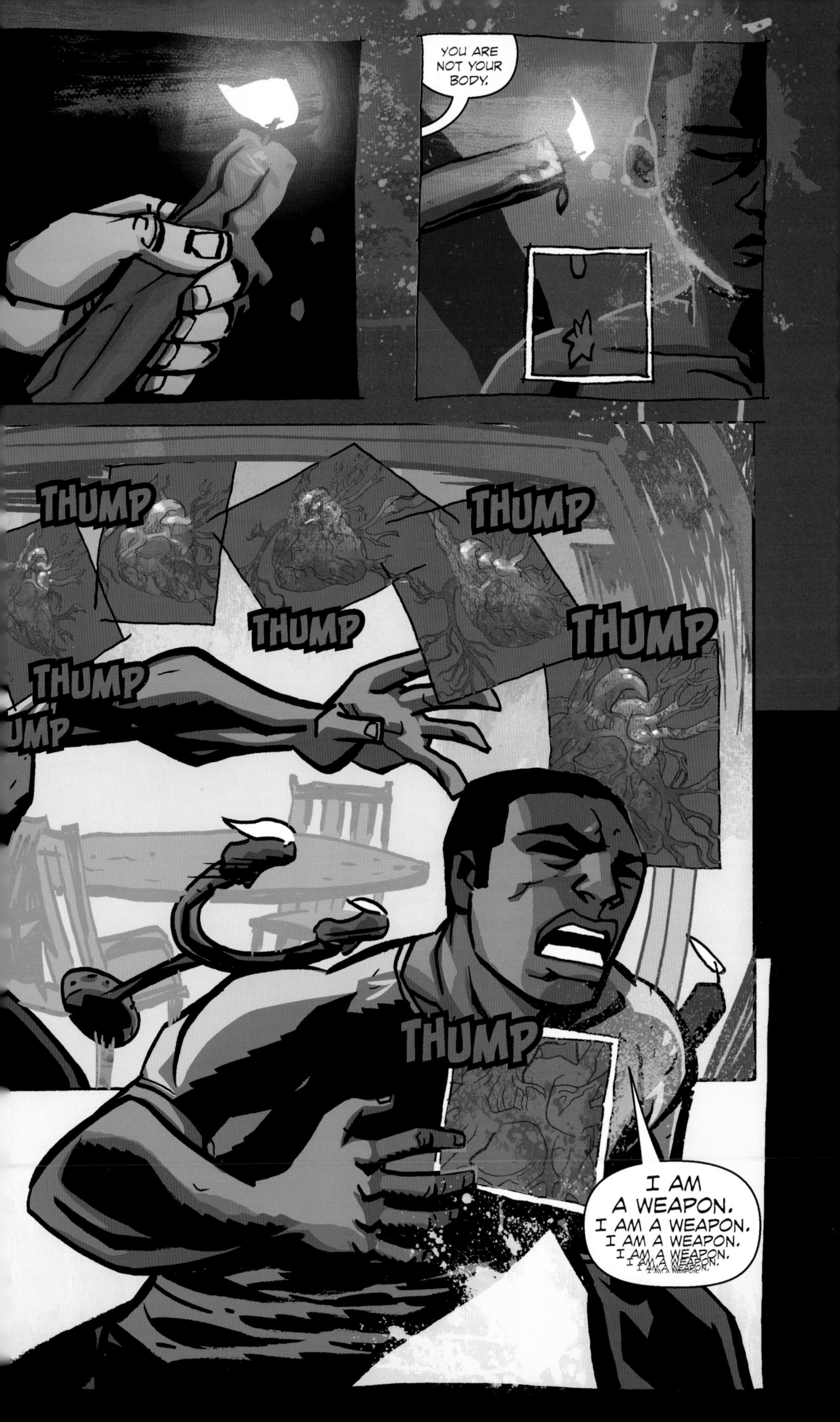
YOU ARE NOT YOUR BODY.
THUMP
THUMP
THUMP
THUMP
THUMP
UMP
THUMP
I AM A WEAPON. I AM A WEAPON. I AM A WEAPON. I AM A WEAPON.

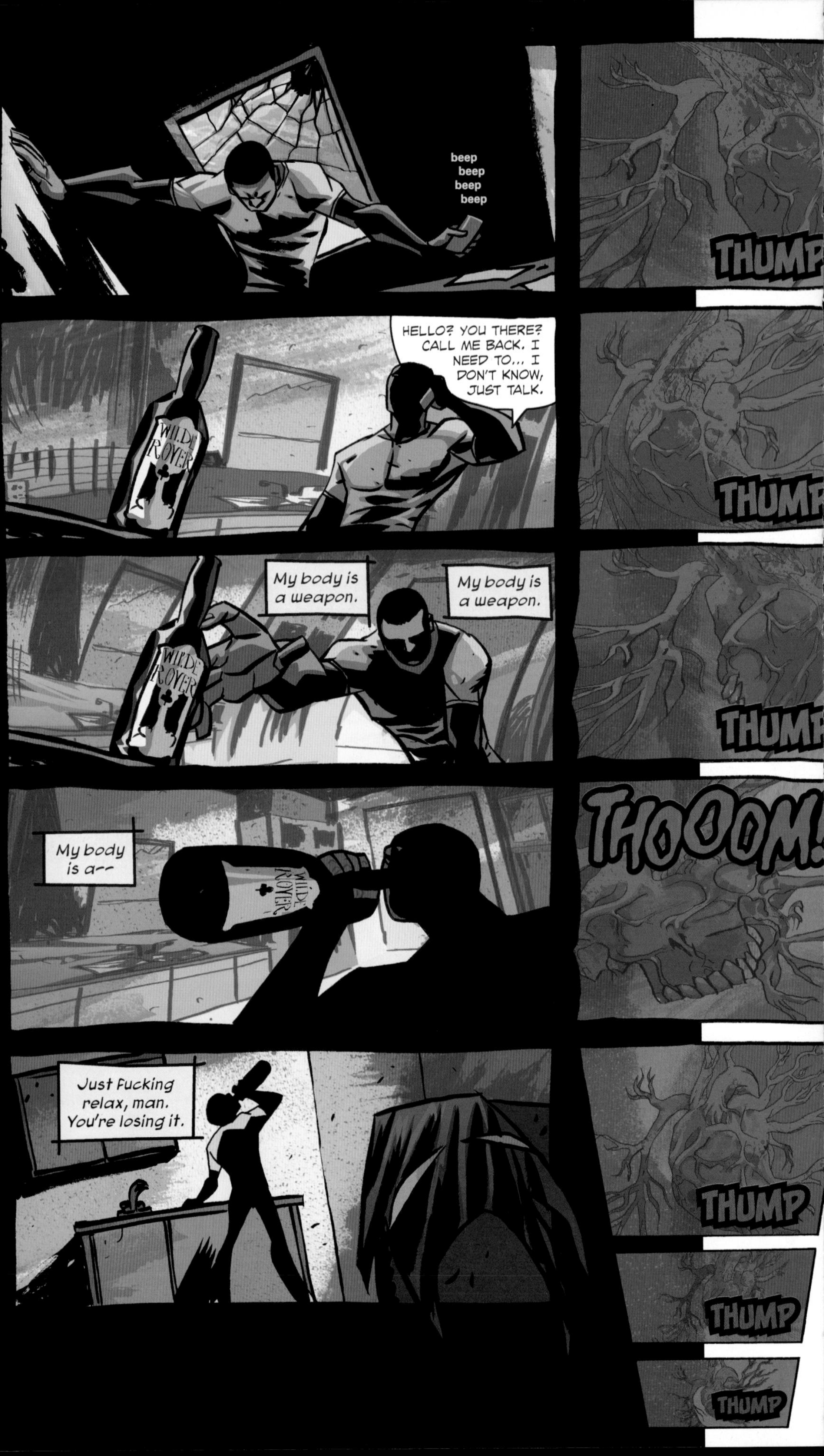

beep
beep
beep
beep
THUMP
HELLO? YOU THERE? CALL ME BACK. I NEED TO... I DON'T KNOW, JUST TALK.
WILDE ROVER
THUMP
My body is a weapon.
My body is a weapon.
WILDE ROVER
THUMP
My body is a--
WILDE ROVER
THOOOM!
Just fucking relax, man. You're losing it.
THUMP
THUMP
THUMP

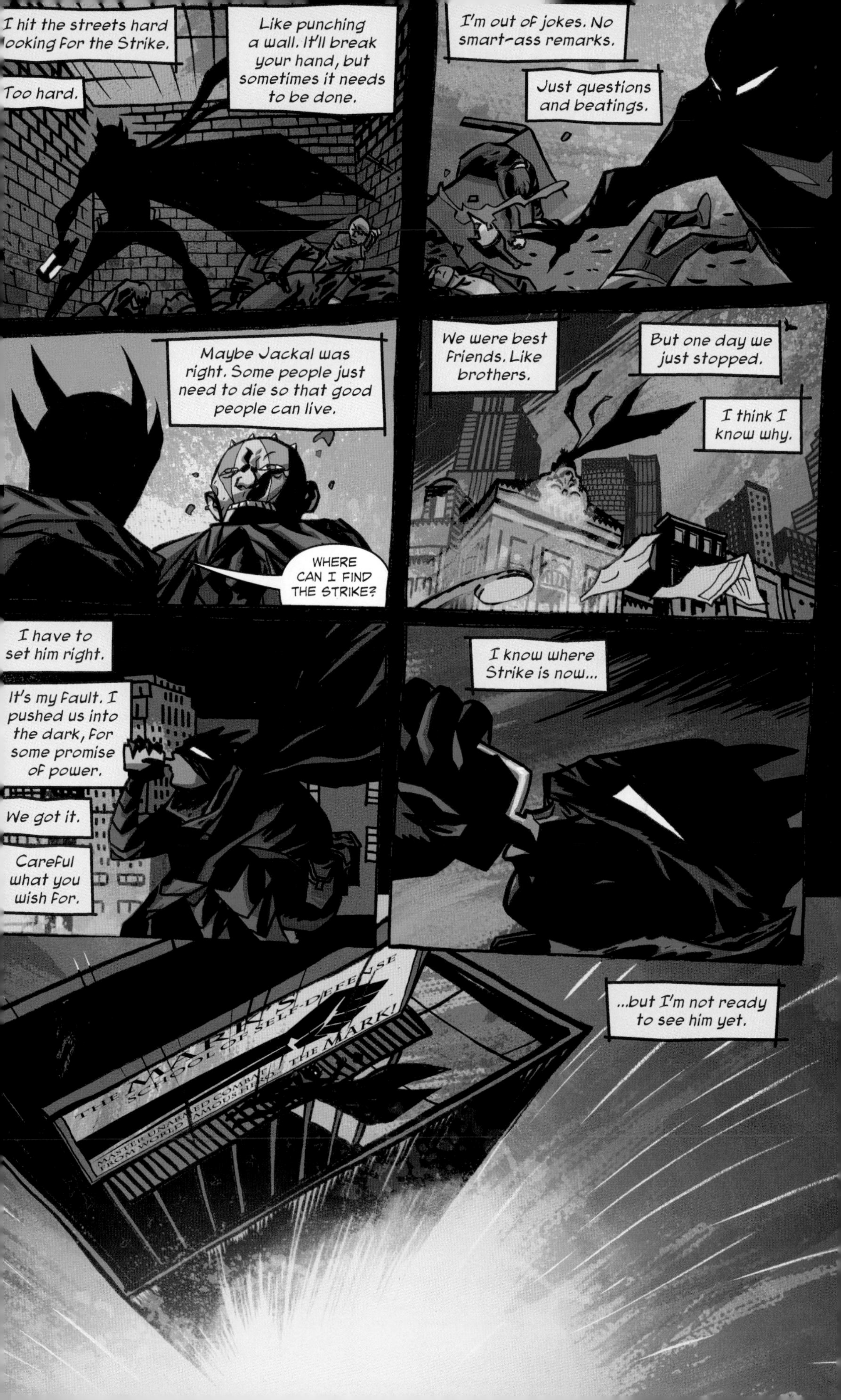
I hit the streets hard looking for the Strike.
Too hard.
Like punching a wall. It'll break your hand, but sometimes it needs to be done.
I'm out of jokes. No smart-ass remarks.
Just questions and beatings.
Maybe Jackal was right. Some people just need to die so that good people can live.
WHERE CAN I FIND THE STRIKE?
We were best friends. Like brothers.
But one day we just stopped.
I think I know why.
I have to set him right.
It's my fault. I pushed us into the dark, for some promise of power.
We got it.
Careful what you wish for.
I know where Strike is now...
...but I'm not ready to see him yet.
THE MARK'S
SCHOOL OF SELF-DEFENSE
MASTER UNARMED COMBAT
THE MARK!

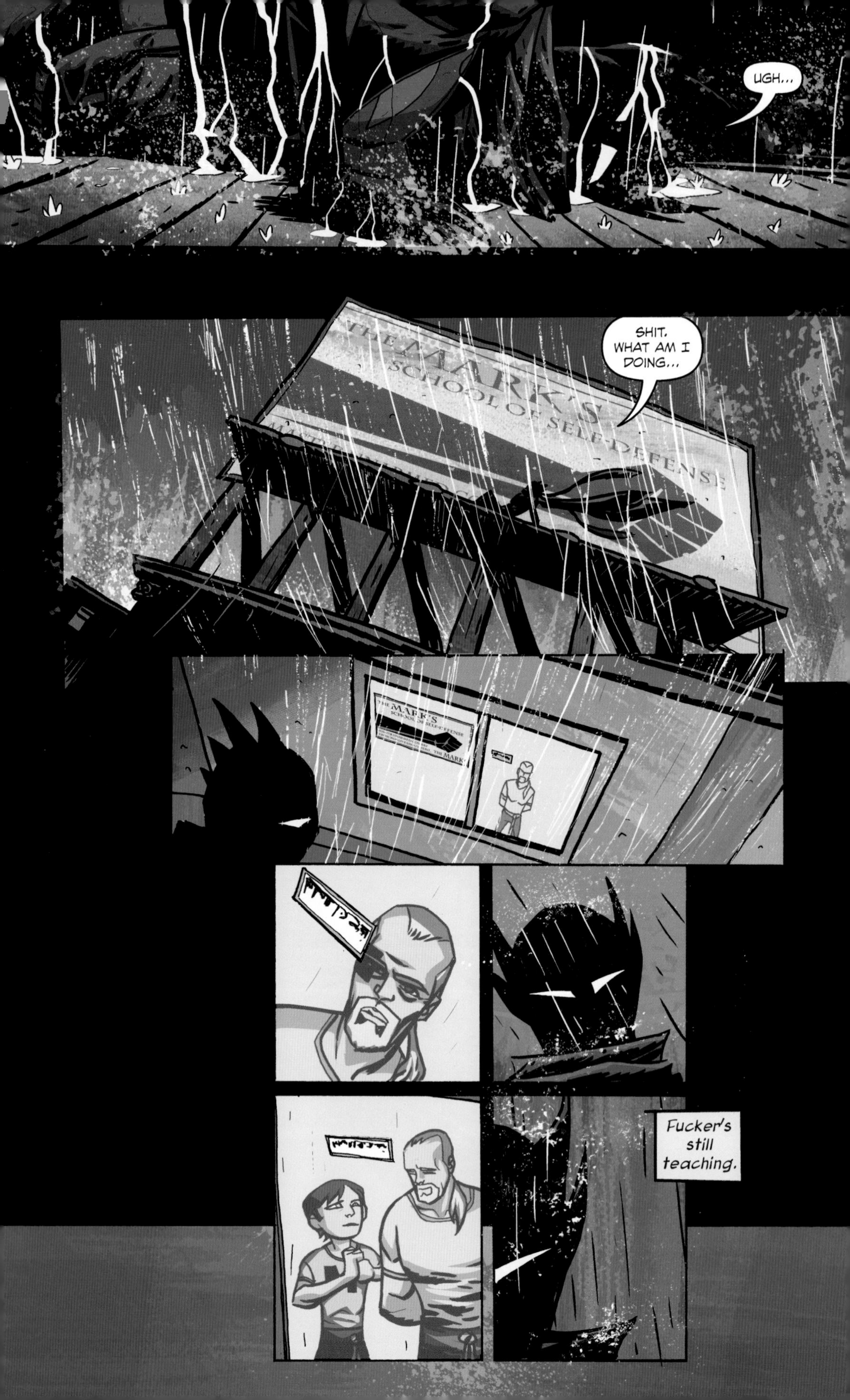
UGH...
THE MARK'S
SCHOOL OF SELF-DEFENSE
SHIT. WHAT AM I DOING...
Fucker's still teaching.

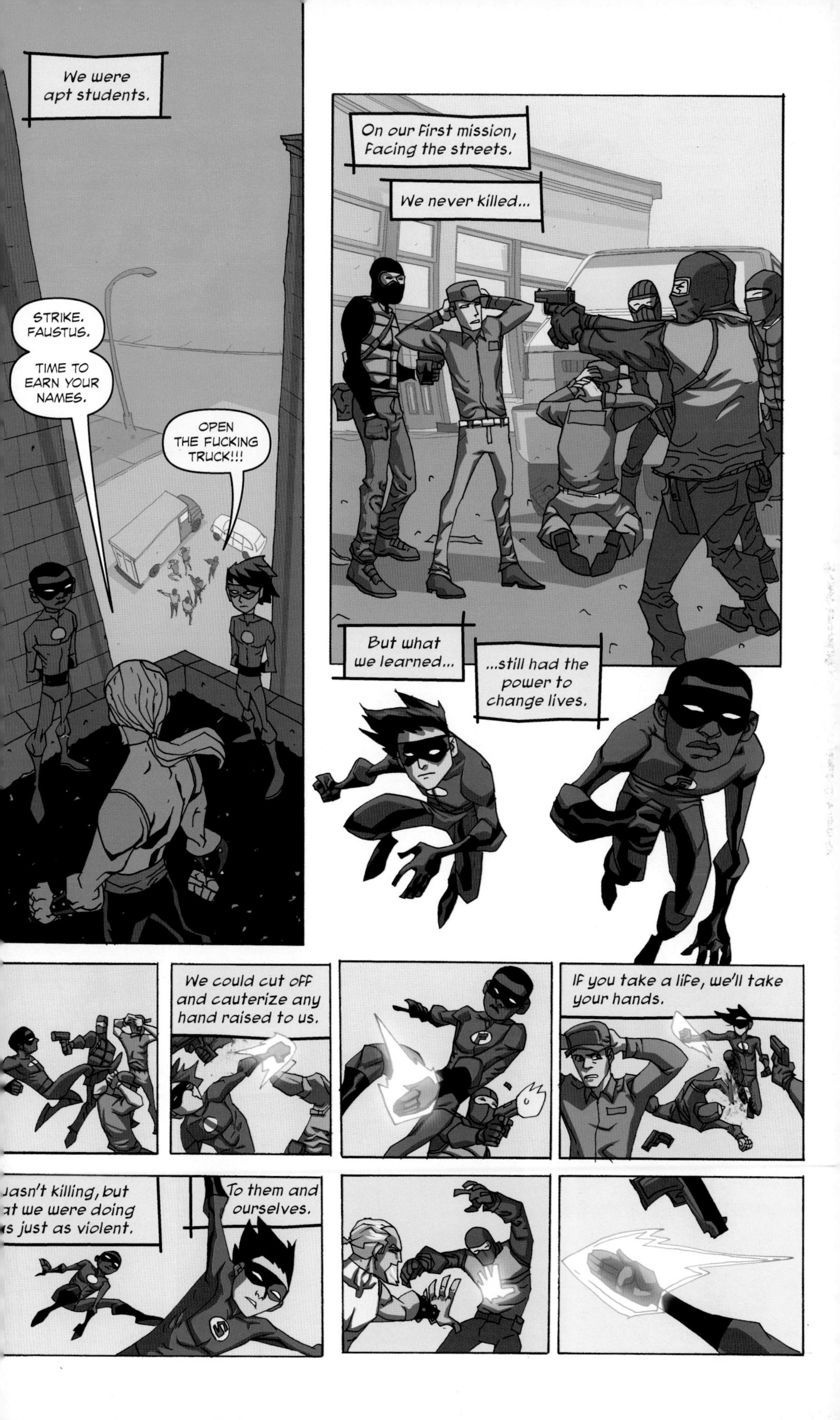

We were apt students.
STRIKE. FAUSTUS.
TIME TO EARN YOUR NAMES.
OPEN THE FUCKING TRUCK!!!
On our first mission, facing the streets.
We never killed...
But what we learned...
...still had the power to change lives.
We could cut off and cauterize any hand raised to us.
If you take a life, we'll take your hands.
asn't killing, but at we were doing s just as violent.
To them and ourselves.

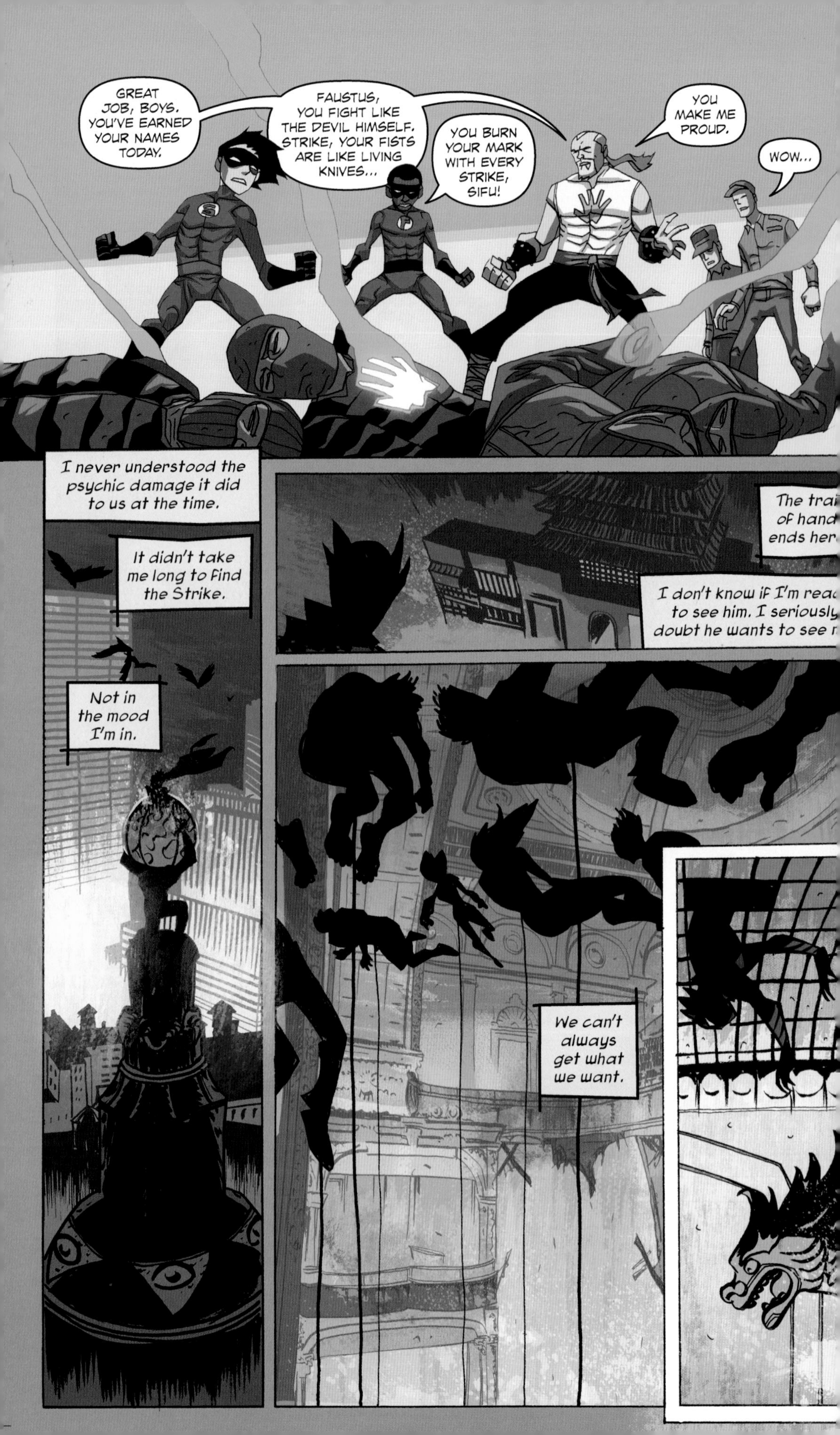
GREAT JOB, BOYS. YOU'VE EARNED YOUR NAMES TODAY.
FAUSTUS, YOU FIGHT LIKE THE DEVIL HIMSELF. STRIKE, YOUR FISTS ARE LIKE LIVING KNIVES...
YOU BURN YOUR MARK WITH EVERY STRIKE, SIFU!
YOU MAKE ME PROUD.
WOW...
I never understood the psychic damage it did to us at the time.
It didn't take me long to find the Strike.
Not in the mood I'm in.
The trai of hand ends her
I don't know if I'm rea to see him. I seriously doubt he wants to see
We can't always get what we want.

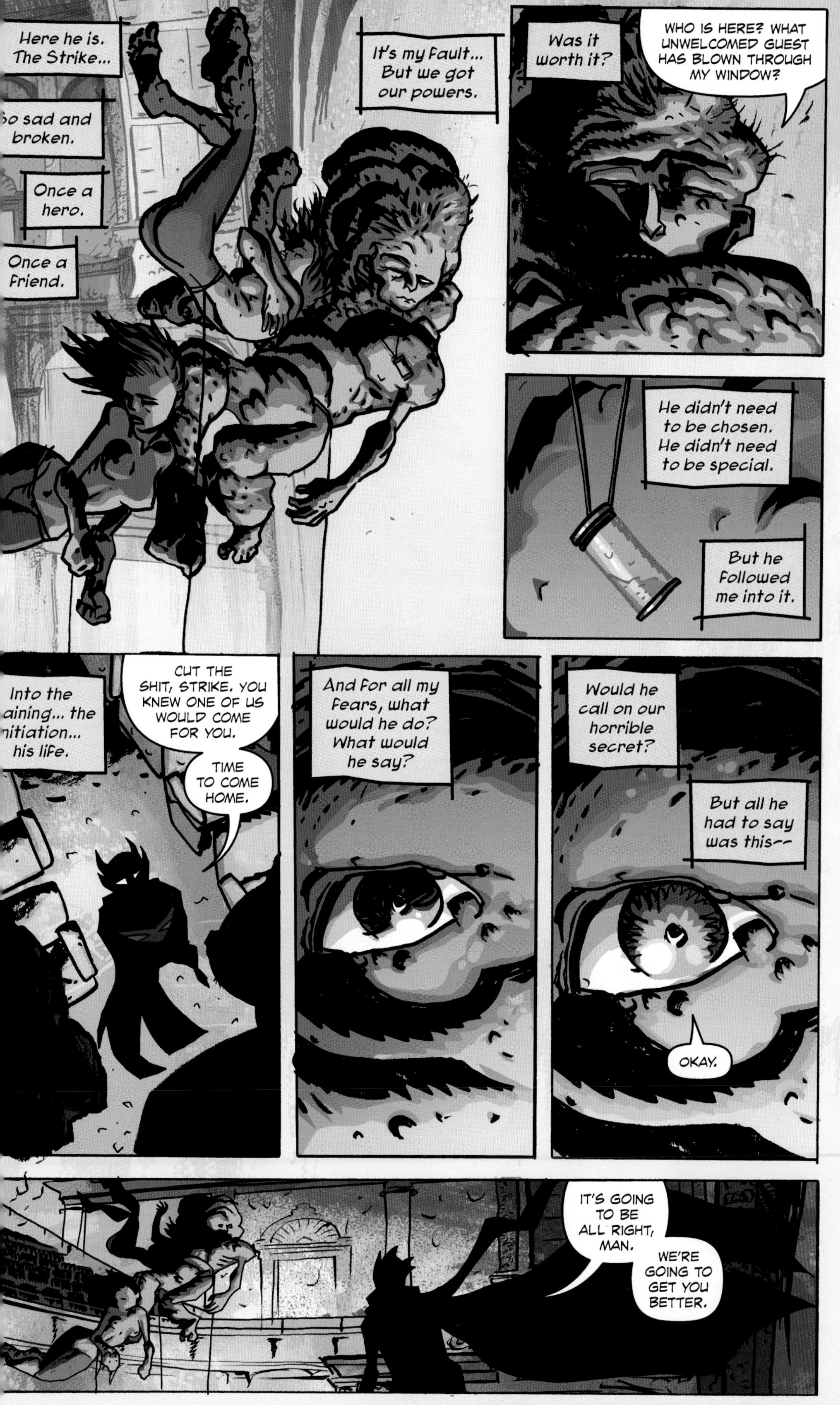

Here he is. The Strike...
So sad and broken.
Once a hero.
Once a friend.
It's my fault... But we got our powers.
Was it worth it?
WHO IS HERE? WHAT UNWELCOMED GUEST HAS BLOWN THROUGH MY WINDOW?
He didn't need to be chosen. He didn't need to be special.
But he followed me into it.
Into the aining... the nitiation... his life.
CUT THE SHIT, STRIKE. YOU KNEW ONE OF US WOULD COME FOR YOU.
TIME TO COME HOME.
And for all my fears, what would he do? What would he say?
Would he call on our horrible secret?
But all he had to say was this--
OKAY.
IT'S GOING TO BE ALL RIGHT, MAN.
WE'RE GOING TO GET YOU BETTER.

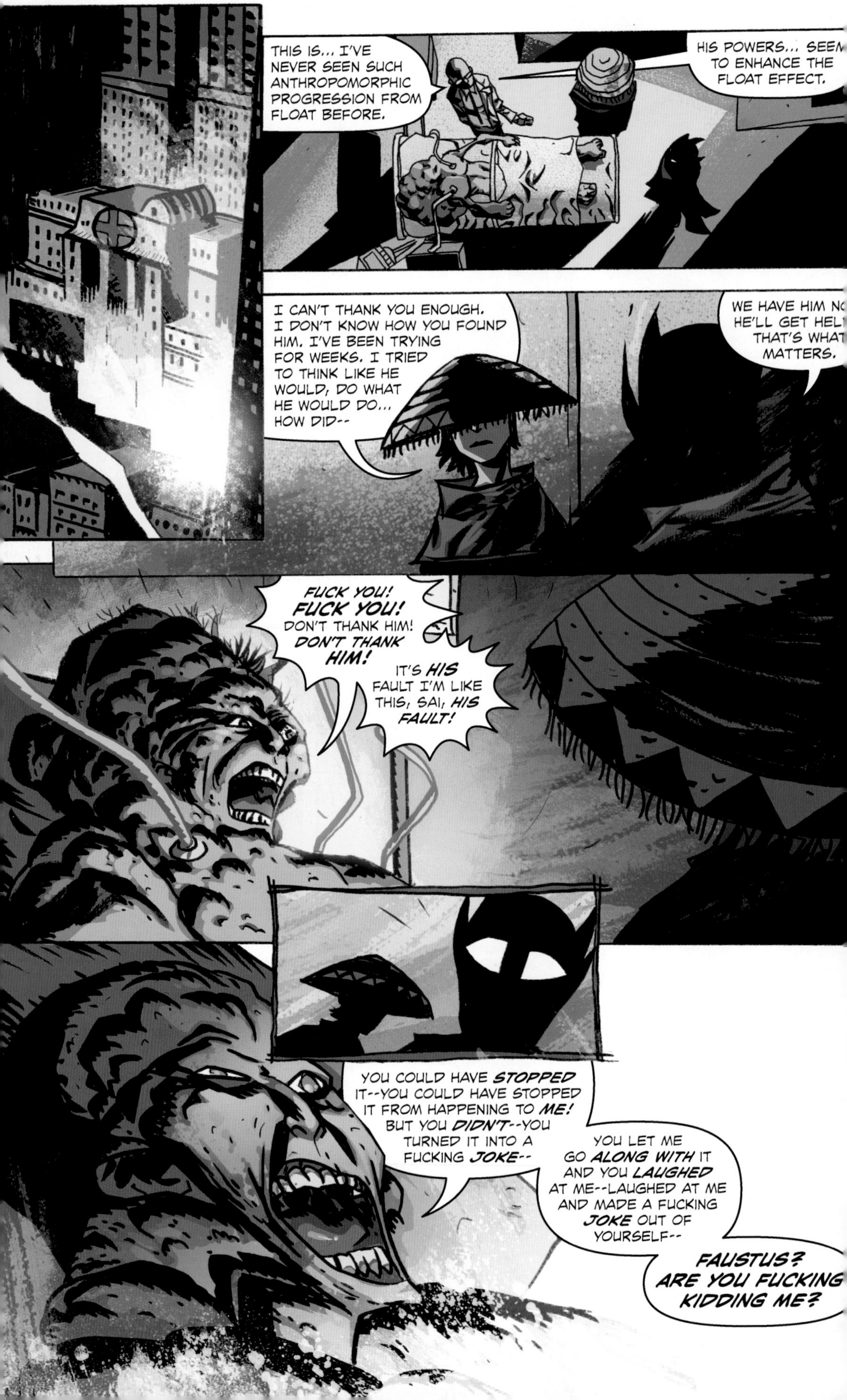
THIS IS... I'VE NEVER SEEN SUCH ANTHROPOMORPHIC PROGRESSION FROM FLOAT BEFORE.
HIS POWERS... SEEM TO ENHANCE THE FLOAT EFFECT.
I CAN'T THANK YOU ENOUGH. I DON'T KNOW HOW YOU FOUND HIM. I'VE BEEN TRYING FOR WEEKS. I TRIED TO THINK LIKE HE WOULD, DO WHAT HE WOULD DO... HOW DID--
WE HAVE HIM NO HE'LL GET HEL THAT'S WHAT MATTERS.
FUCK YOU! FUCK YOU! DON'T THANK HIM! DON'T THANK HIM!
IT'S HIS FAULT I'M LIKE THIS, SAI, HIS FAULT!
YOU COULD HAVE STOPPED IT--YOU COULD HAVE STOPPED IT FROM HAPPENING TO ME! BUT YOU DIDN'T--YOU TURNED IT INTO A FUCKING JOKE--
YOU LET ME GO ALONG WITH IT AND YOU LAUGHED AT ME--LAUGHED AT ME AND MADE A FUCKING JOKE OUT OF YOURSELF--
FAUSTUS? ARE YOU FUCKING KIDDING ME?

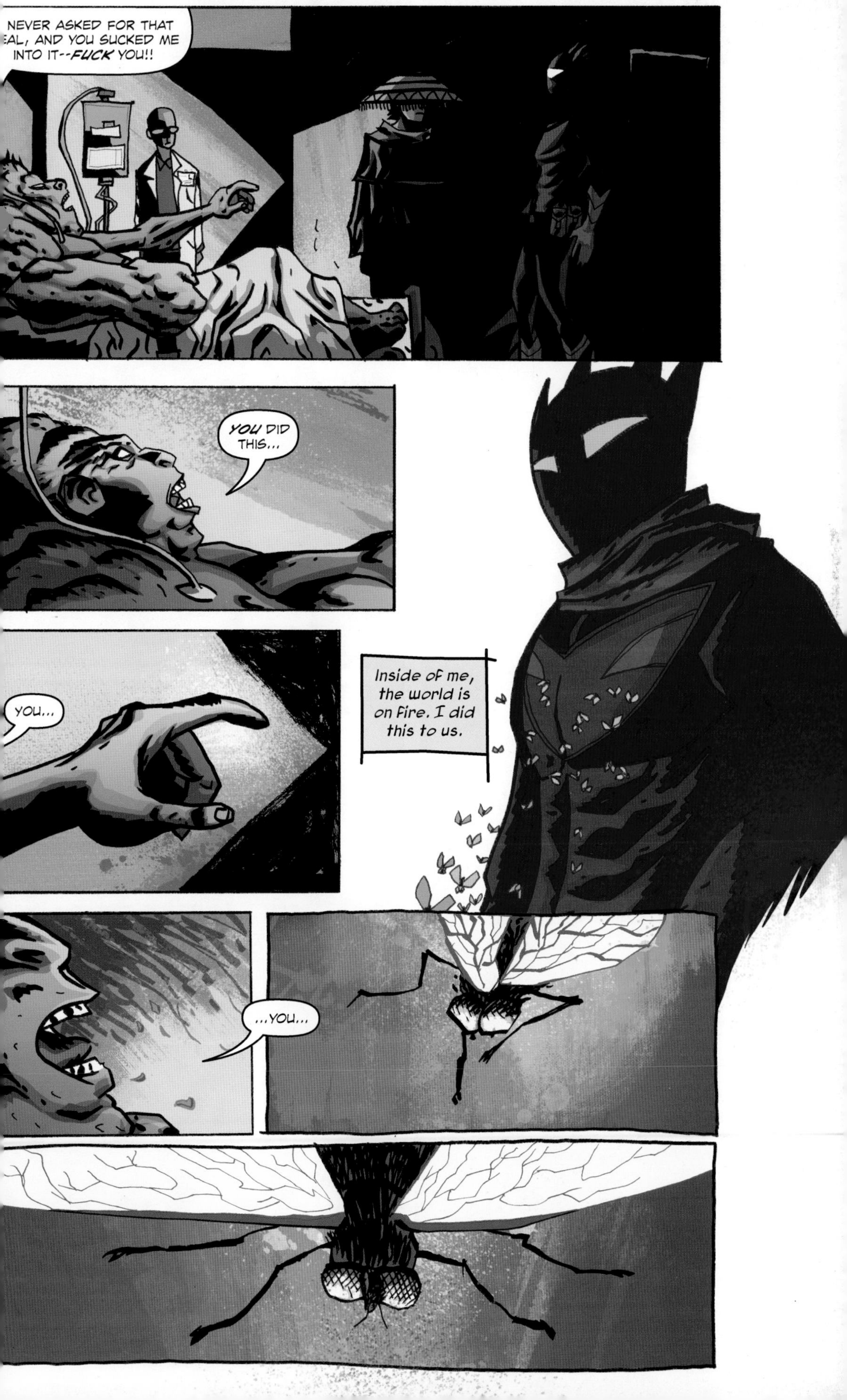
NEVER ASKED FOR THAT
EAL, AND YOU SUCKED ME
INTO IT--FUCK YOU!!
YOU DID THIS...
Inside of me, the world is on fire. I did this to us.
YOU...
...YOU...

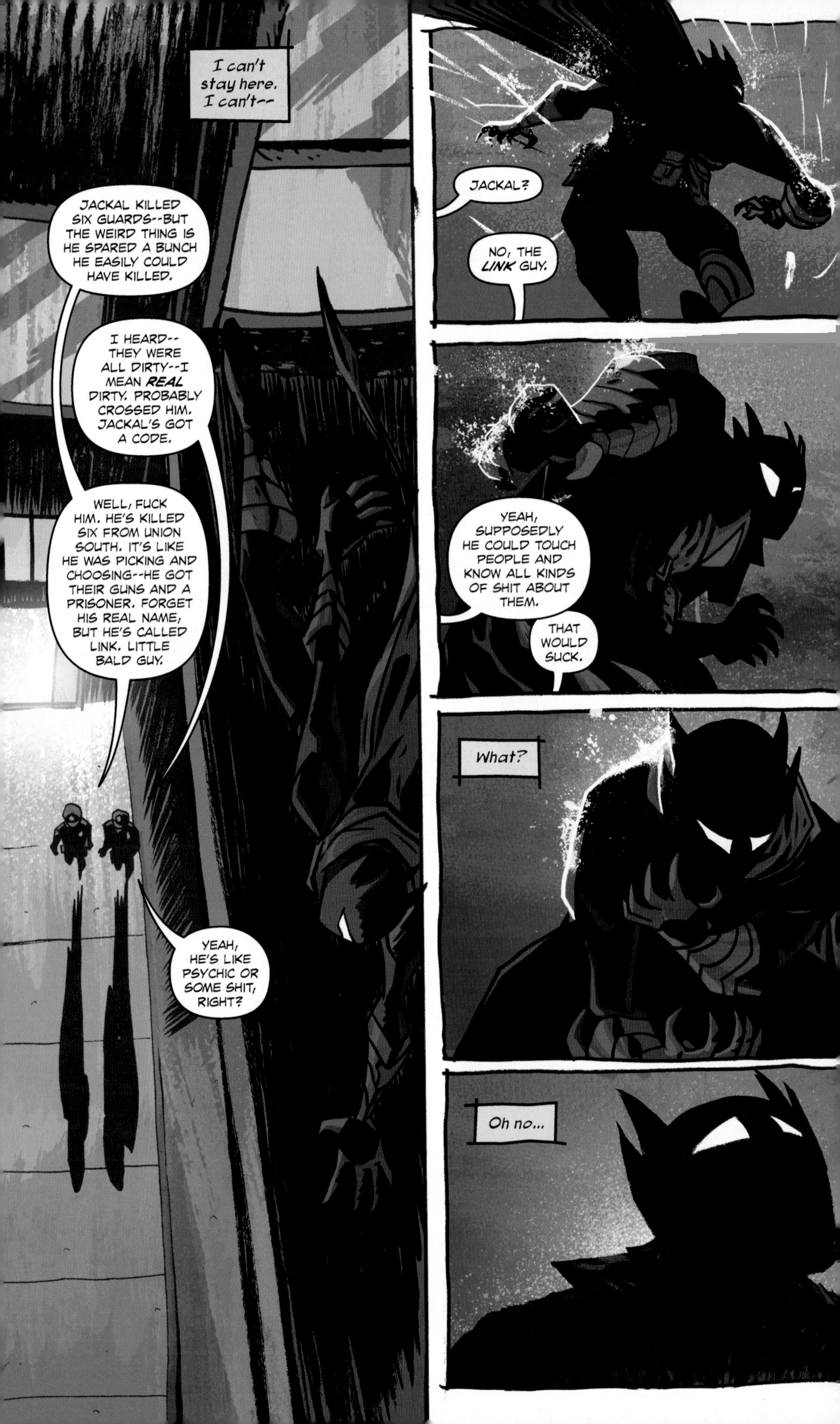
I can't stay here. I can't--
JACKAL KILLED SIX GUARDS--BUT THE WEIRD THING IS HE SPARED A BUNCH HE EASILY COULD HAVE KILLED.
I HEARD--THEY WERE ALL DIRTY--I MEAN REAL DIRTY. PROBABLY CROSSED HIM. JACKAL'S GOT A CODE.
WELL, FUCK HIM. HE'S KILLED SIX FROM UNION SOUTH. IT'S LIKE HE WAS PICKING AND CHOOSING--HE GOT THEIR GUNS AND A PRISONER. FORGET HIS REAL NAME, BUT HE'S CALLED LINK. LITTLE BALD GUY.
YEAH, HE'S LIKE PSYCHIC OR SOME SHIT, RIGHT?
JACKAL?
NO, THE LINK GUY.
YEAH, SUPPOSEDLY HE COULD TOUCH PEOPLE AND KNOW ALL KINDS OF SHIT ABOUT THEM.
THAT WOULD SUCK.
What?
Oh no...

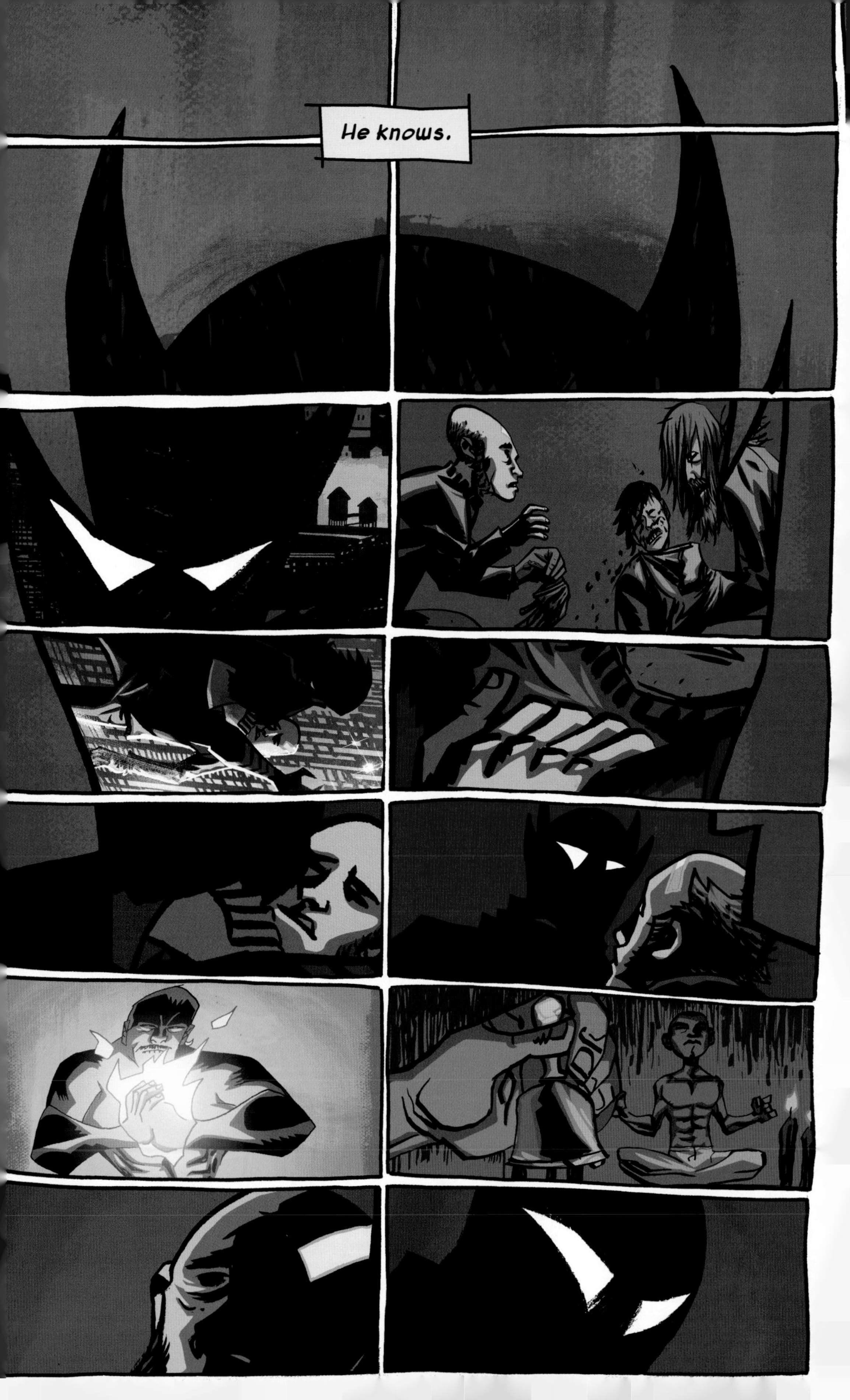
He knows.

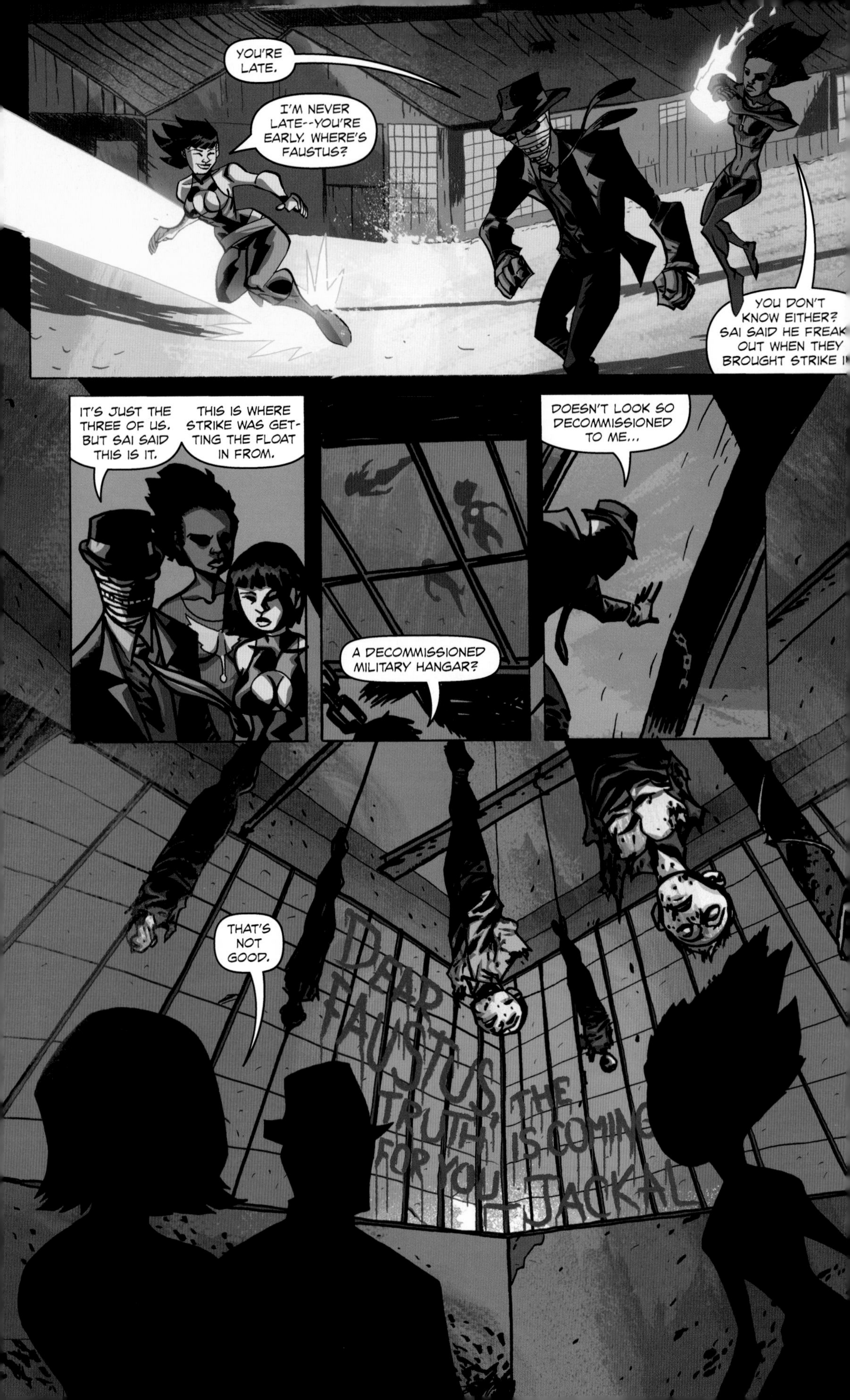
YOU'RE LATE.
I'M NEVER LATE--YOU'RE EARLY. WHERE'S FAUSTUS?
YOU DON'T KNOW EITHER? SAI SAID HE FREAK OUT WHEN THEY BROUGHT STRIKE I
IT'S JUST THE THREE OF US. BUT SAI SAID THIS IS IT.
THIS IS WHERE STRIKE WAS GETTING THE FLOAT IN FROM.
A DECOMMISSIONED MILITARY HANGAR?
DOESN'T LOOK SO DECOMMISSIONED TO ME...
THAT'S NOT GOOD.
DEAR FAUSTUS, THE TRUTH IS COMING FOR YOU --JACKAL

CHAPTER FOUR

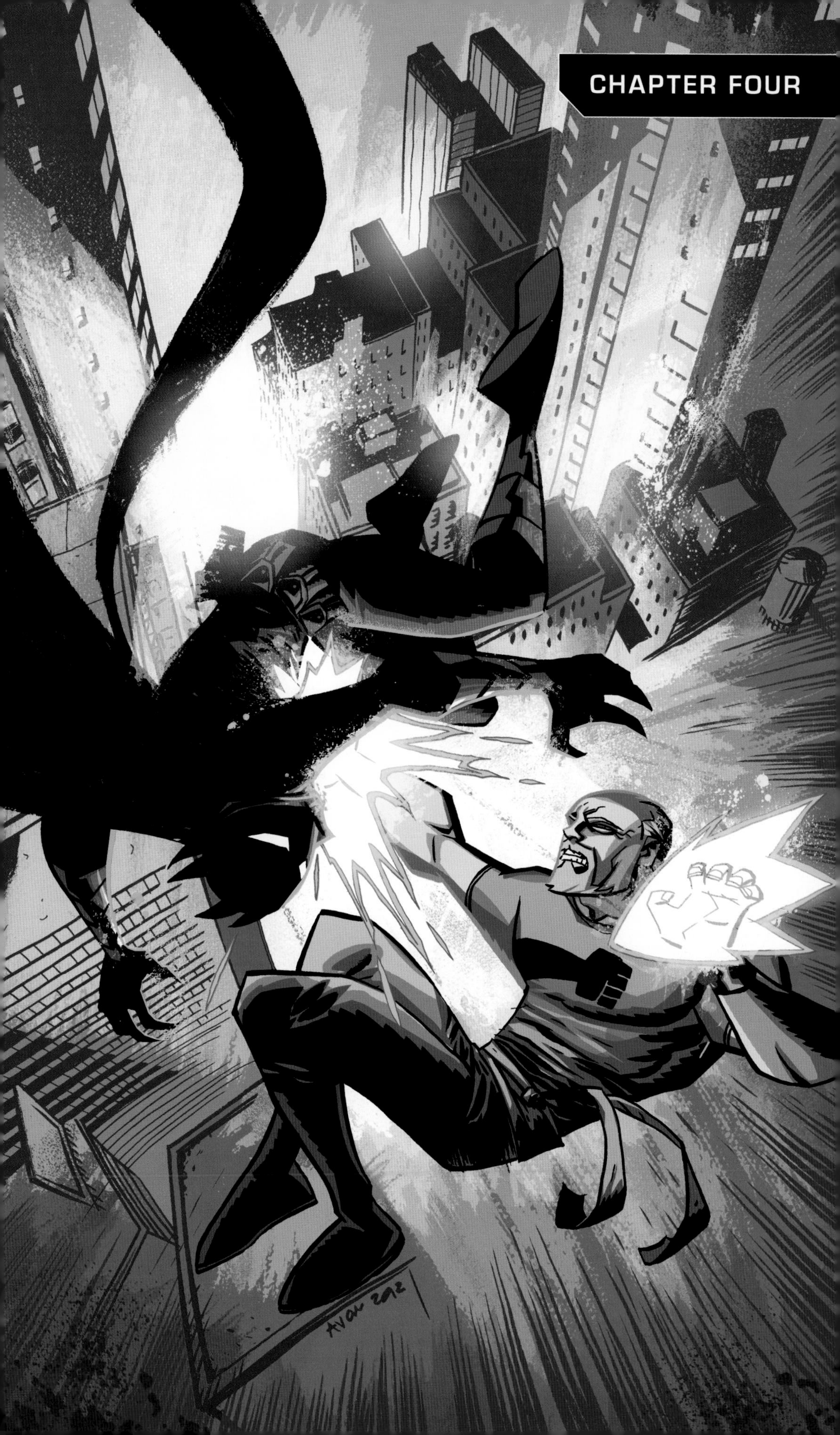

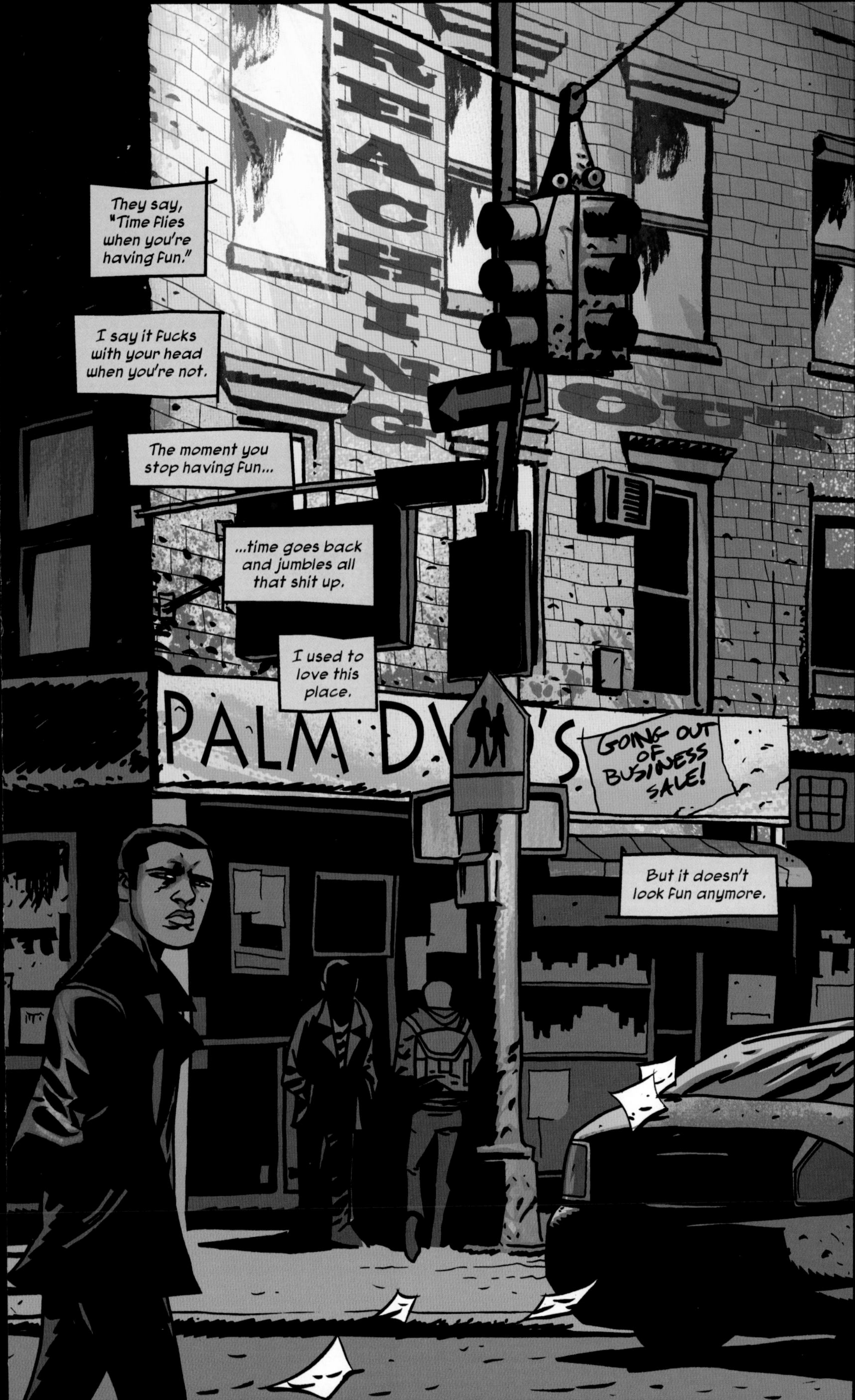
They say, "Time flies when you're having fun."
I say it fucks with your head when you're not.
The moment you stop having fun...
...time goes back and jumbles all that shit up.
I used to love this place.
GOING OUT OF BUSINESS SALE!
But it doesn't look fun anymore.

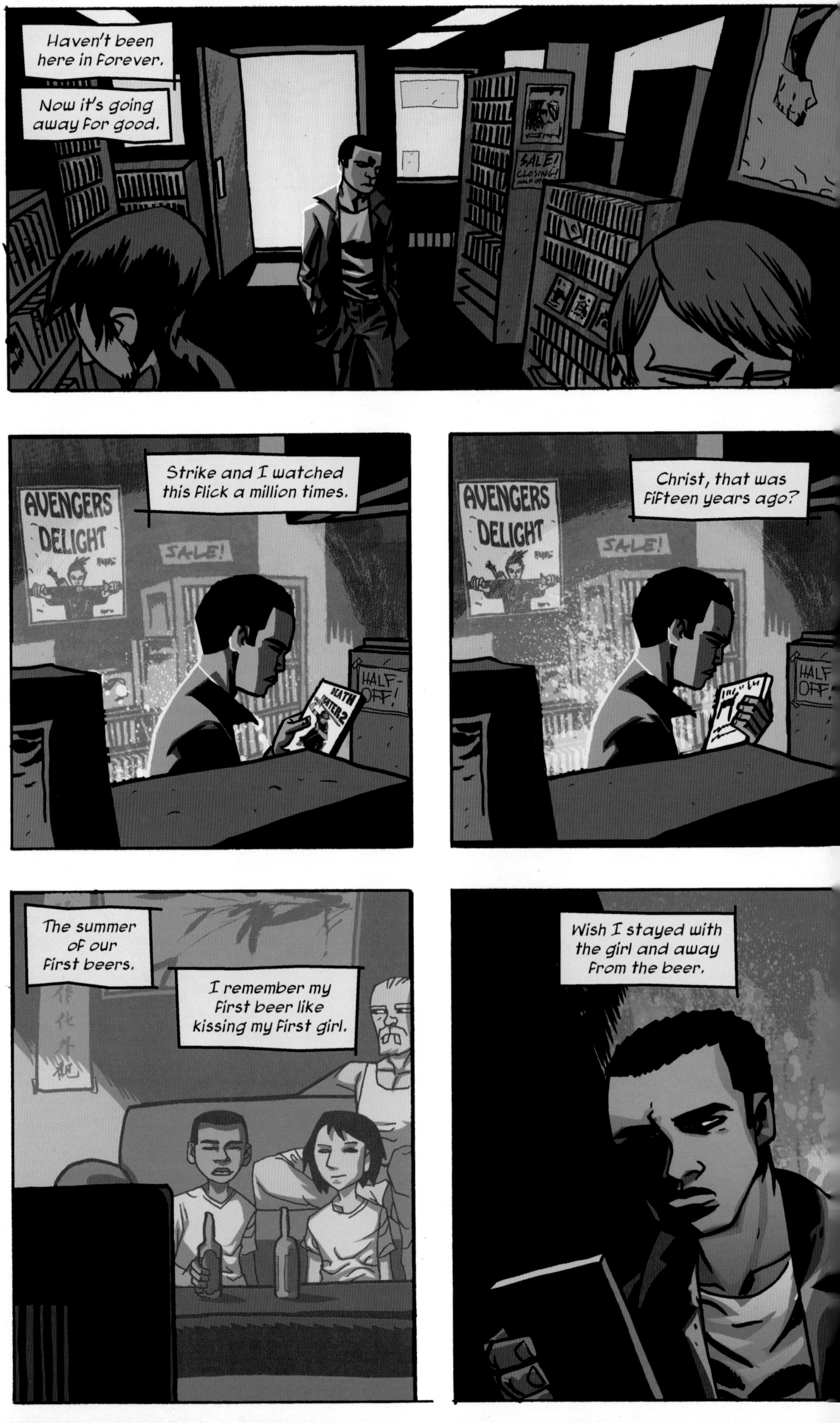

Haven't been here in forever.
Now it's going away for good.
SALE! CLOSING!
AVENGERS DELIGHT
SALE!
Strike and I watched this flick a million times.
DEATH FIGHTER 2
HALF-OFF!
AVENGERS DELIGHT
SALE!
Christ, that was fifteen years ago?
HALF OFF
The summer of our first beers.
I remember my first beer like kissing my first girl.
Wish I stayed with the girl and away from the beer.

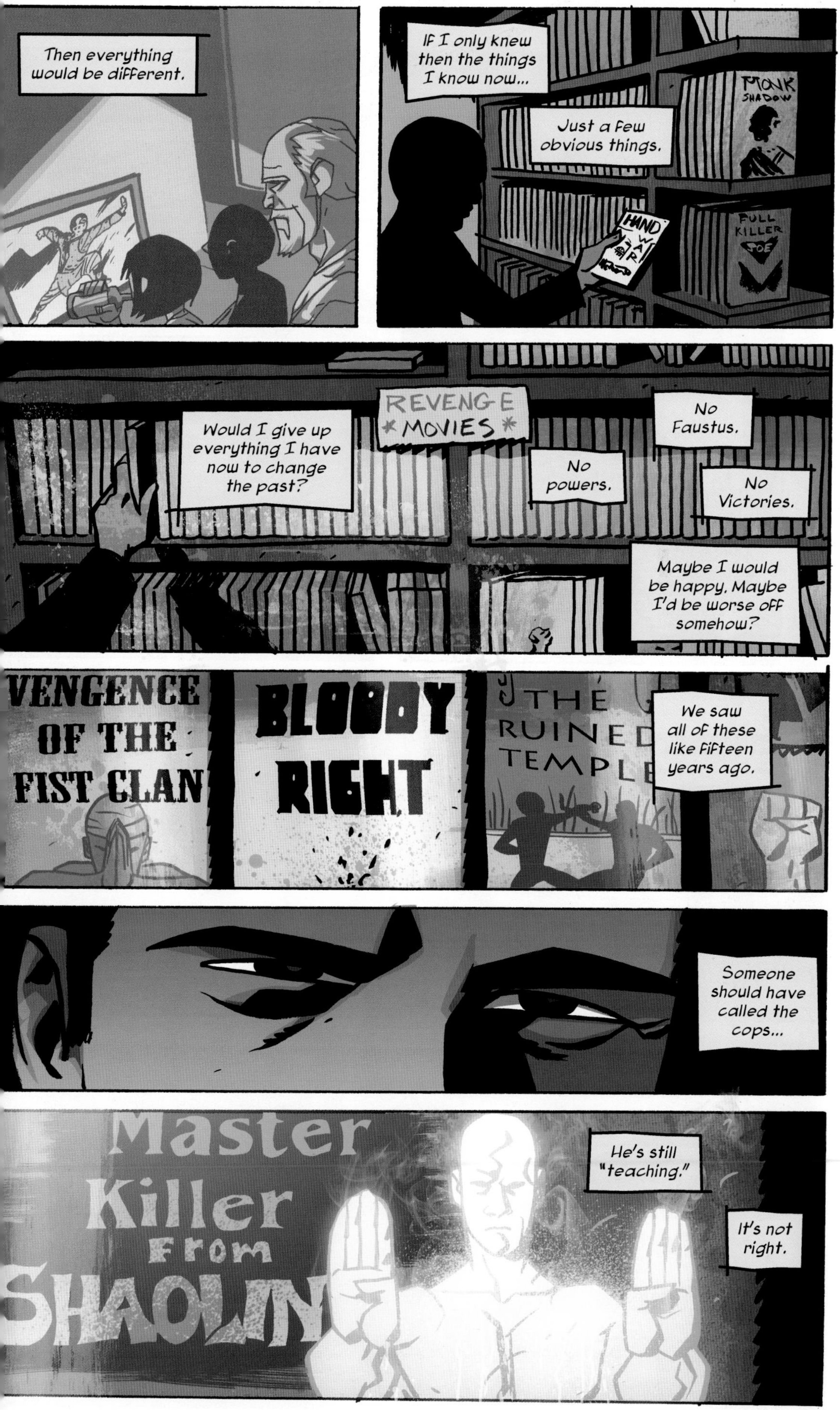
Then everything would be different.
If I only knew then the things I know now...
Just a few obvious things.
MONK SHADOW
HAND WAR
FULL KILLER JOE
Would I give up everything I have now to change the past?
REVENGE *MOVIES*
No Faustus.
No powers.
No Victories.
Maybe I would be happy. Maybe I'd be worse off somehow?
VENGENCE OF THE FIST CLAN
BLOODY RIGHT
THE RUINED TEMPLE
We saw all of these like fifteen years ago.
Someone should have called the cops...
Master Killer from SHAOLIN
He's still "teaching."
It's not right.

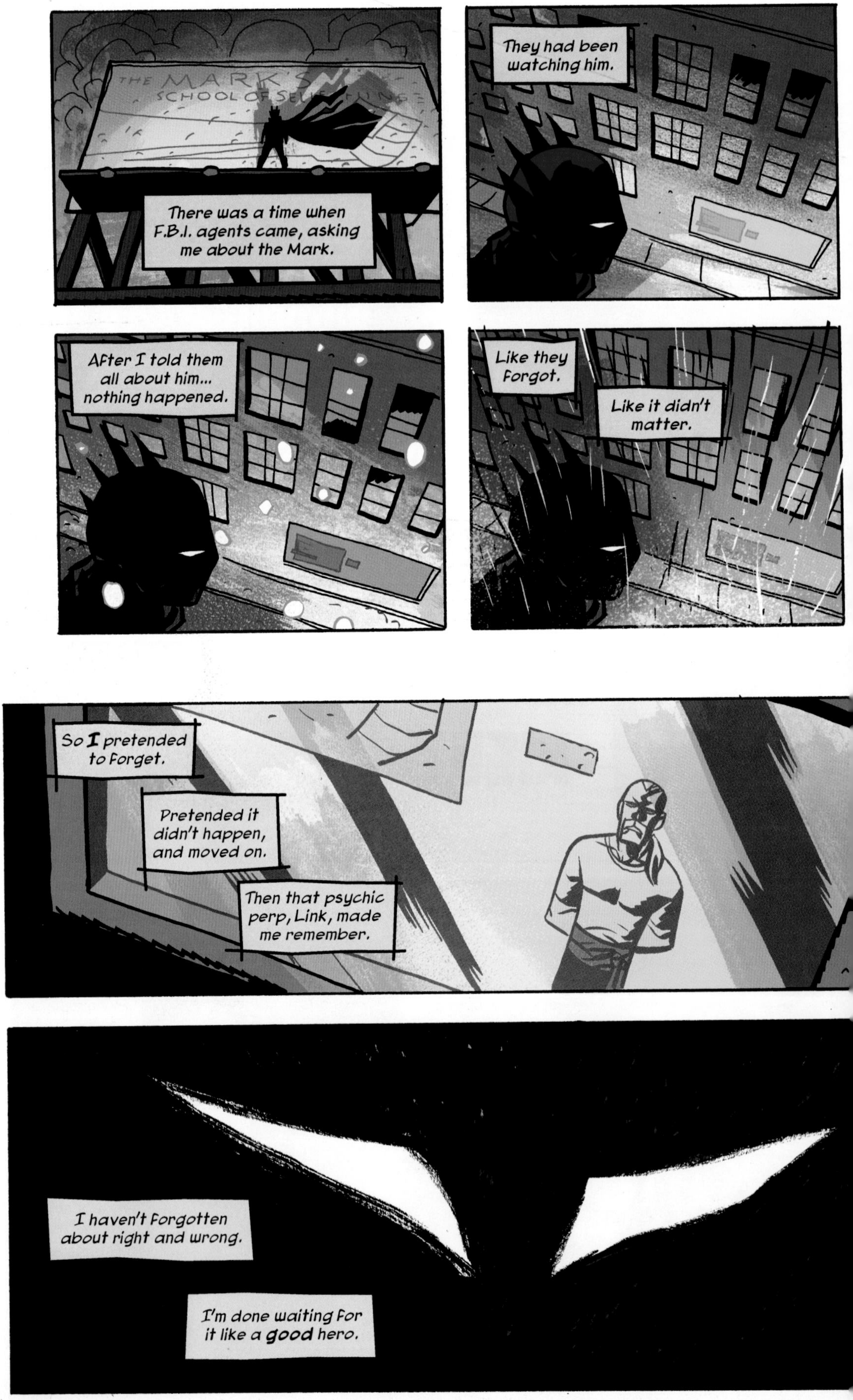
THE MARKS
SCHOOL OF SELF
There was a time when F.B.I. agents came, asking me about the Mark.
They had been watching him.
After I told them all about him... nothing happened.
Like they forgot.
Like it didn't matter.
So I pretended to forget.
Pretended it didn't happen, and moved on.
Then that psychic perp, Link, made me remember.
I haven't forgotten about right and wrong.
I'm done waiting for it like a good hero.

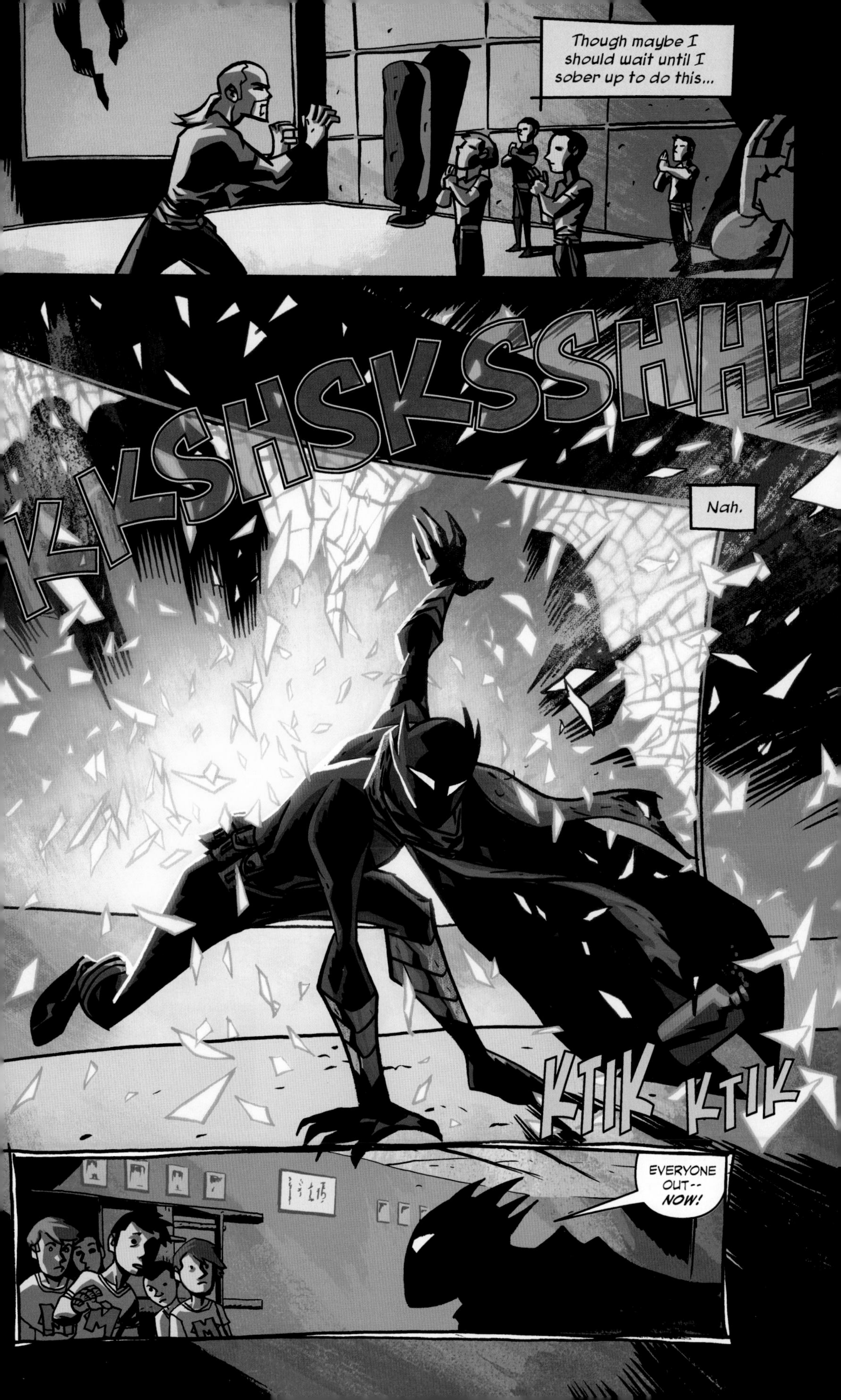
Though maybe I should wait until I sober up to do this...
KKSHSKSSHH!
Nah.
KTIK KTIK
EVERYONE OUT-- NOW!

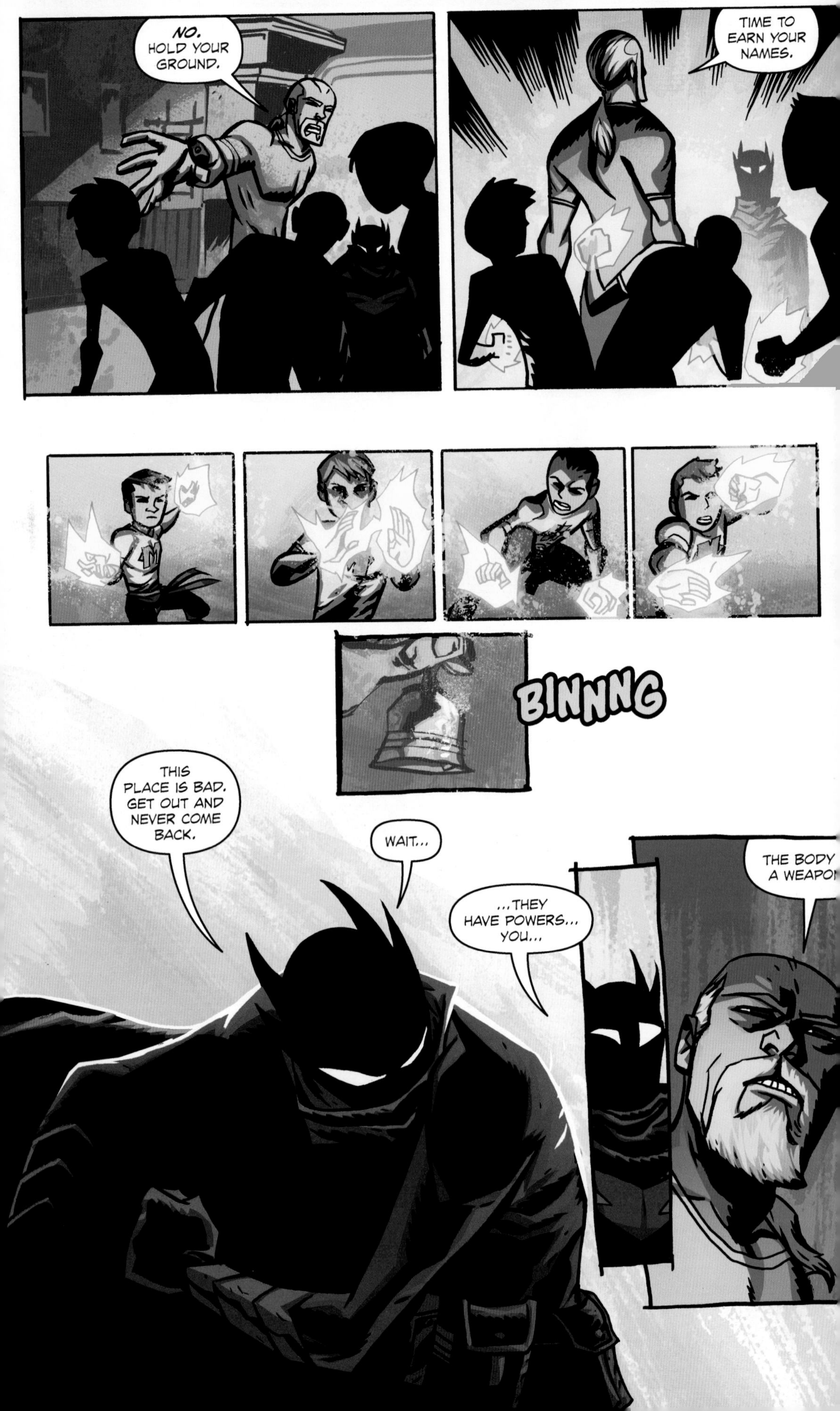
NO. HOLD YOUR GROUND.
TIME TO EARN YOUR NAMES.
BINNNG
THIS PLACE IS BAD. GET OUT AND NEVER COME BACK.
WAIT...
...THEY HAVE POWERS... YOU...
THE BODY
A WEAPO

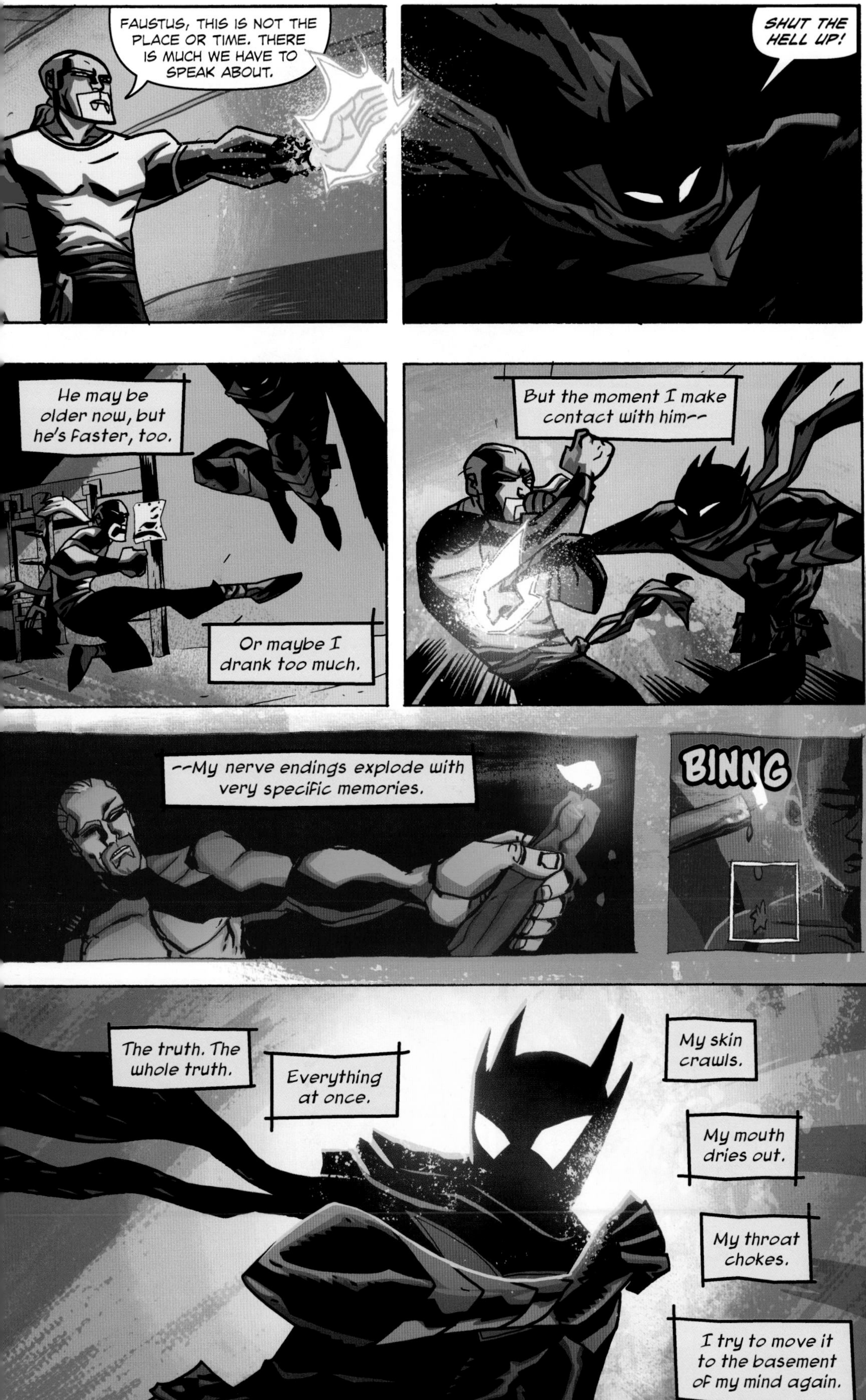
FAUSTUS, THIS IS NOT THE PLACE OR TIME. THERE IS MUCH WE HAVE TO SPEAK ABOUT.
SHUT THE HELL UP!
He may be older now, but he's faster, too.
Or maybe I drank too much.
But the moment I make contact with him--
--My nerve endings explode with very specific memories.
BINNG
The truth. The whole truth.
Everything at once.
My skin crawls.
My mouth dries out.
My throat chokes.
I try to move it to the basement of my mind again.

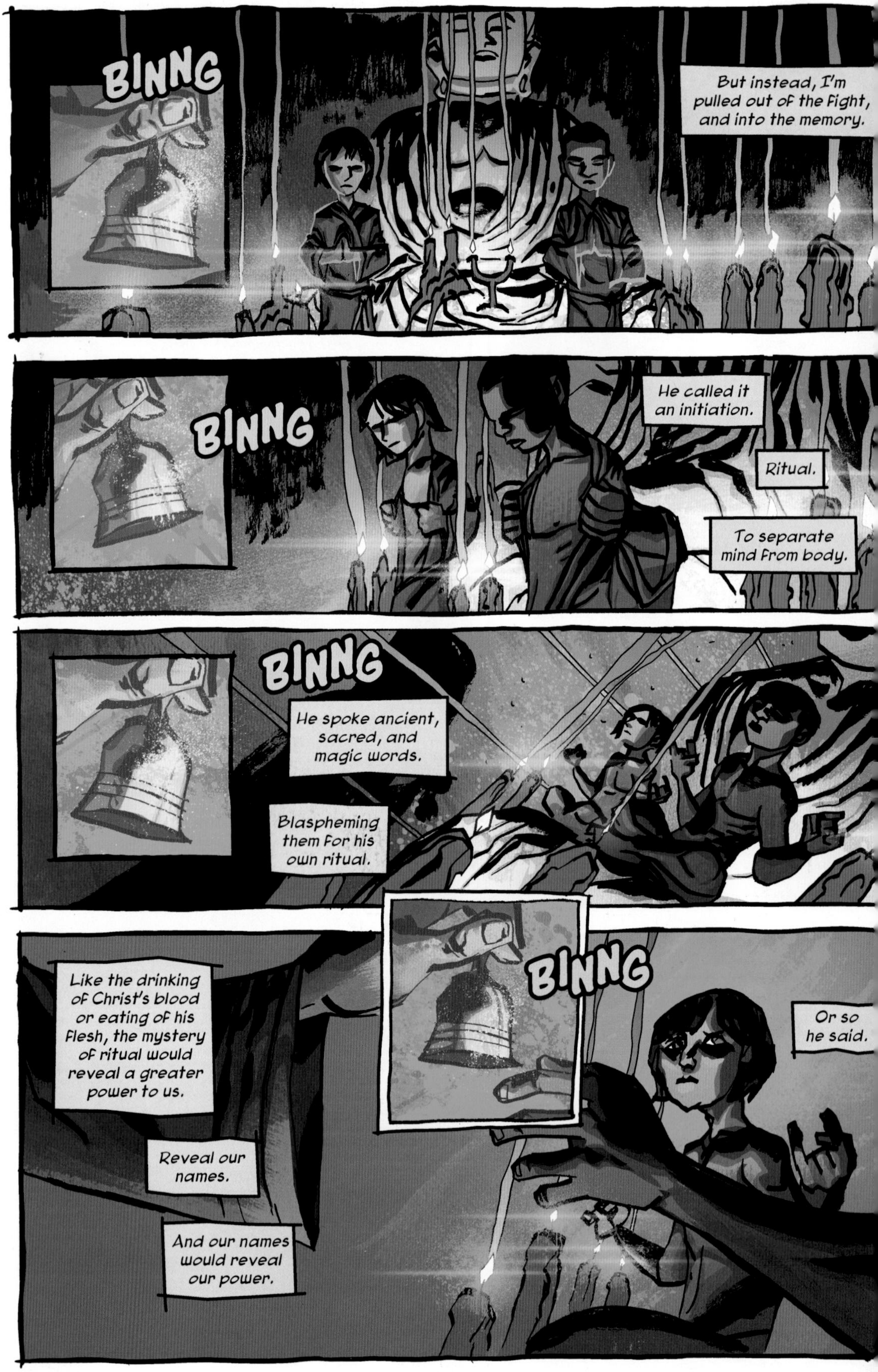
BINNG
But instead, I'm pulled out of the fight, and into the memory.
BINNG
He called it an initiation.
Ritual.
To separate mind from body.
BINNG
He spoke ancient, sacred, and magic words.
Blaspheming them for his own ritual.
Like the drinking of Christ's blood or eating of his flesh, the mystery of ritual would reveal a greater power to us.
BINNG
Or so he said.
Reveal our names.
And our names would reveal our power.

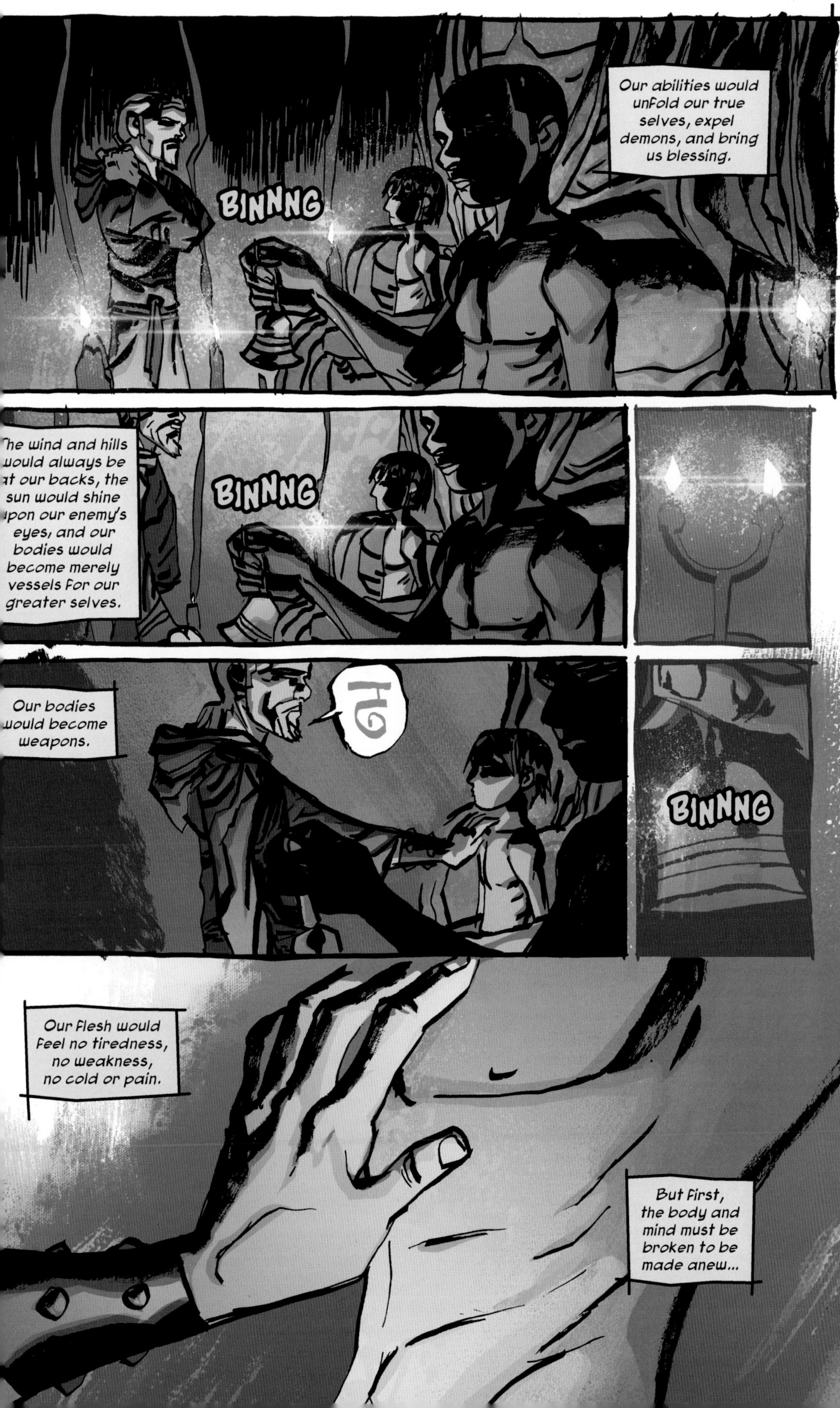
Our abilities would unfold our true selves, expel demons, and bring us blessing.
BINNNG
The wind and hills would always be at our backs, the sun would shine upon our enemy's eyes, and our bodies would become merely vessels for our greater selves.
BINNNG
Our bodies would become weapons.
BINNNG
Our flesh would feel no tiredness, no weakness, no cold or pain.
But first, the body and mind must be broken to be made anew...

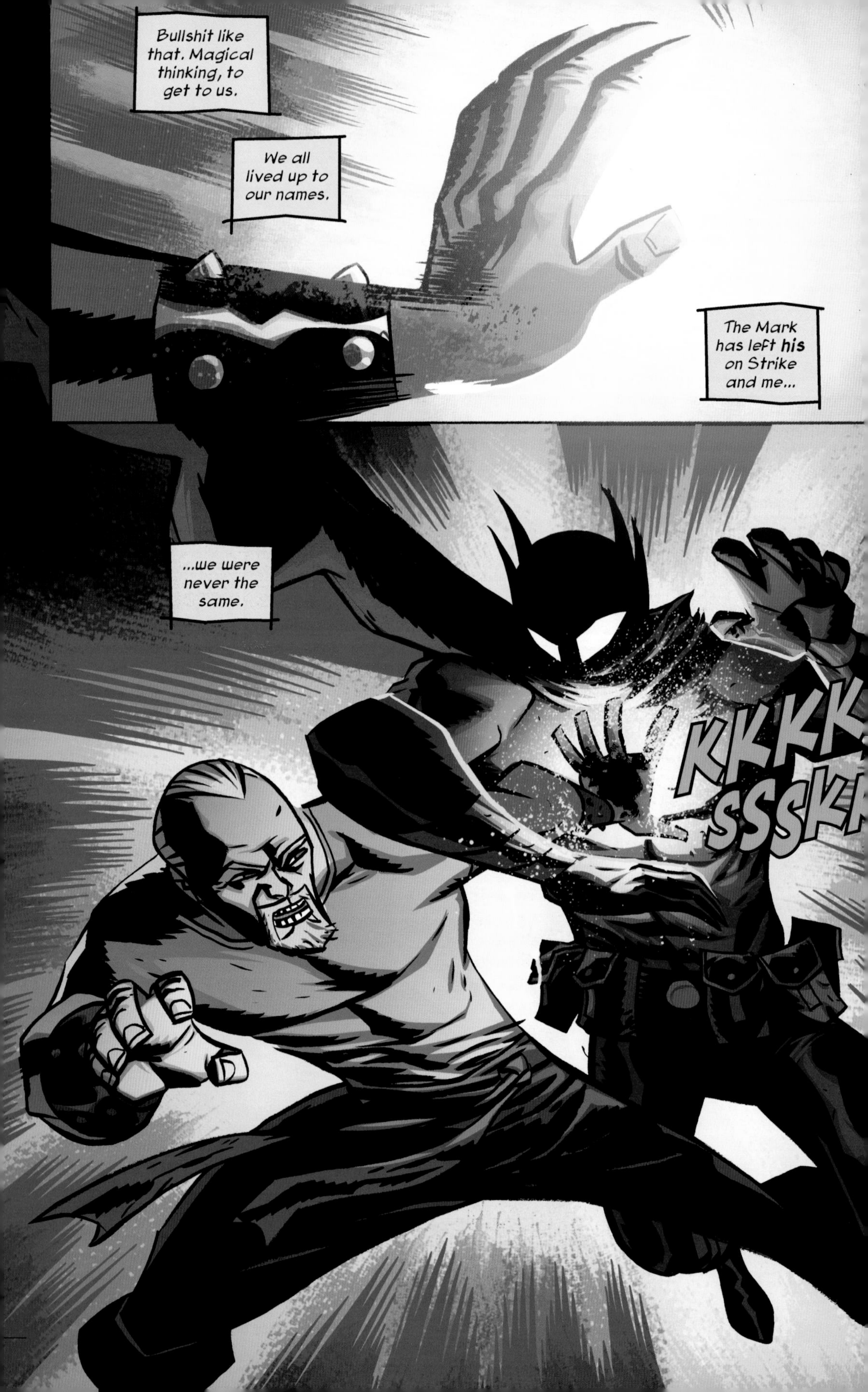

Bullshit like that. Magical thinking, to get to us.
We all lived up to our names.
The Mark has left **his** on Strike and me...
...we were never the same.
KKKK
SSSK

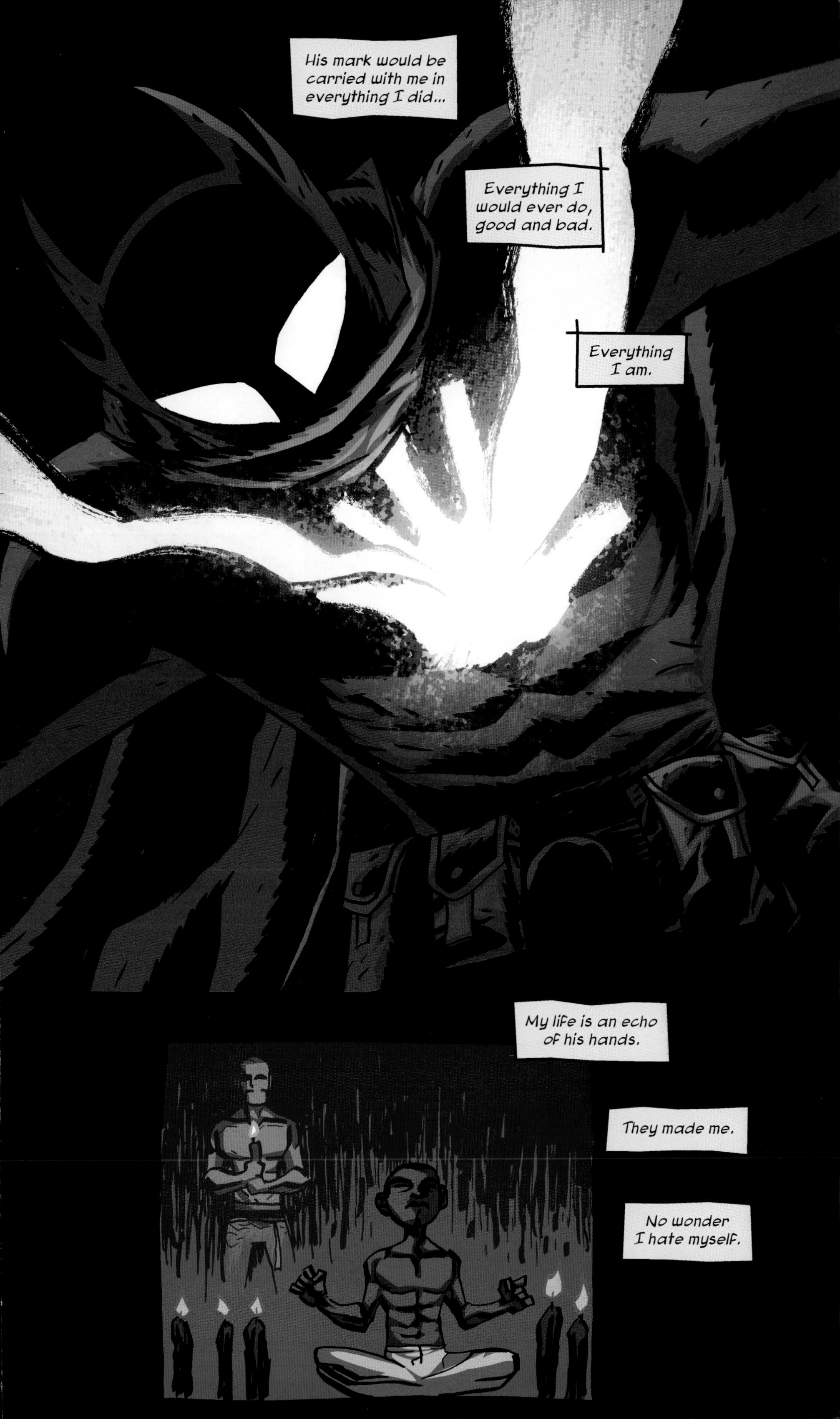
His mark would be carried with me in everything I did...
Everything I would ever do, good and bad.
Everything I am.
My life is an echo of his hands.
They made me.
No wonder I hate myself.

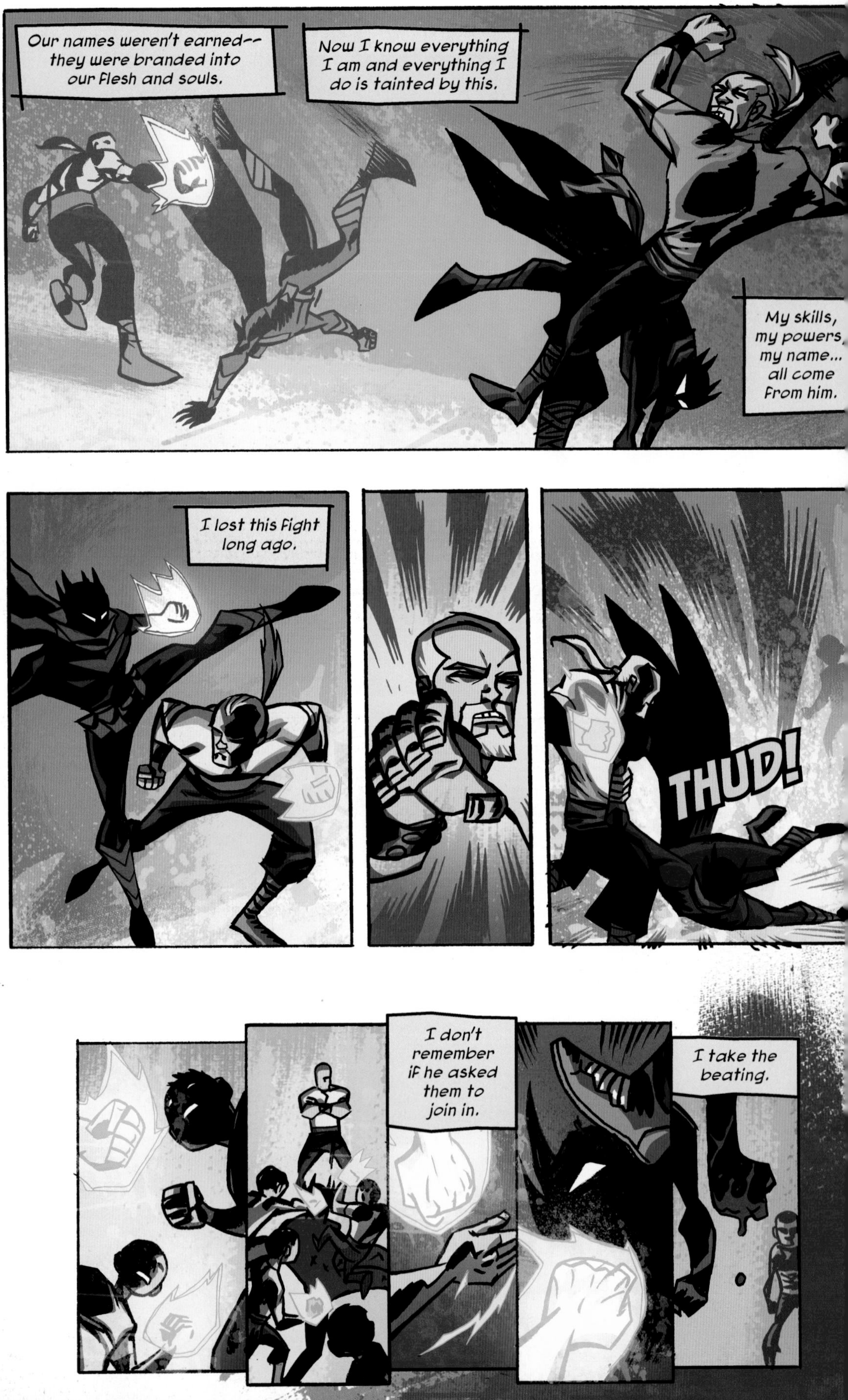

Our names weren't earned-- they were branded into our flesh and souls.
Now I know everything I am and everything I do is tainted by this.
My skills, my powers, my name... all come from him.
I lost this fight long ago.
THUD!
I don't remember if he asked them to join in.
I take the beating.

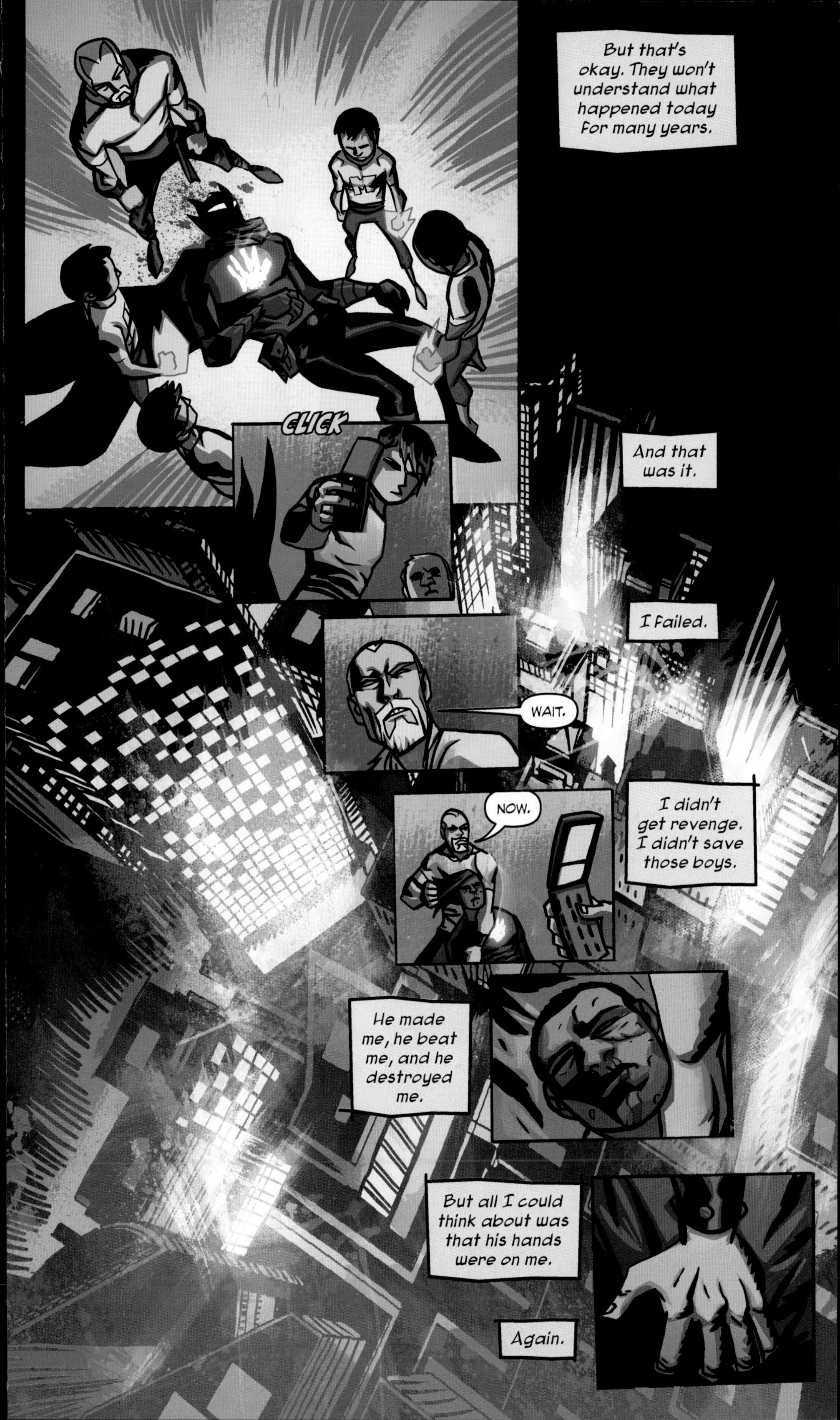
But that's okay. They won't understand what happened today for many years.
CLICK
And that was it.
I failed.
WAIT.
NOW.
I didn't get revenge. I didn't save those boys.
He made me, he beat me, and he destroyed me.
But all I could think about was that his hands were on me.
Again.

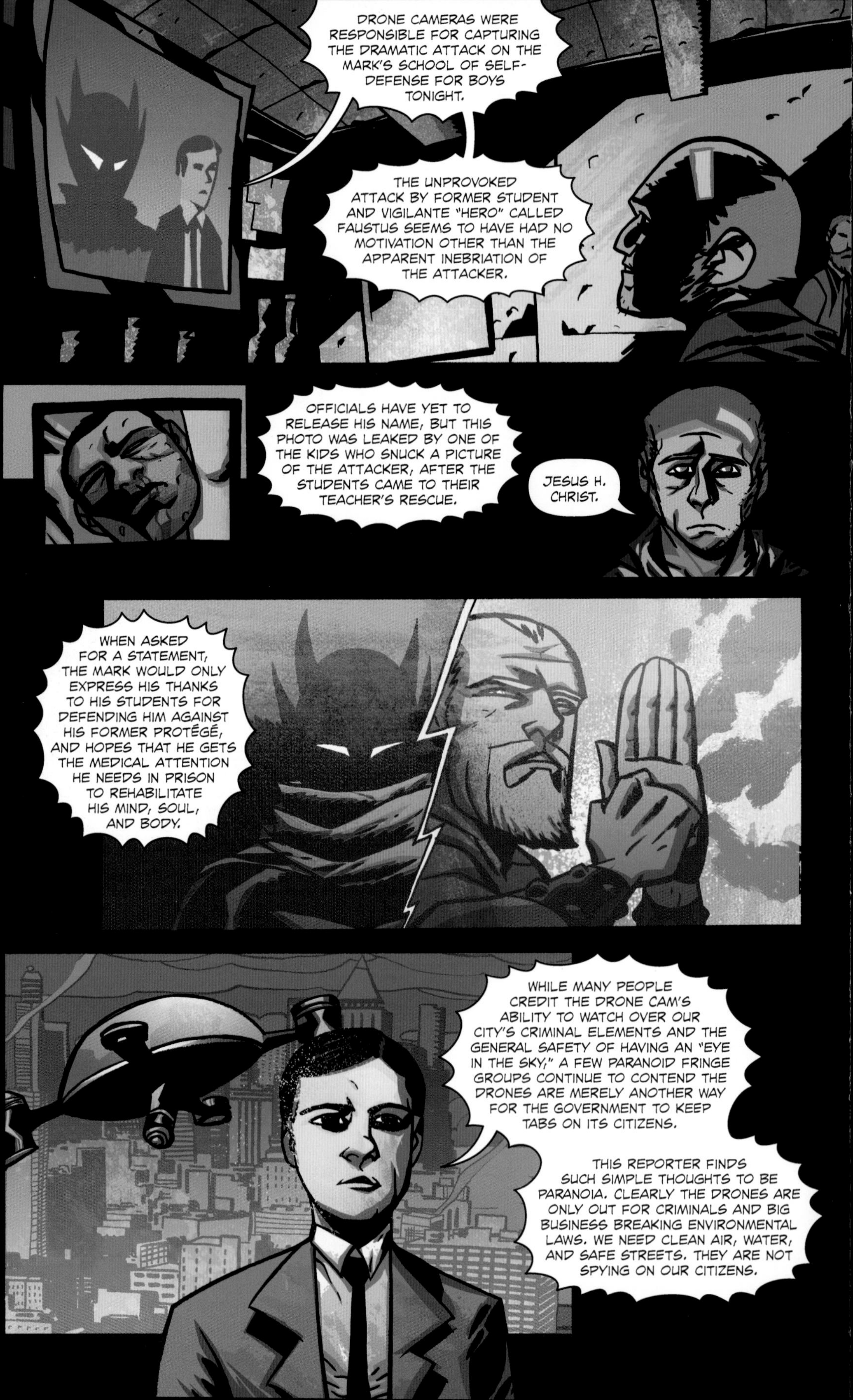
DRONE CAMERAS WERE RESPONSIBLE FOR CAPTURING THE DRAMATIC ATTACK ON THE MARK'S SCHOOL OF SELF-DEFENSE FOR BOYS TONIGHT.
THE UNPROVOKED ATTACK BY FORMER STUDENT AND VIGILANTE "HERO" CALLED FAUSTUS SEEMS TO HAVE HAD NO MOTIVATION OTHER THAN THE APPARENT INEBRIATION OF THE ATTACKER.
OFFICIALS HAVE YET TO RELEASE HIS NAME, BUT THIS PHOTO WAS LEAKED BY ONE OF THE KIDS WHO SNUCK A PICTURE OF THE ATTACKER, AFTER THE STUDENTS CAME TO THEIR TEACHER'S RESCUE.
JESUS H. CHRIST.
WHEN ASKED FOR A STATEMENT, THE MARK WOULD ONLY EXPRESS HIS THANKS TO HIS STUDENTS FOR DEFENDING HIM AGAINST HIS FORMER PROTÉGÉ, AND HOPES THAT HE GETS THE MEDICAL ATTENTION HE NEEDS IN PRISON TO REHABILITATE HIS MIND, SOUL, AND BODY.
WHILE MANY PEOPLE CREDIT THE DRONE CAM'S ABILITY TO WATCH OVER OUR CITY'S CRIMINAL ELEMENTS AND THE GENERAL SAFETY OF HAVING AN "EYE IN THE SKY," A FEW PARANOID FRINGE GROUPS CONTINUE TO CONTEND THE DRONES ARE MERELY ANOTHER WAY FOR THE GOVERNMENT TO KEEP TABS ON ITS CITIZENS.
THIS REPORTER FINDS SUCH SIMPLE THOUGHTS TO BE PARANOIA. CLEARLY THE DRONES ARE ONLY OUT FOR CRIMINALS AND BIG BUSINESS BREAKING ENVIRONMENTAL LAWS. WE NEED CLEAN AIR, WATER, AND SAFE STREETS. THEY ARE NOT SPYING ON OUR CITIZENS.

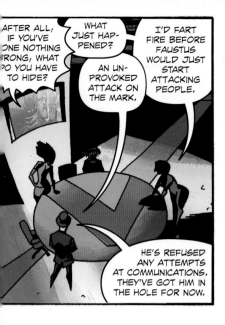

AFTER ALL, IF YOU'VE DONE NOTHING WRONG, WHAT DO YOU HAVE TO HIDE?

WHAT JUST HAPPENED?

AN UNPROVOKED ATTACK ON THE MARK.

I'D FART FIRE BEFORE FAUSTUS WOULD JUST START ATTACKING PEOPLE.

HE'S REFUSED ANY ATTEMPTS AT COMMUNICATIONS. THEY'VE GOT HIM IN THE HOLE FOR NOW.

DO YOU KNOW ANYTHING ABOUT THIS, SAI? ALL THIS HISTORY WITH YOUR BROTHER STRIKE AND FAUSTUS HAS BEEN DUG UP RECENTLY. IS THIS SOME KIND OF HONOR THING?

MY BROTHER'S MIND IS AS A BROKEN MIRROR. UNTIL WE SPEAK WITH FAUSTUS, THERE IS NO CLEAR PATH TO THIS RIDDLE.

LET'S GET TO THE MARK AND BEAT SOME ANSWERS OUT OF HIM.

AND BEAT HIM, WHY? THERE IS NO EVIDENCE OF--

EVIDENCE? FAUSTUS IS ONE OF US!

IF WE'RE HANDING OUT A BEAT-DOWN, WE NEED TO AT LEAST KNOW WHY--SO WE KNOW WHAT QUESTIONS TO ASK, WHAT TO LOOK FOR.

SAI AND I KNOW THE MARK BEST. LET'S START BY TALKING TO HIM. SAI IS EXCELLENT AT READING BODY LANGUAGE AND *TELLS*. HE'LL KNOW IF THE MARK IS HIDING ANYTHING.

WHATEVER. LOGIC SUCKS.

CALL ME AT "BEAT O' CLOCK."

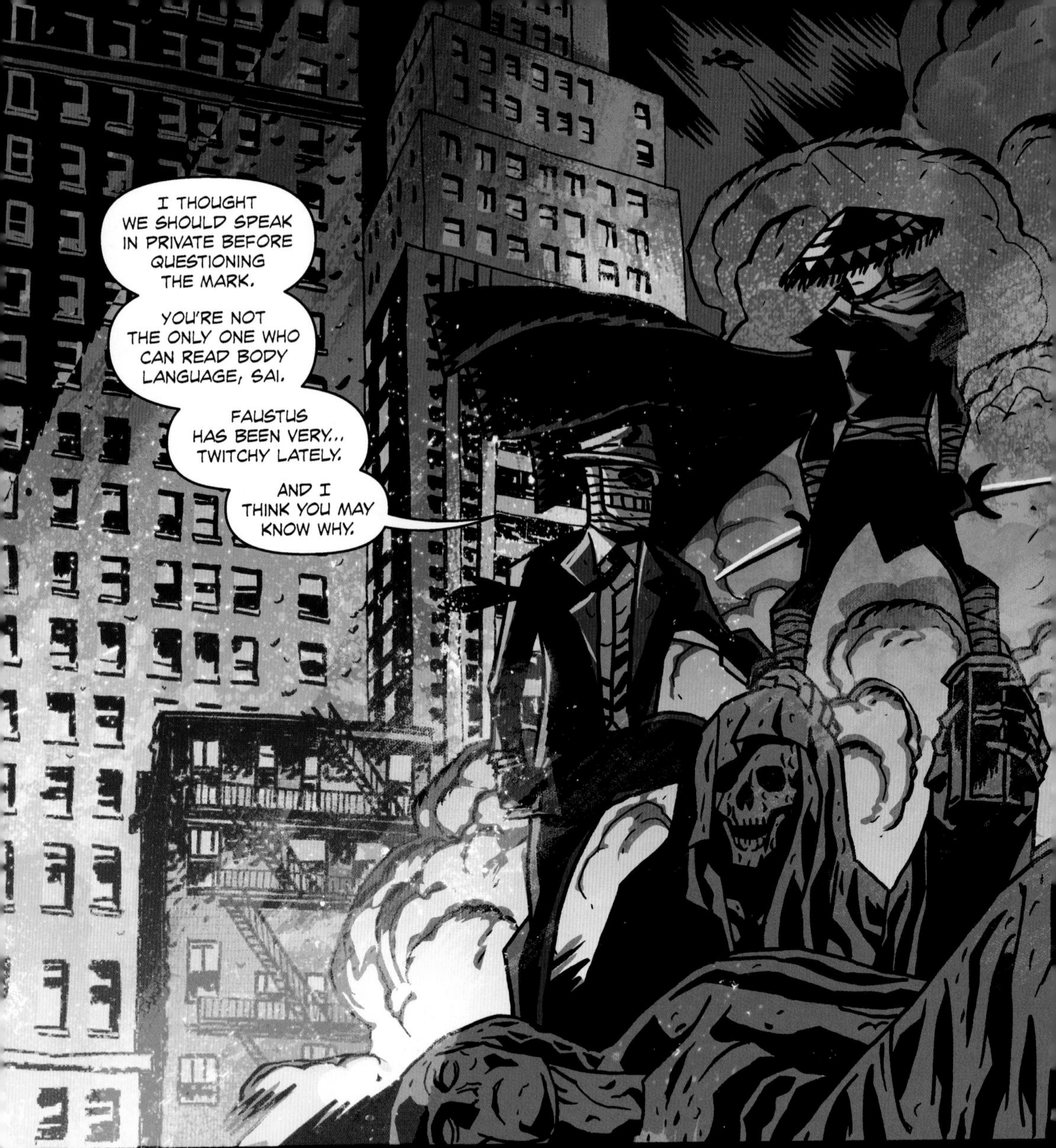
I THOUGHT WE SHOULD SPEAK IN PRIVATE BEFORE QUESTIONING THE MARK.
YOU'RE NOT THE ONLY ONE WHO CAN READ BODY LANGUAGE, SAI.
FAUSTUS HAS BEEN VERY... TWITCHY LATELY.
AND I THINK YOU MAY KNOW WHY.

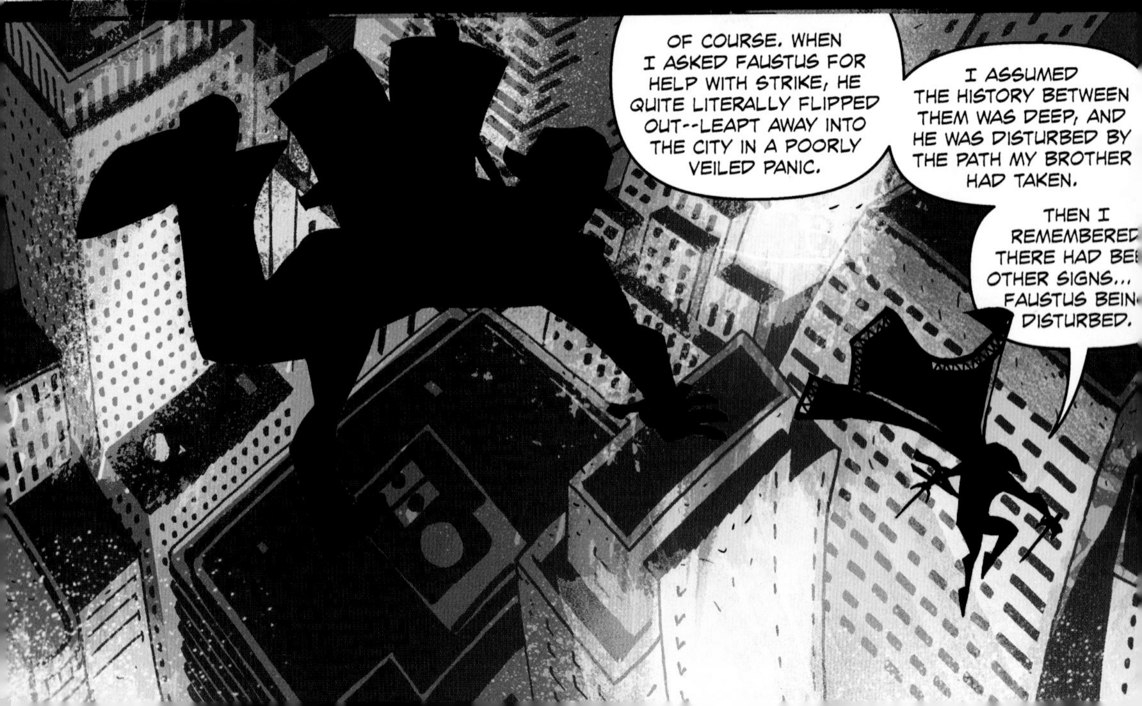
OF COURSE. WHEN I ASKED FAUSTUS FOR HELP WITH STRIKE, HE QUITE LITERALLY FLIPPED OUT--LEAPT AWAY INTO THE CITY IN A POORLY VEILED PANIC.
I ASSUMED THE HISTORY BETWEEN THEM WAS DEEP, AND HE WAS DISTURBED BY THE PATH MY BROTHER HAD TAKEN.
THEN I REMEMBERED THERE HAD BE OTHER SIGNS... FAUSTUS BEIN DISTURBED.

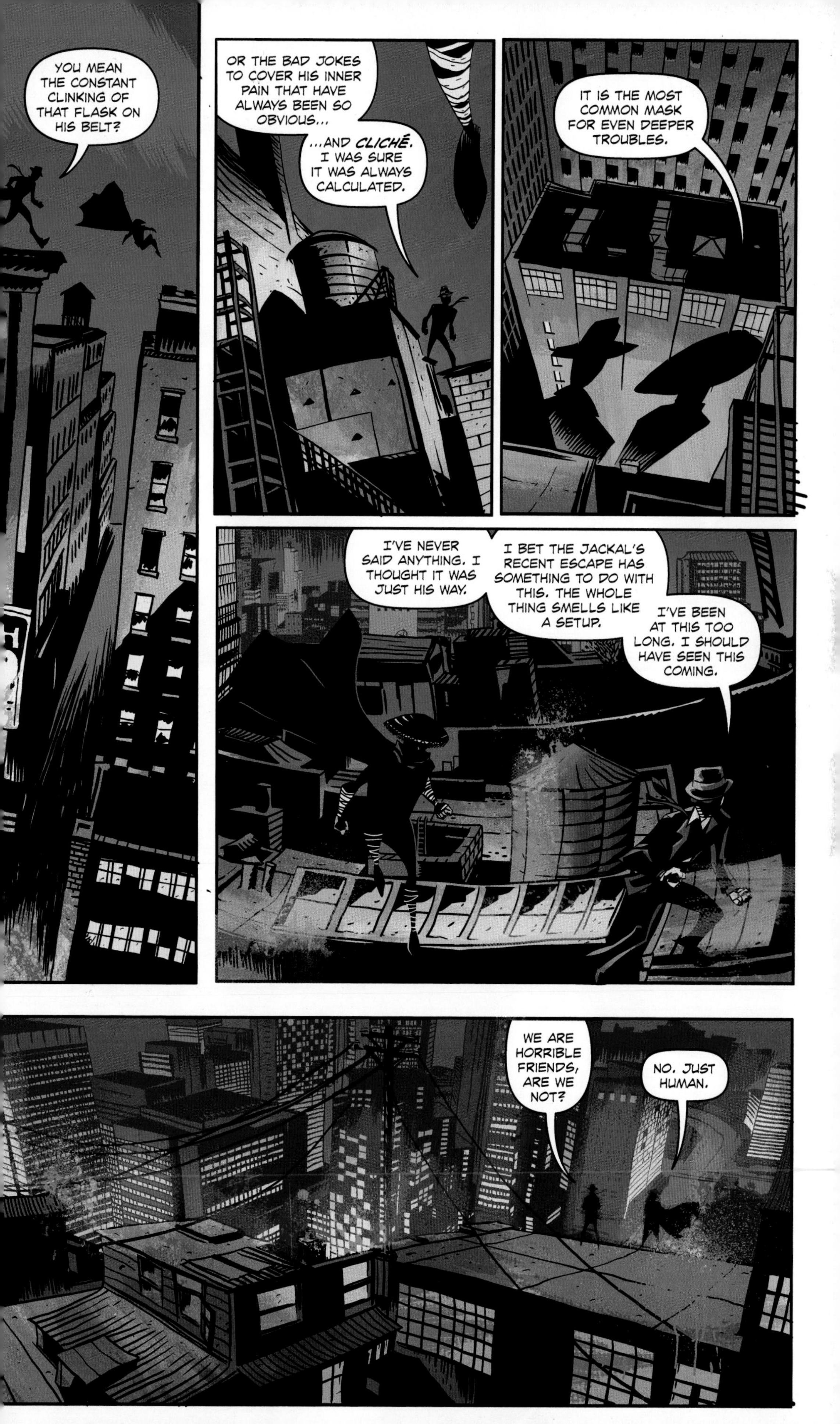
YOU MEAN THE CONSTANT CLINKING OF THAT FLASK ON HIS BELT?
OR THE BAD JOKES TO COVER HIS INNER PAIN THAT HAVE ALWAYS BEEN SO OBVIOUS...
...AND *CLICHÉ.* I WAS SURE IT WAS ALWAYS CALCULATED.
IT IS THE MOST COMMON MASK FOR EVEN DEEPER TROUBLES.
I'VE NEVER SAID ANYTHING. I THOUGHT IT WAS JUST HIS WAY.
I BET THE JACKAL'S RECENT ESCAPE HAS SOMETHING TO DO WITH THIS. THE WHOLE THING SMELLS LIKE A SETUP.
I'VE BEEN AT THIS TOO LONG. I SHOULD HAVE SEEN THIS COMING.
WE ARE HORRIBLE FRIENDS, ARE WE NOT?
NO. JUST HUMAN.

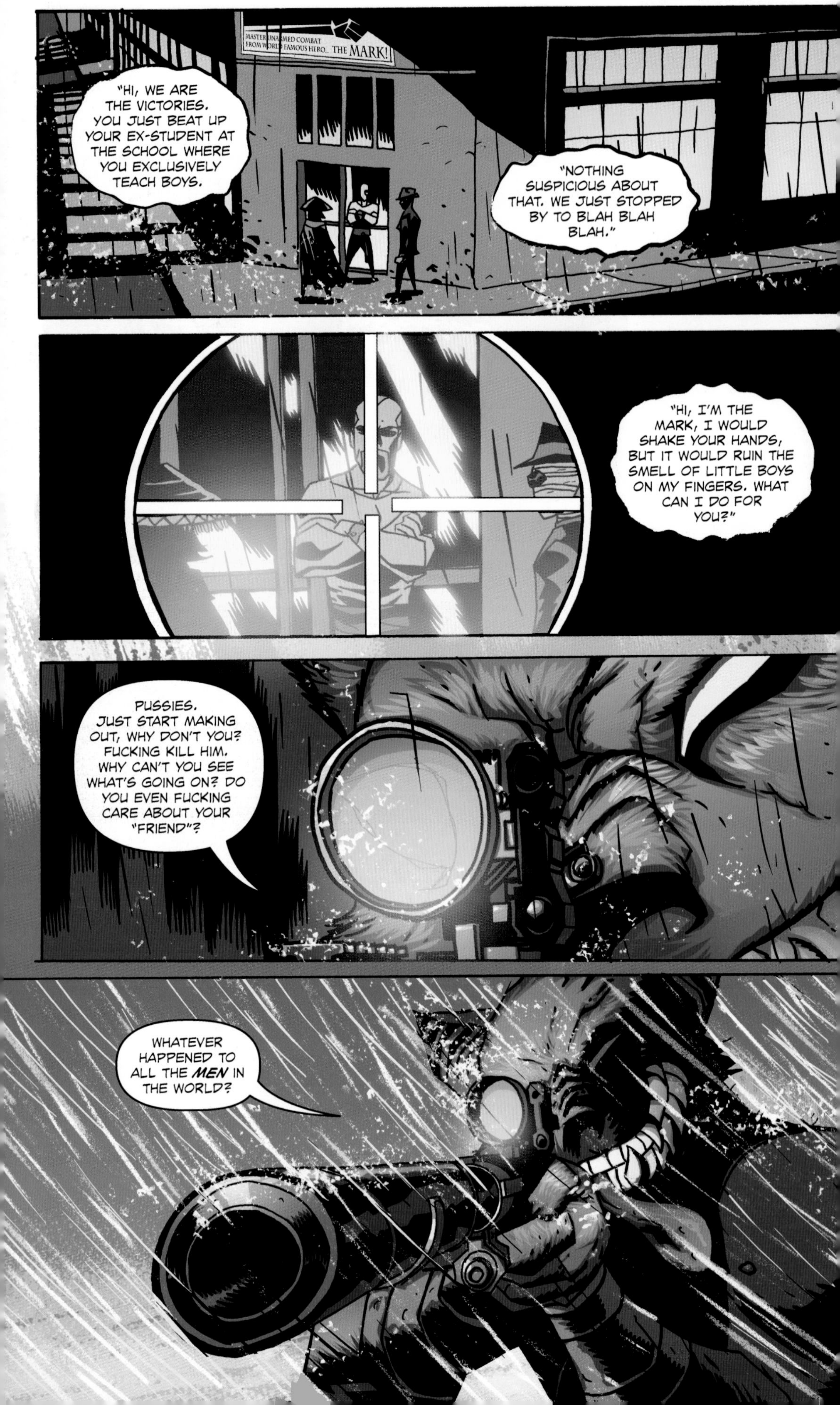
MASTER UNARMED COMBAT FROM WORLD FAMOUS HERO... THE MARK!
"HI, WE ARE THE VICTORIES. YOU JUST BEAT UP YOUR EX-STUDENT AT THE SCHOOL WHERE YOU EXCLUSIVELY TEACH BOYS.
"NOTHING SUSPICIOUS ABOUT THAT. WE JUST STOPPED BY TO BLAH BLAH BLAH."
"HI, I'M THE MARK, I WOULD SHAKE YOUR HANDS, BUT IT WOULD RUIN THE SMELL OF LITTLE BOYS ON MY FINGERS. WHAT CAN I DO FOR YOU?"
PUSSIES. JUST START MAKING OUT, WHY DON'T YOU? FUCKING KILL HIM. WHY CAN'T YOU SEE WHAT'S GOING ON? DO YOU EVEN FUCKING CARE ABOUT YOUR "FRIEND"?
WHATEVER HAPPENED TO ALL THE ***MEN*** IN THE WORLD?

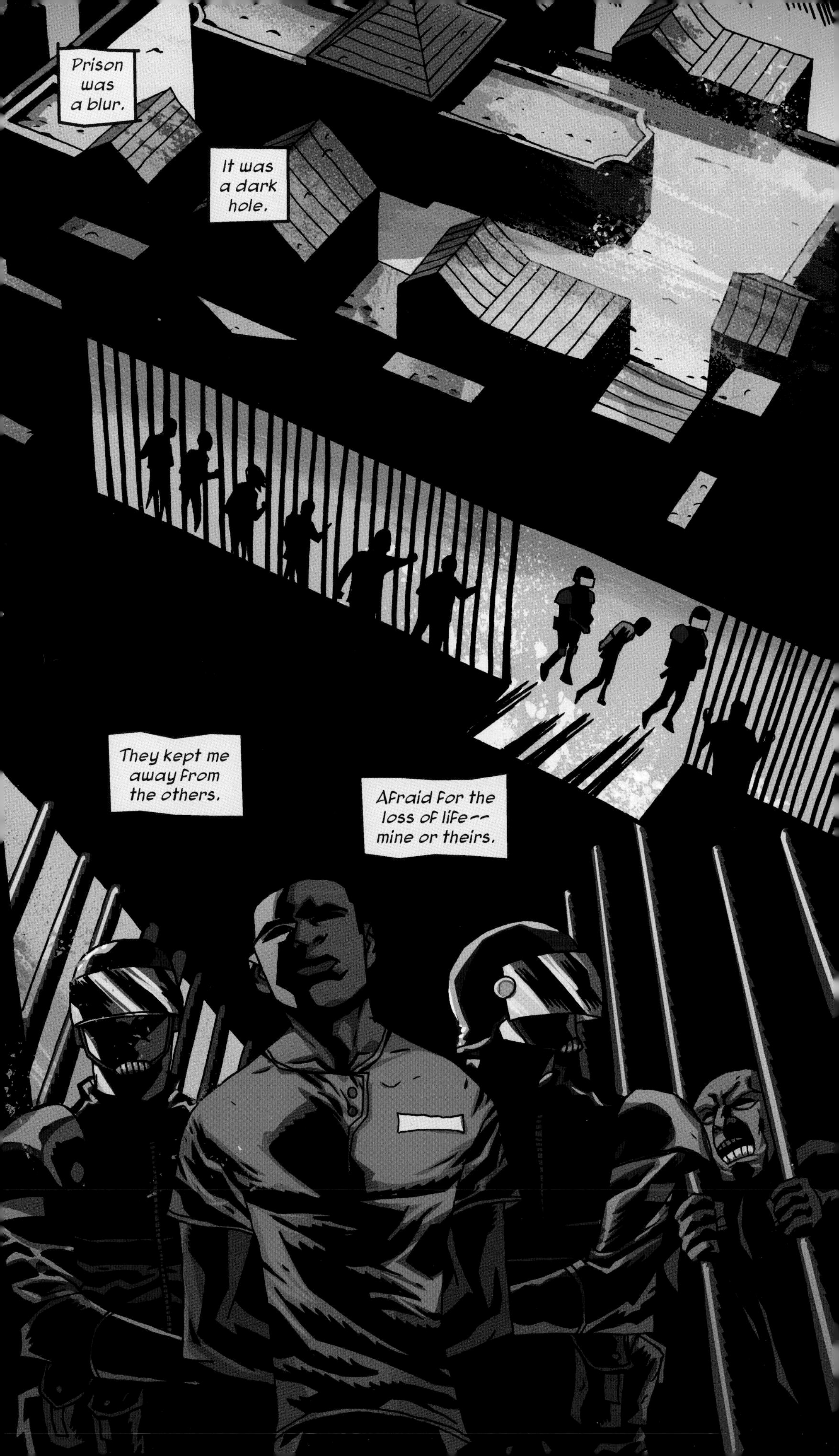
Prison was a blur.
It was a dark hole.
They kept me away from the others.
Afraid for the loss of life--mine or theirs.

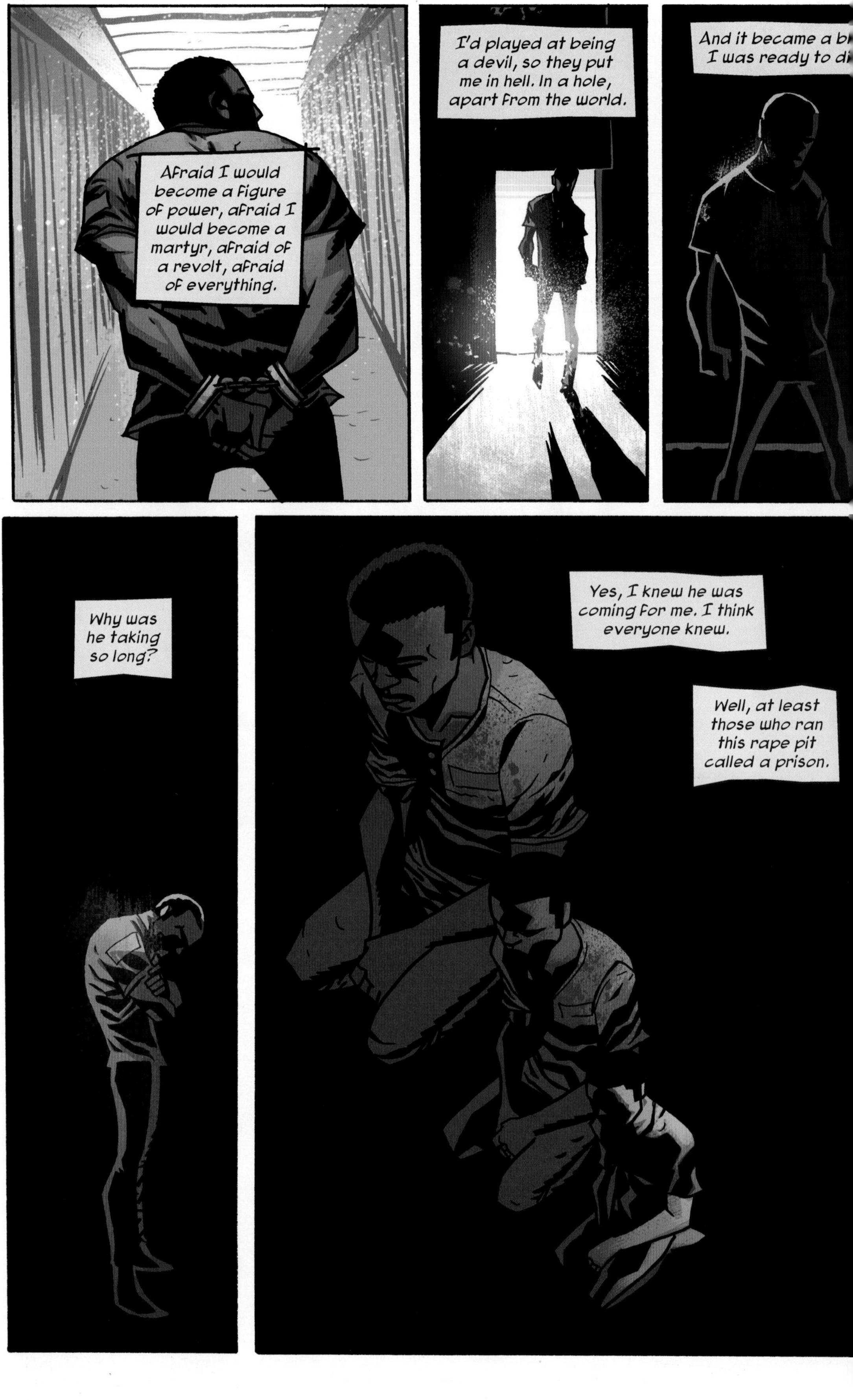
Afraid I would become a figure of power, afraid I would become a martyr, afraid of a revolt, afraid of everything.
I'd played at being a devil, so they put me in hell. In a hole, apart from the world.
And it became a
I was ready to
Why was he taking so long?
Yes, I knew he was coming for me. I think everyone knew.
Well, at least those who ran this rape pit called a prison.

He bribed, blackmailed, or forced someone in the prison to disable the alarm system for him.

KRKKTKT

KKRACKT

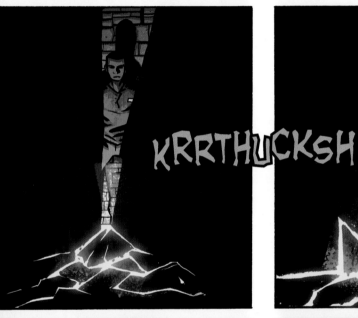

KRRTHUCKSH

I saw this coming.

KTHOOM!

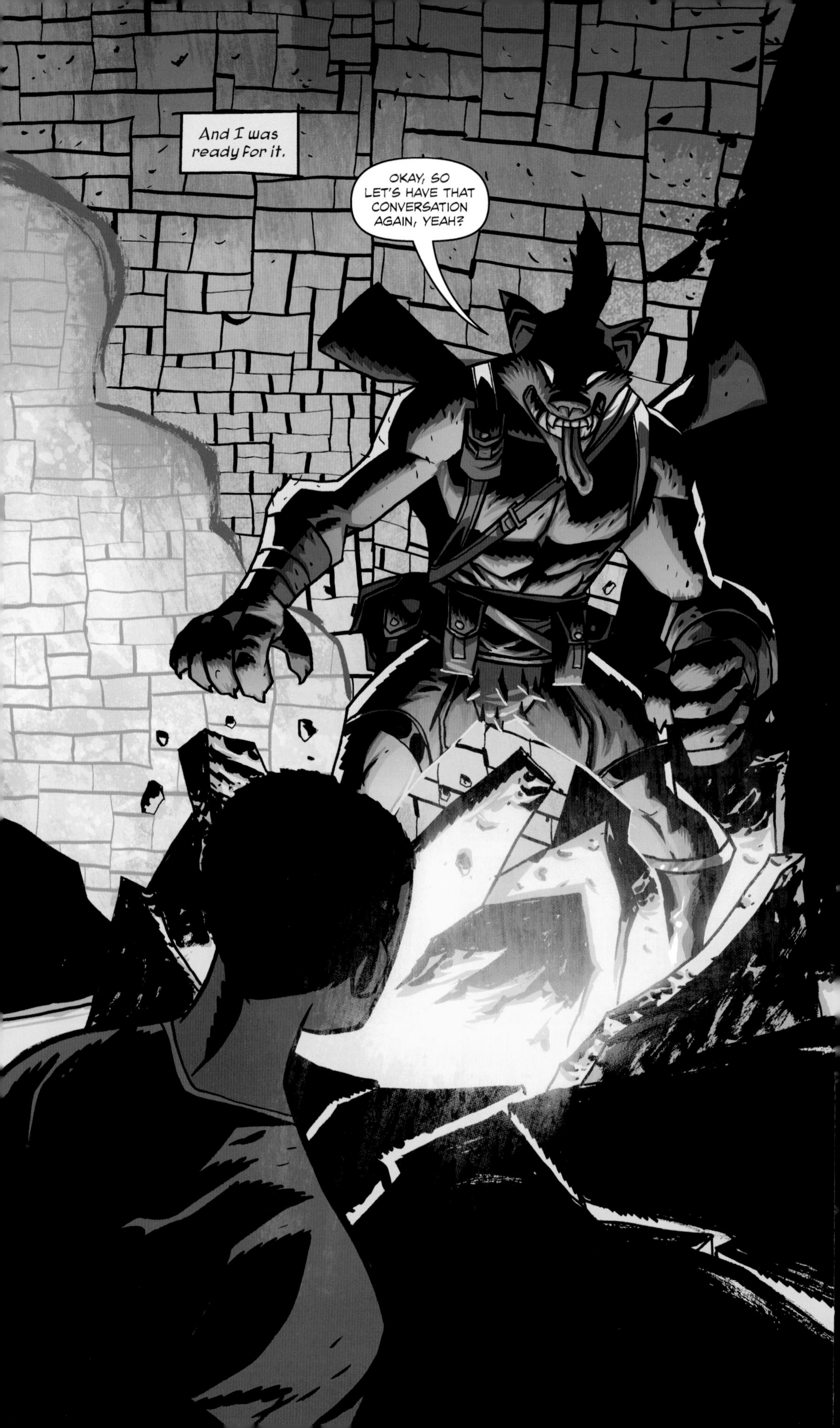
And I was ready for it.
OKAY, SO LET'S HAVE THAT CONVERSATION AGAIN, YEAH?

CHAPTER FIVE

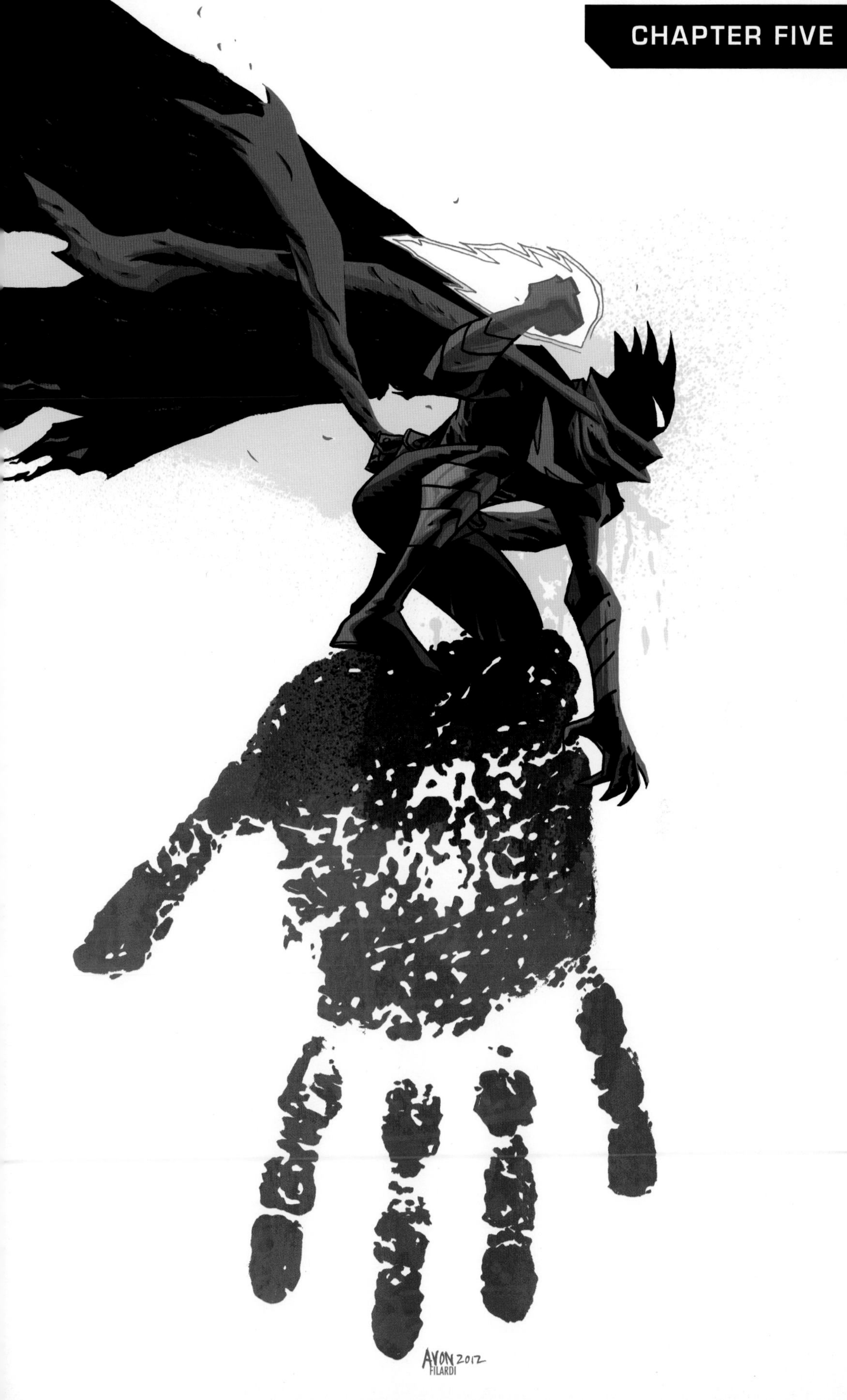
AVON 2012
FILARDI

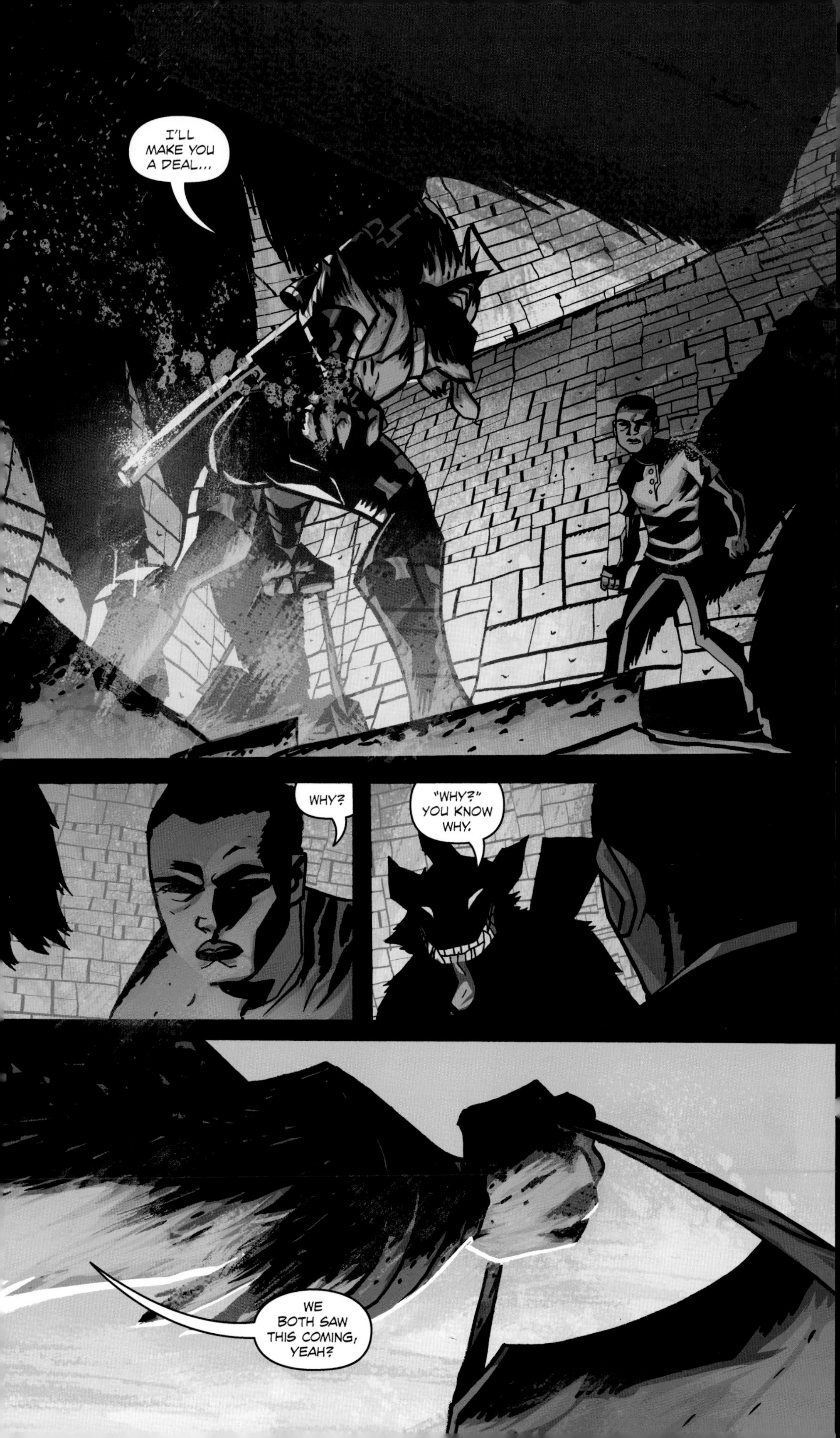
I'LL MAKE YOU A DEAL...
WHY?
"WHY?" YOU KNOW WHY.
WE BOTH SAW THIS COMING, YEAH?

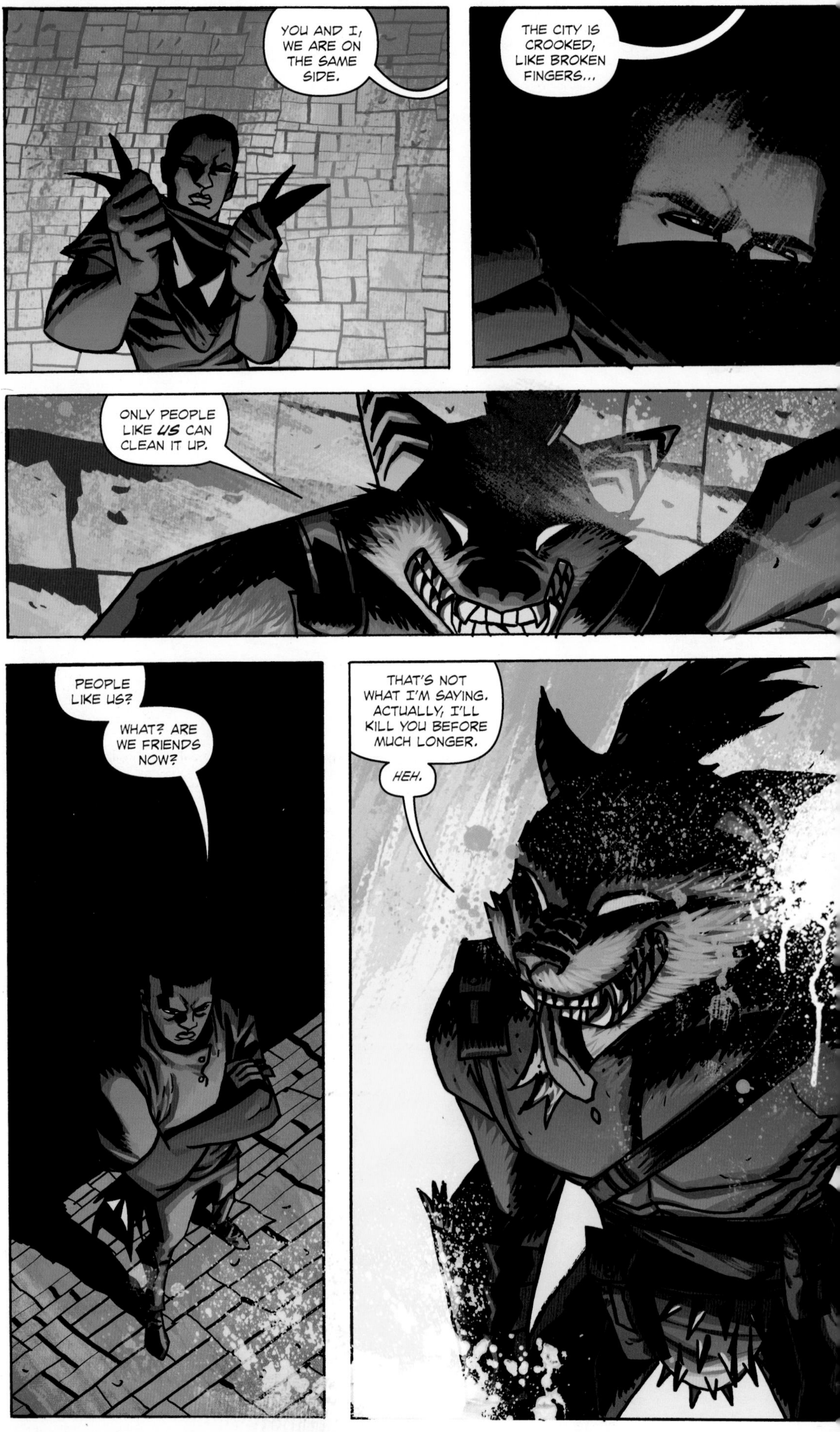
YOU AND I, WE ARE ON THE SAME SIDE.
THE CITY IS CROOKED, LIKE BROKEN FINGERS...
ONLY PEOPLE LIKE *US* CAN CLEAN IT UP.
PEOPLE LIKE US?
WHAT? ARE WE FRIENDS NOW?
THAT'S NOT WHAT I'M SAYING. ACTUALLY, I'LL KILL YOU BEFORE MUCH LONGER.
HEH.

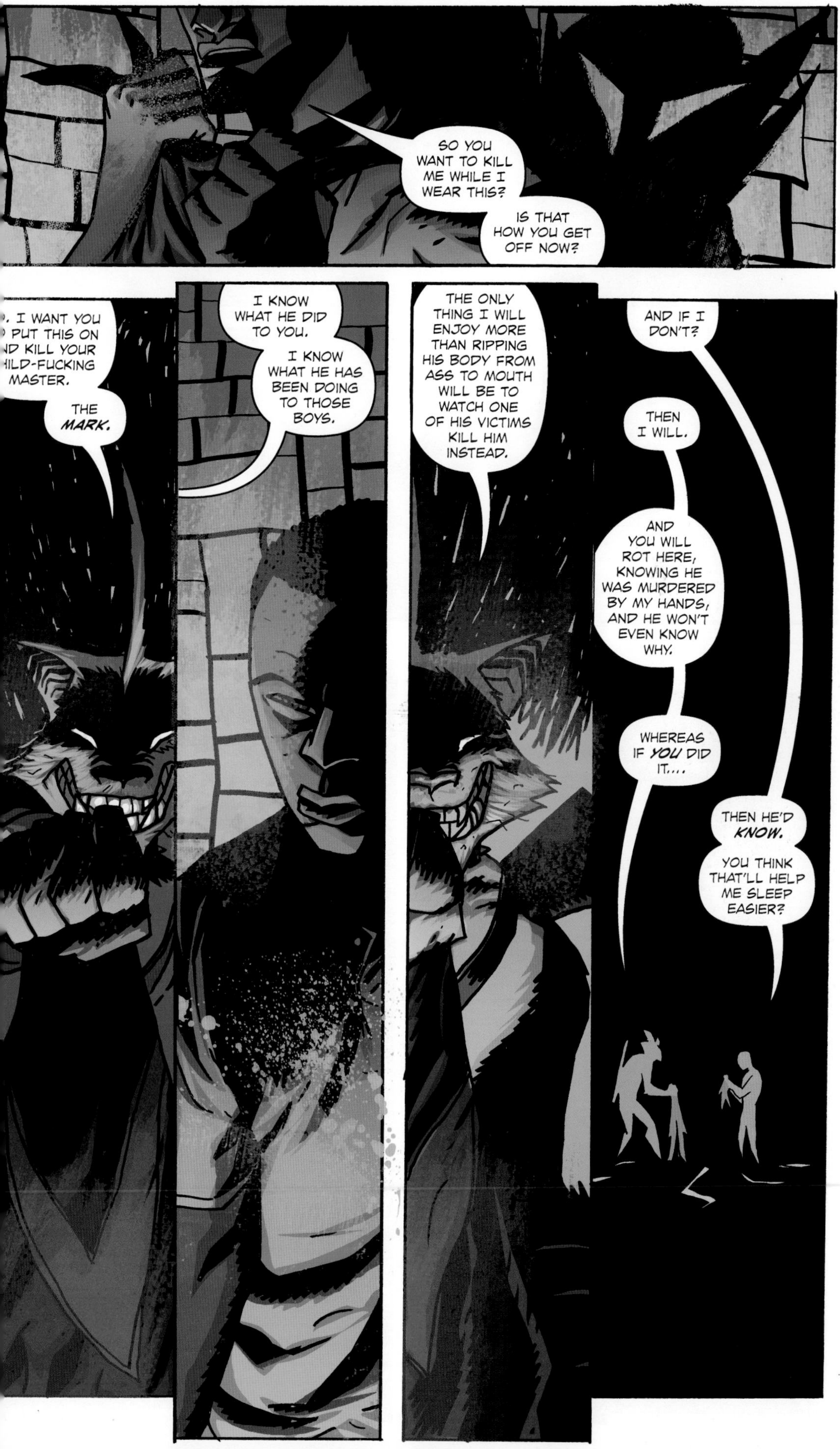
SO YOU WANT TO KILL ME WHILE I WEAR THIS?
IS THAT HOW YOU GET OFF NOW?
. I WANT YOU PUT THIS ON ND KILL YOUR HILD-FUCKING MASTER.
THE *MARK.*
I KNOW WHAT HE DID TO YOU.
I KNOW WHAT HE HAS BEEN DOING TO THOSE BOYS.
THE ONLY THING I WILL ENJOY MORE THAN RIPPING HIS BODY FROM ASS TO MOUTH WILL BE TO WATCH ONE OF HIS VICTIMS KILL HIM INSTEAD.
AND IF I DON'T?
THEN I WILL.
AND YOU WILL ROT HERE, KNOWING HE WAS MURDERED BY MY HANDS, AND HE WON'T EVEN KNOW WHY.
WHEREAS IF *YOU* DID IT....
THEN HE'D *KNOW.*
YOU THINK THAT'LL HELP ME SLEEP EASIER?

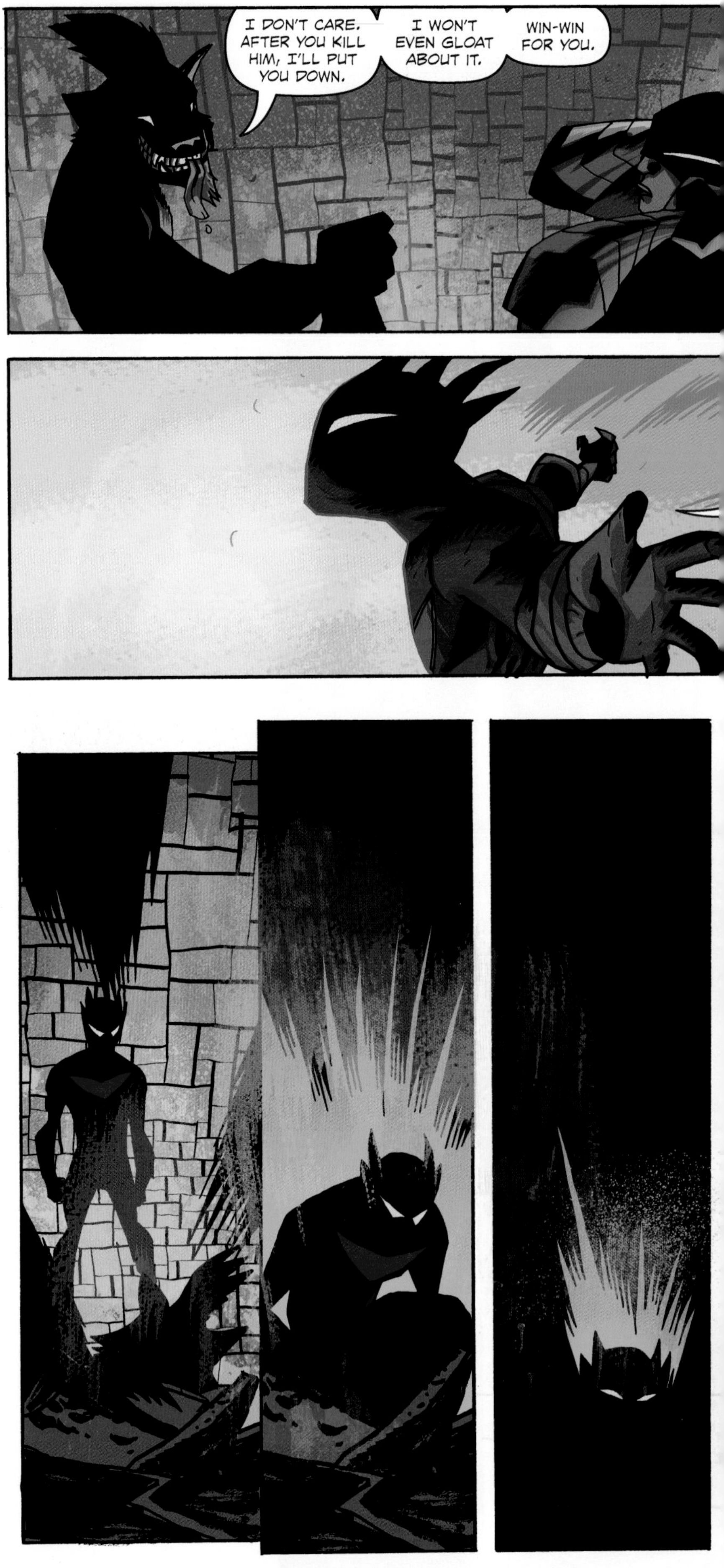
I DON'T CARE. AFTER YOU KILL HIM, I'LL PUT YOU DOWN.
I WON'T EVEN GLOAT ABOUT IT.
WIN-WIN FOR YOU.

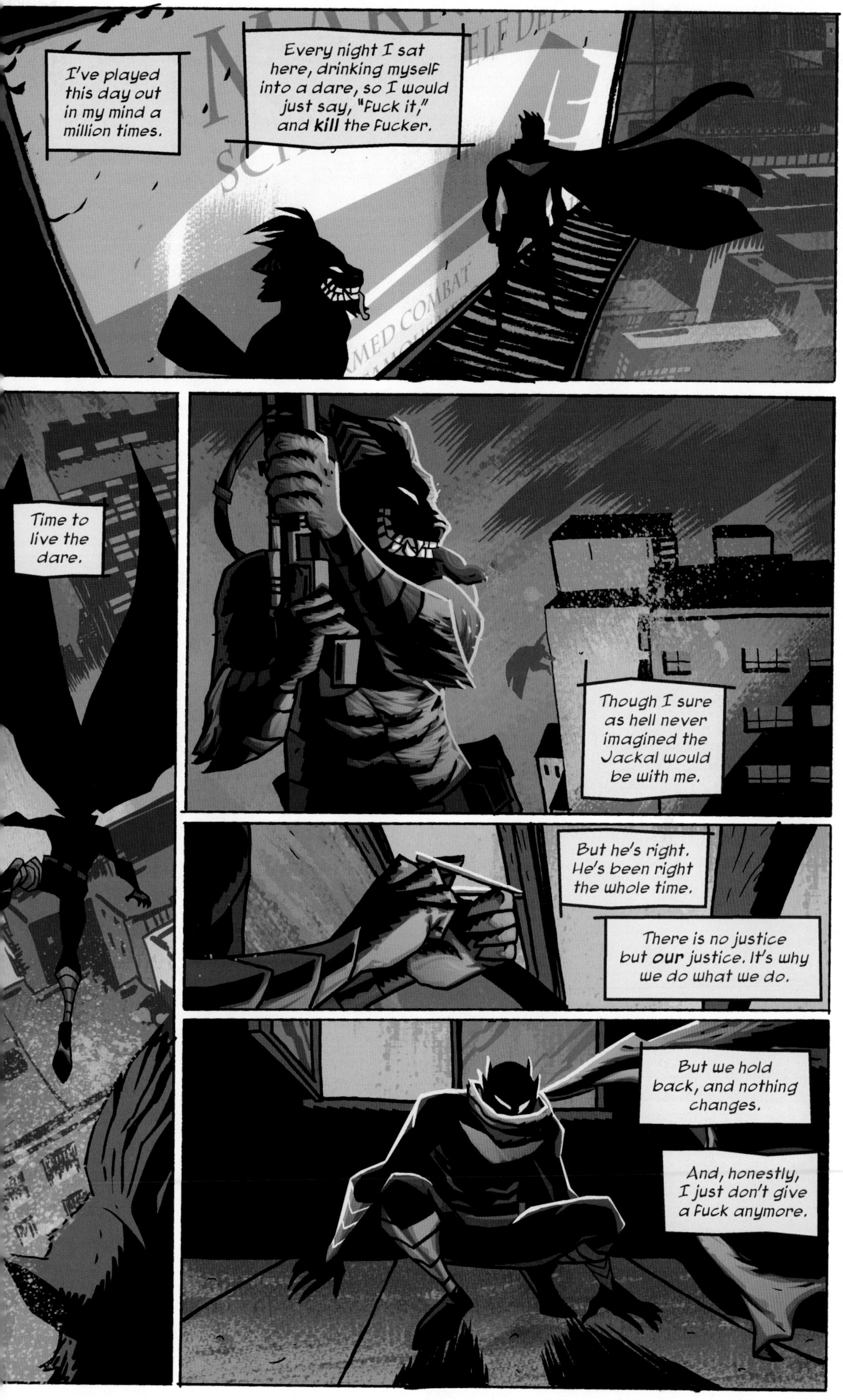
I've played this day out in my mind a million times.
Every night I sat here, drinking myself into a dare, so I would just say, "Fuck it," and **kill** the fucker.
MED COMBAT
Time to live the dare.
Though I sure as hell never imagined the Jackal would be with me.
But he's right. He's been right the whole time.
There is no justice but **our** justice. It's why we do what we do.
But we hold back, and nothing changes.
And, honestly, I just don't give a fuck anymore.

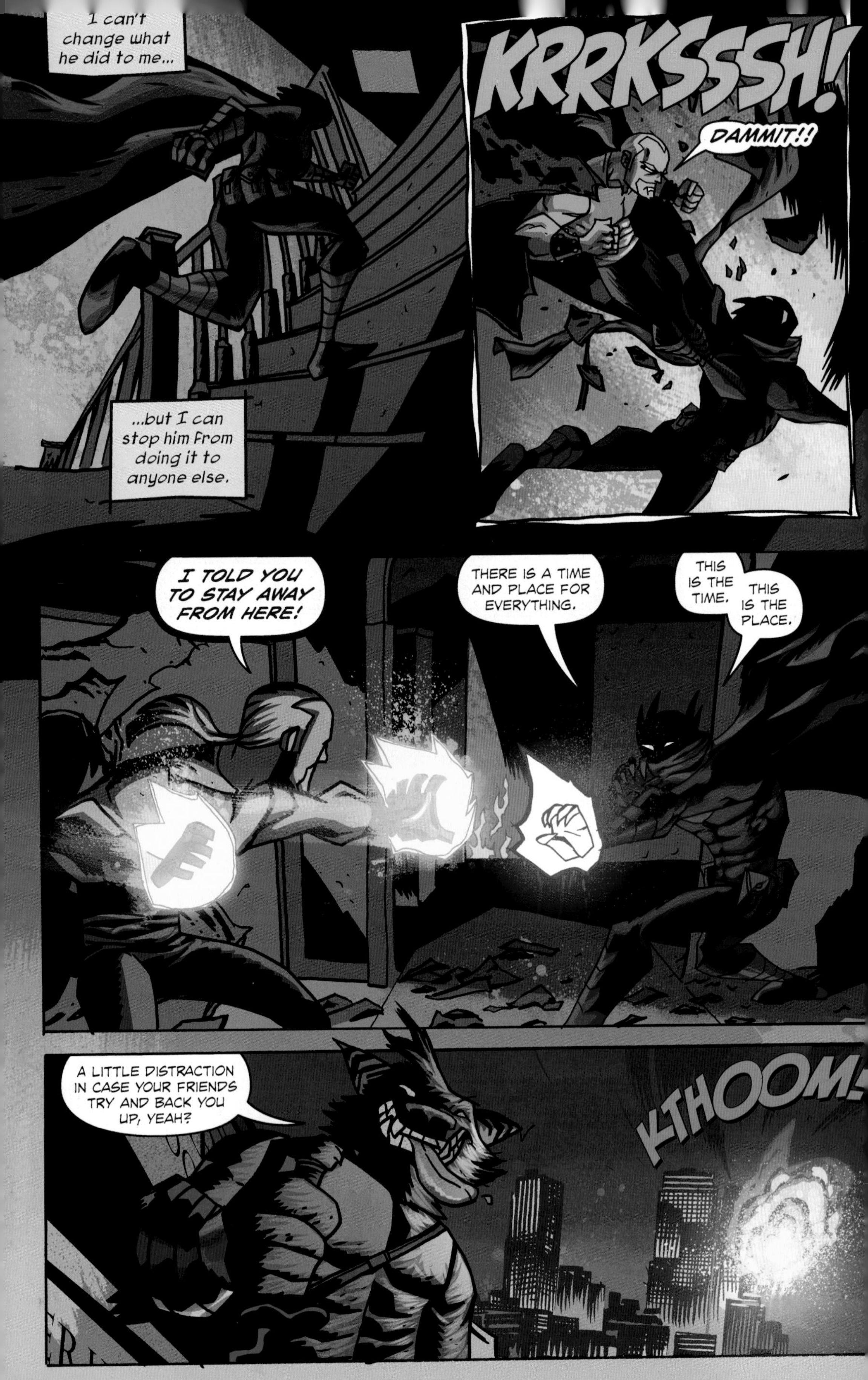

I can't change what he did to me...
KRRKSSSH!
DAMMIT!!
...but I can stop him from doing it to anyone else.
I TOLD YOU TO STAY AWAY FROM HERE!
THERE IS A TIME AND PLACE FOR EVERYTHING.
THIS IS THE TIME.
THIS IS THE PLACE.
A LITTLE DISTRACTION IN CASE YOUR FRIENDS TRY AND BACK YOU UP, YEAH?
KTHOOM!

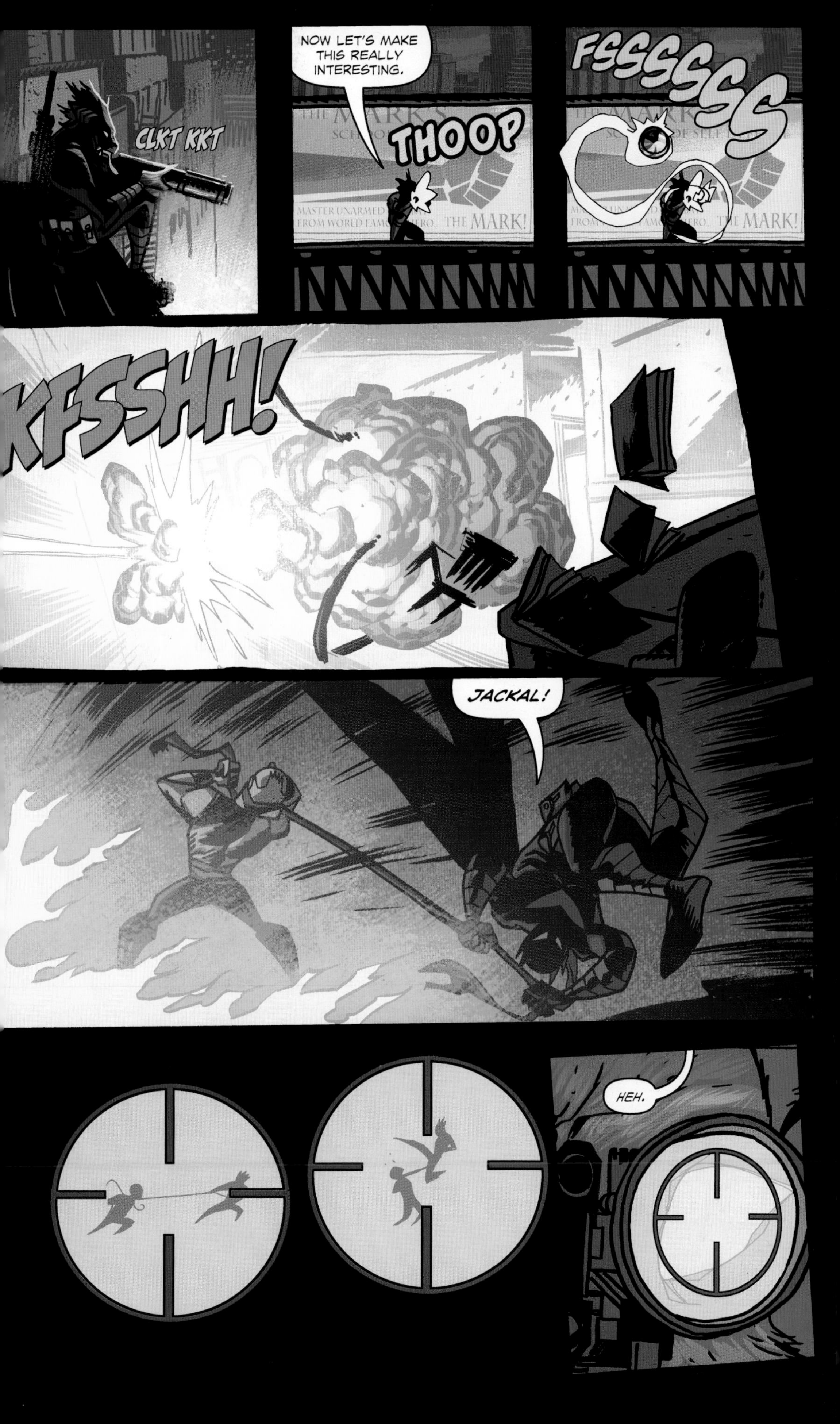
CLKT KKT
NOW LET'S MAKE THIS REALLY INTERESTING.
THE MARK'S SCHOOL
MASTER UNARMED FROM WORLD FAMOUS HERO... THE MARK!
THOOP
FSSSSSSS
KFSSHH!
JACKAL!
HEH.

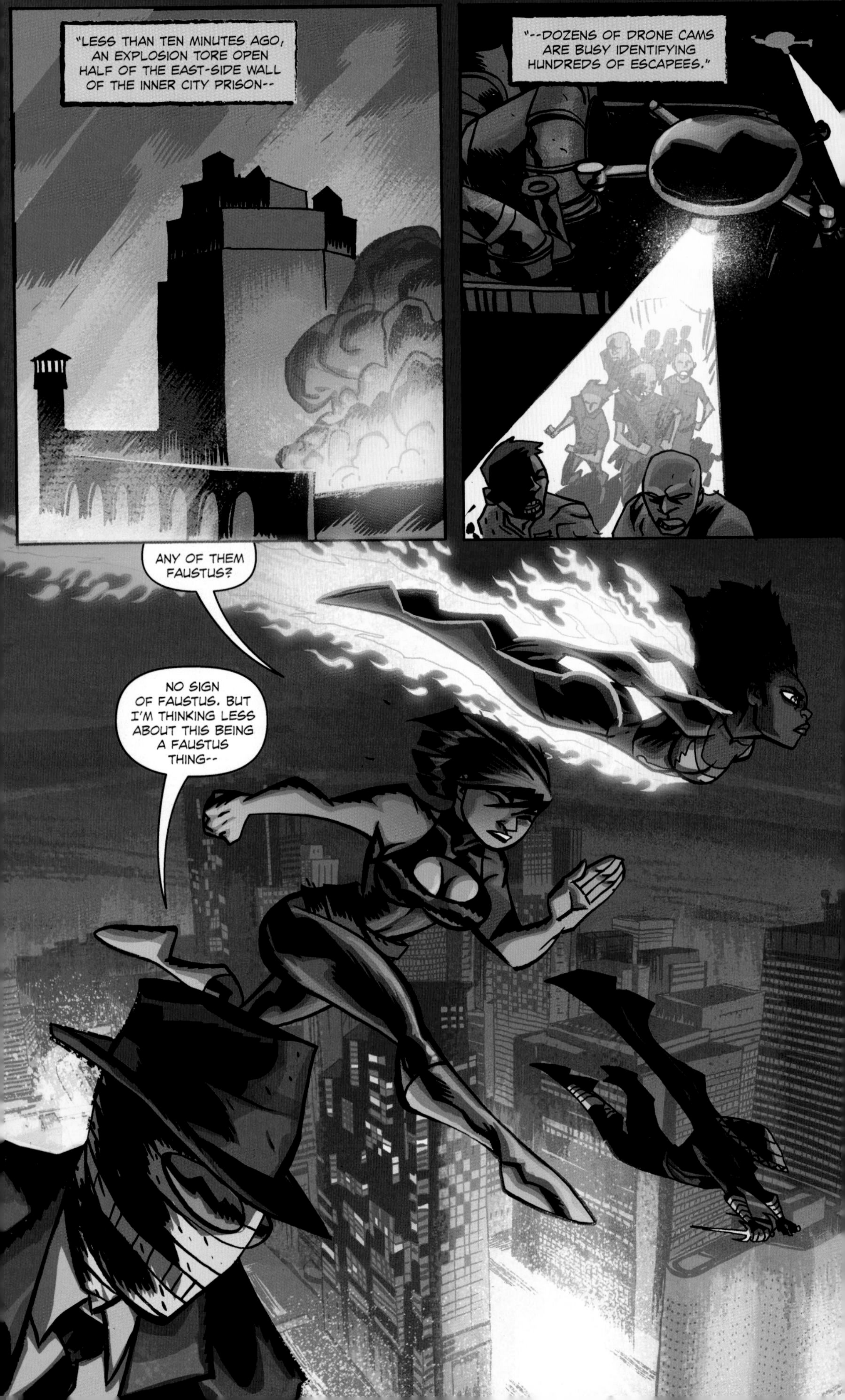
"LESS THAN TEN MINUTES AGO, AN EXPLOSION TORE OPEN HALF OF THE EAST-SIDE WALL OF THE INNER CITY PRISON--
"--DOZENS OF DRONE CAMS ARE BUSY IDENTIFYING HUNDREDS OF ESCAPEES."
ANY OF THEM FAUSTUS?
NO SIGN OF FAUSTUS. BUT I'M THINKING LESS ABOUT THIS BEING A FAUSTUS THING--

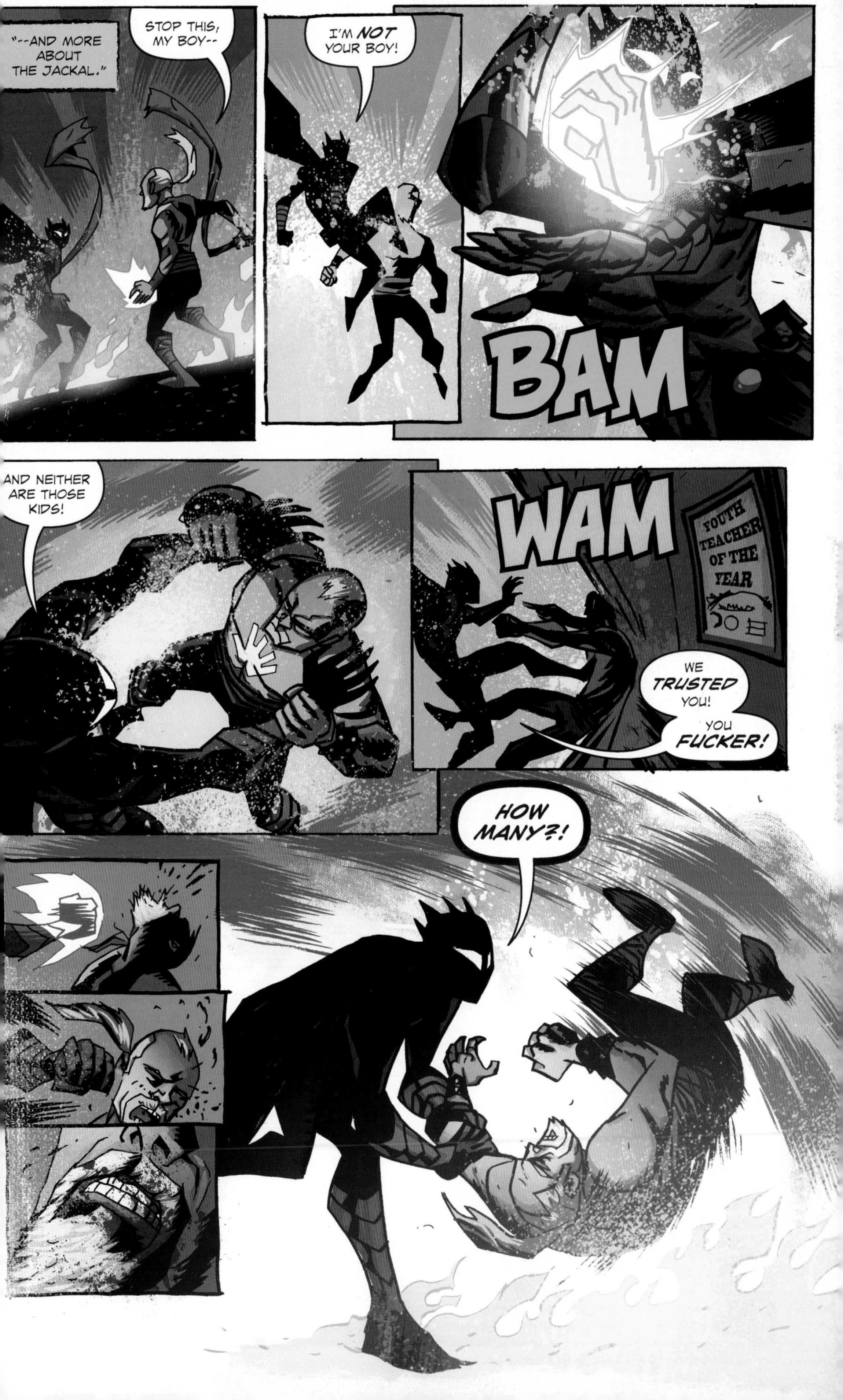
"--AND MORE ABOUT THE JACKAL."
STOP THIS, MY BOY--
I'M NOT YOUR BOY!
BAM
AND NEITHER ARE THOSE KIDS!
WAM
YOUTH TEACHER OF THE YEAR
WE TRUSTED YOU!
YOU FUCKER!
HOW MANY?!

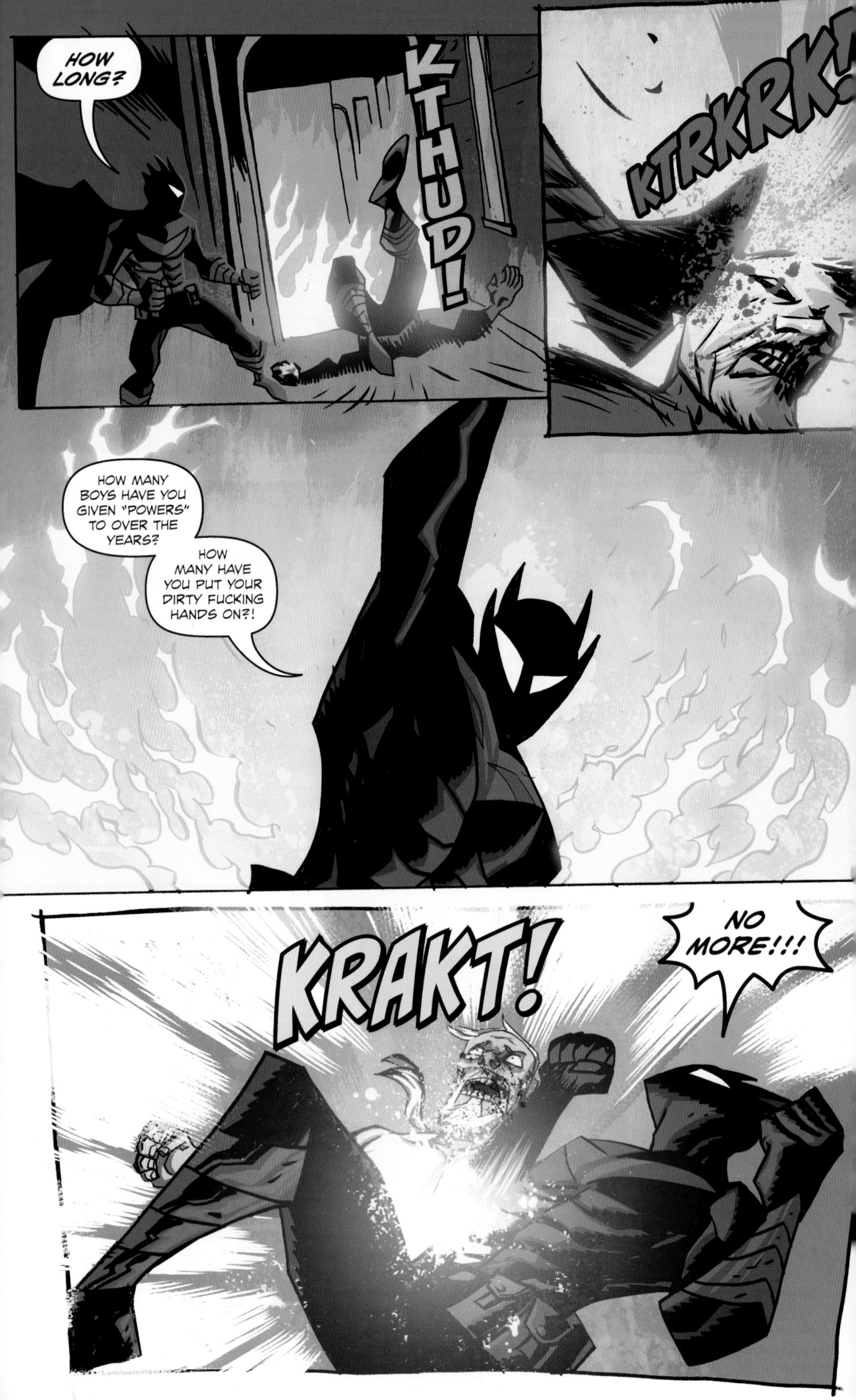
HOW LONG?
KTHUD!
KTRKRK!
HOW MANY BOYS HAVE YOU GIVEN "POWERS" TO OVER THE YEARS?
HOW MANY HAVE YOU PUT YOUR DIRTY FUCKING HANDS ON?!
KRAKT!
NO MORE!!!

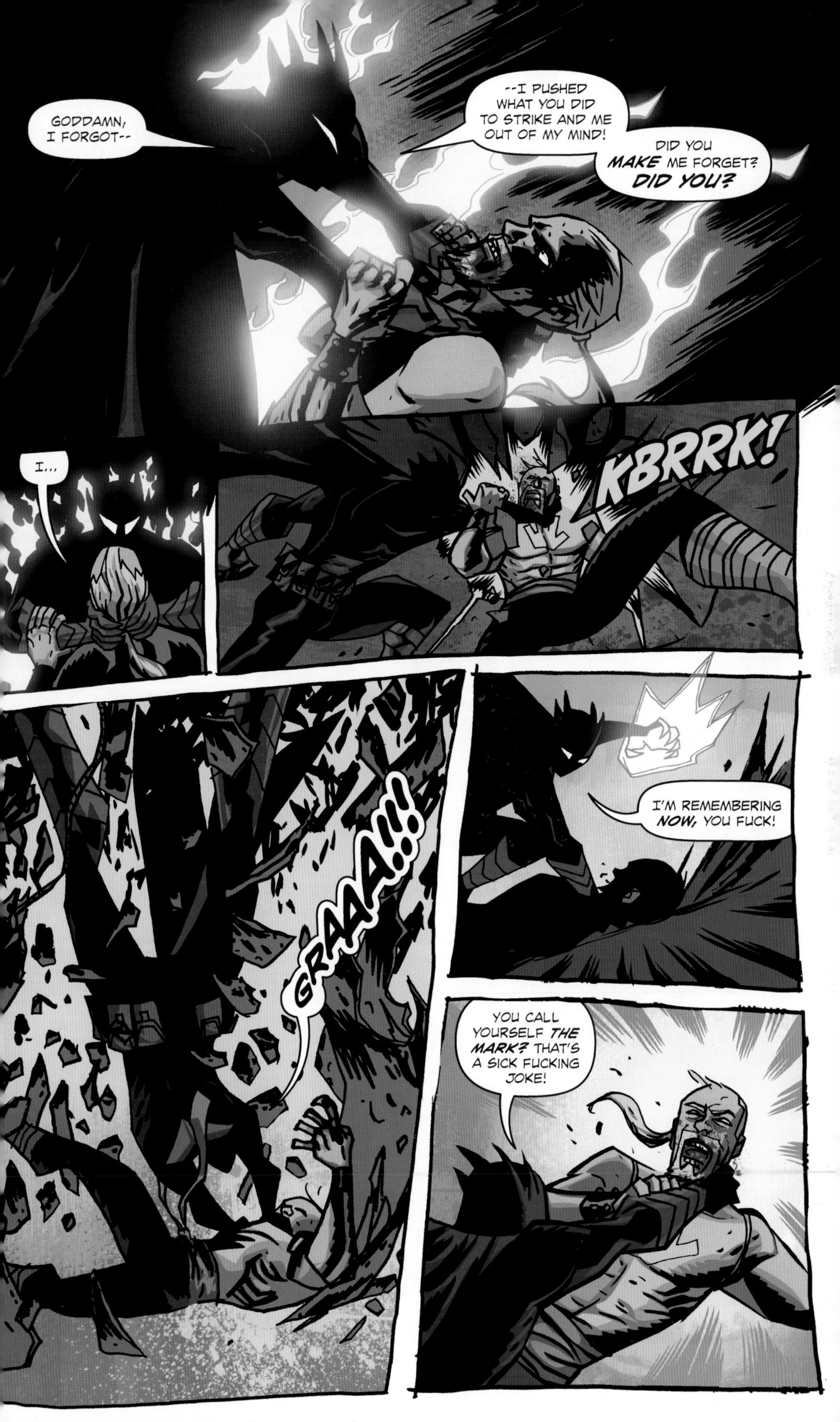
GODDAMN, I FORGOT--
--I PUSHED WHAT YOU DID TO STRIKE AND ME OUT OF MY MIND!
DID YOU MAKE ME FORGET? DID YOU?
I...
KBRRK!
GRAAA!!!
I'M REMEMBERING NOW, YOU FUCK!
YOU CALL YOURSELF THE MARK? THAT'S A SICK FUCKING JOKE!

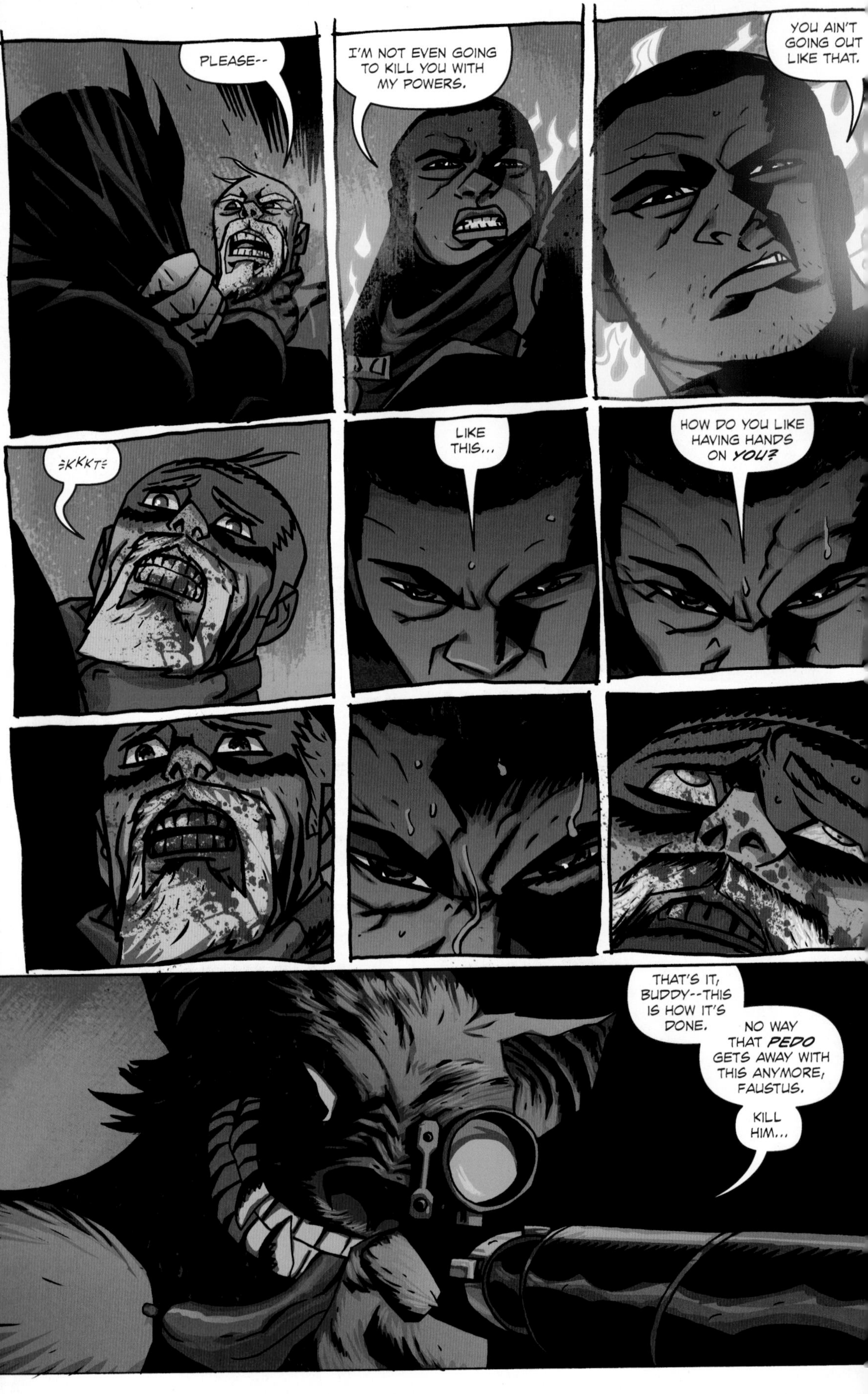
PLEASE--
I'M NOT EVEN GOING TO KILL YOU WITH MY POWERS.
YOU AIN'T GOING OUT LIKE THAT.
KKKT
LIKE THIS...
HOW DO YOU LIKE HAVING HANDS ON *YOU*?
THAT'S IT, BUDDY--THIS IS HOW IT'S DONE.
NO WAY THAT *PEDO* GETS AWAY WITH THIS ANYMORE, FAUSTUS.
KILL HIM...

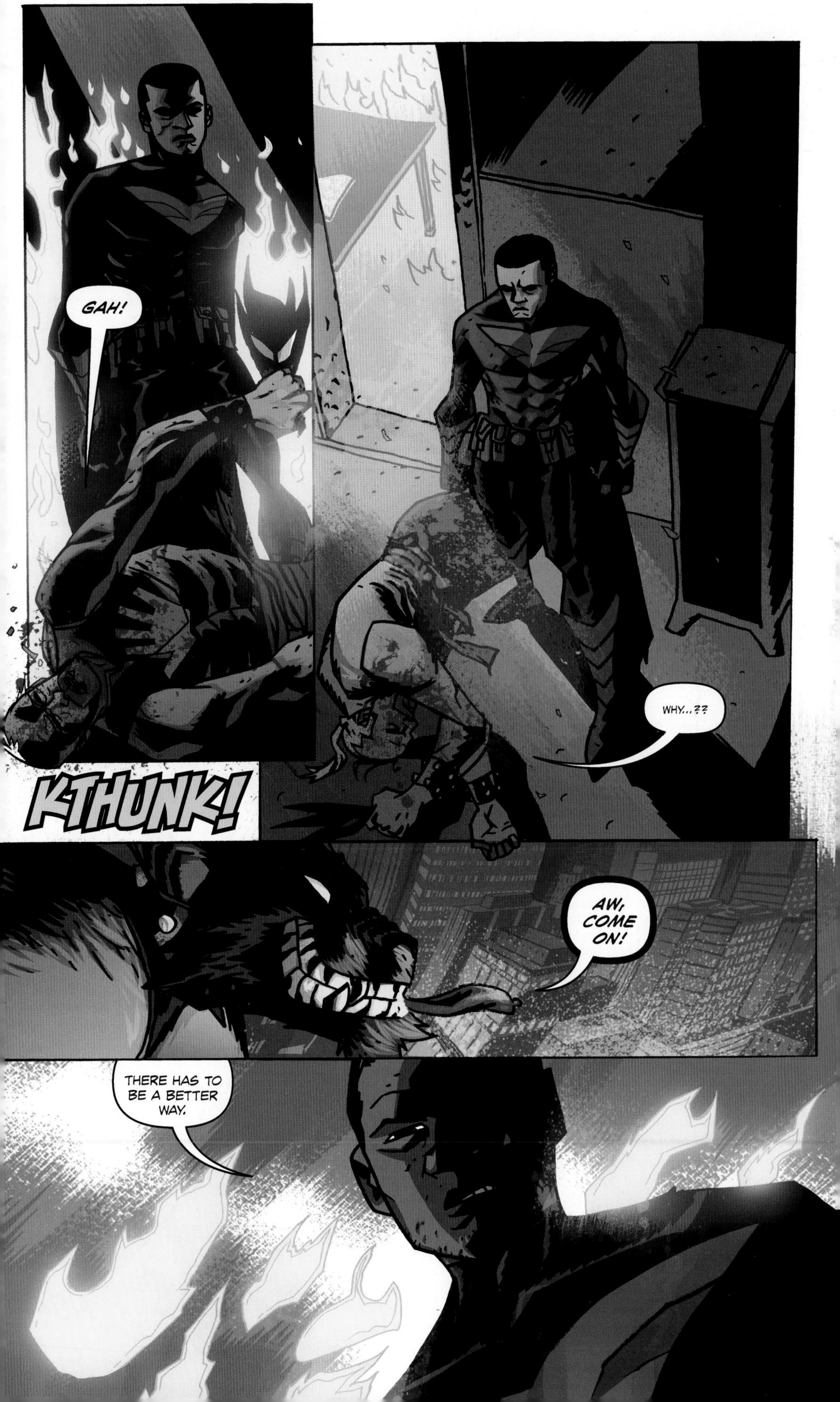
GAH!
KTHUNK!
WHY...??
AW, COME ON!
THERE HAS TO BE A BETTER WAY.

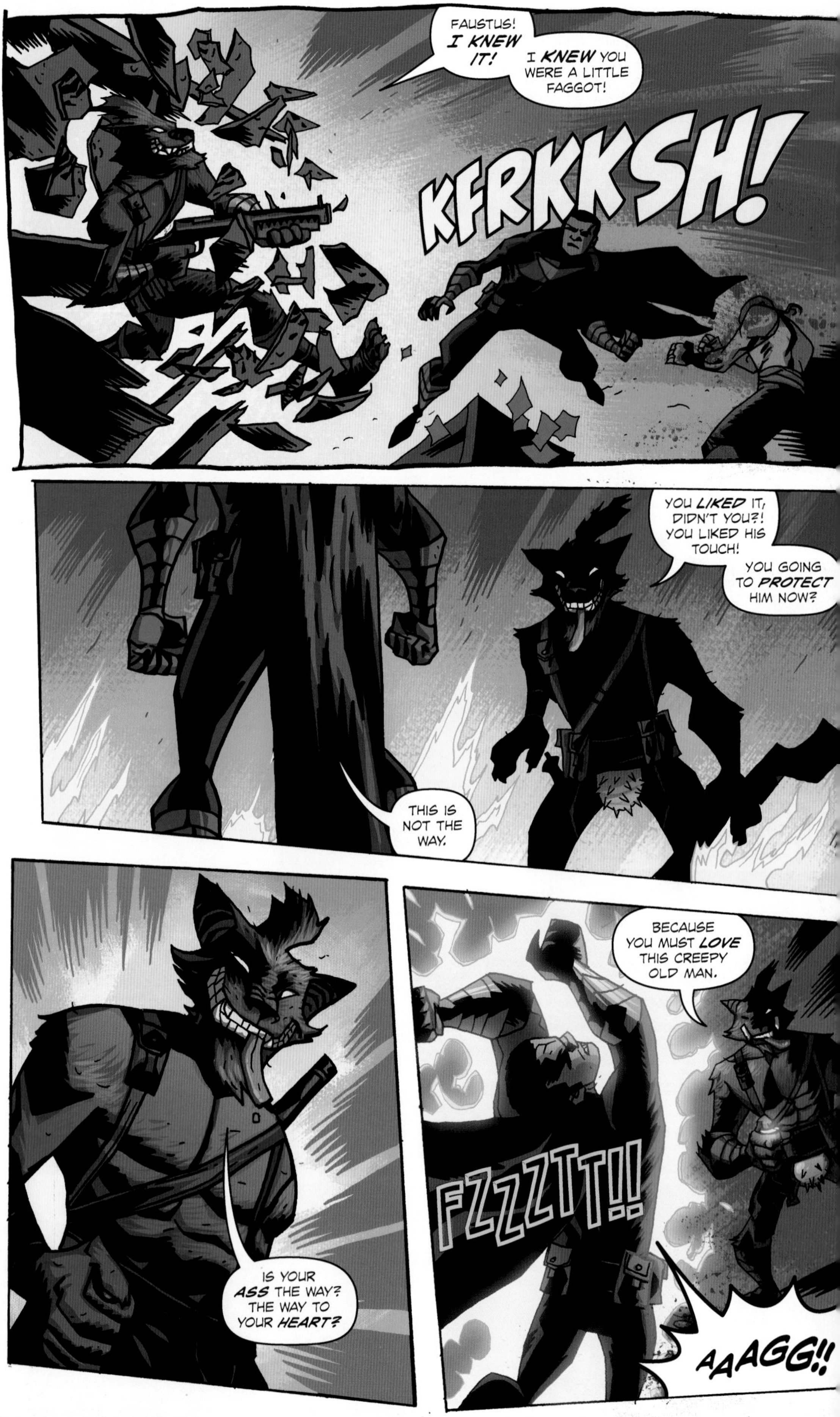
FAUSTUS! I KNEW IT!
I KNEW YOU WERE A LITTLE FAGGOT!
KFRKKSH!
YOU LIKED IT, DIDN'T YOU?! YOU LIKED HIS TOUCH!
YOU GOING TO PROTECT HIM NOW?
THIS IS NOT THE WAY.
IS YOUR ASS THE WAY? THE WAY TO YOUR HEART?
BECAUSE YOU MUST LOVE THIS CREEPY OLD MAN.
FZZZTT!!
AAAGG!!

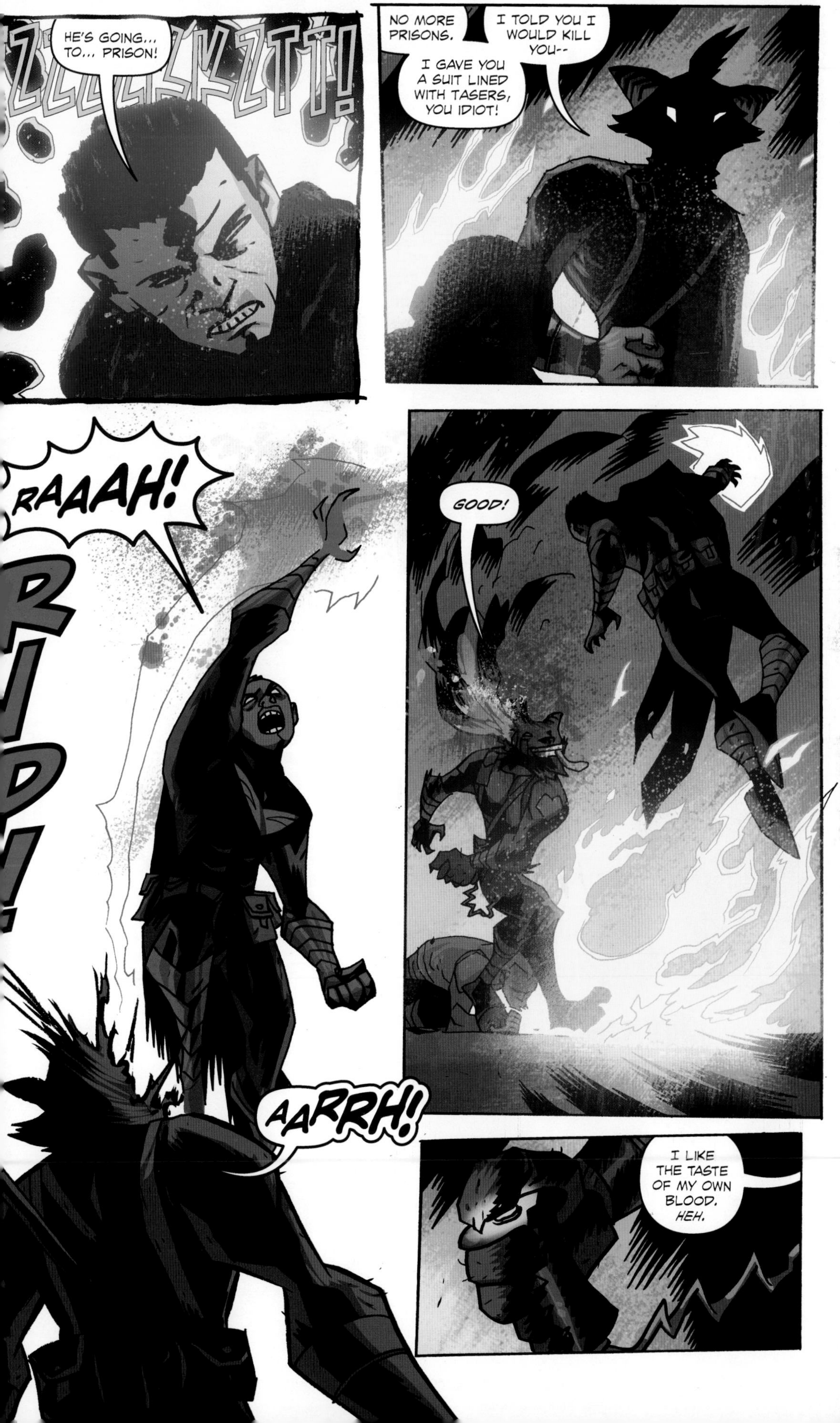
HE'S GOING... TO... PRISON!
NO MORE PRISONS.
I TOLD YOU I WOULD KILL YOU--
I GAVE YOU A SUIT LINED WITH TASERS, YOU IDIOT!
RAAAH!
AARRH!
GOOD!
I LIKE THE TASTE OF MY OWN BLOOD. *HEH.*

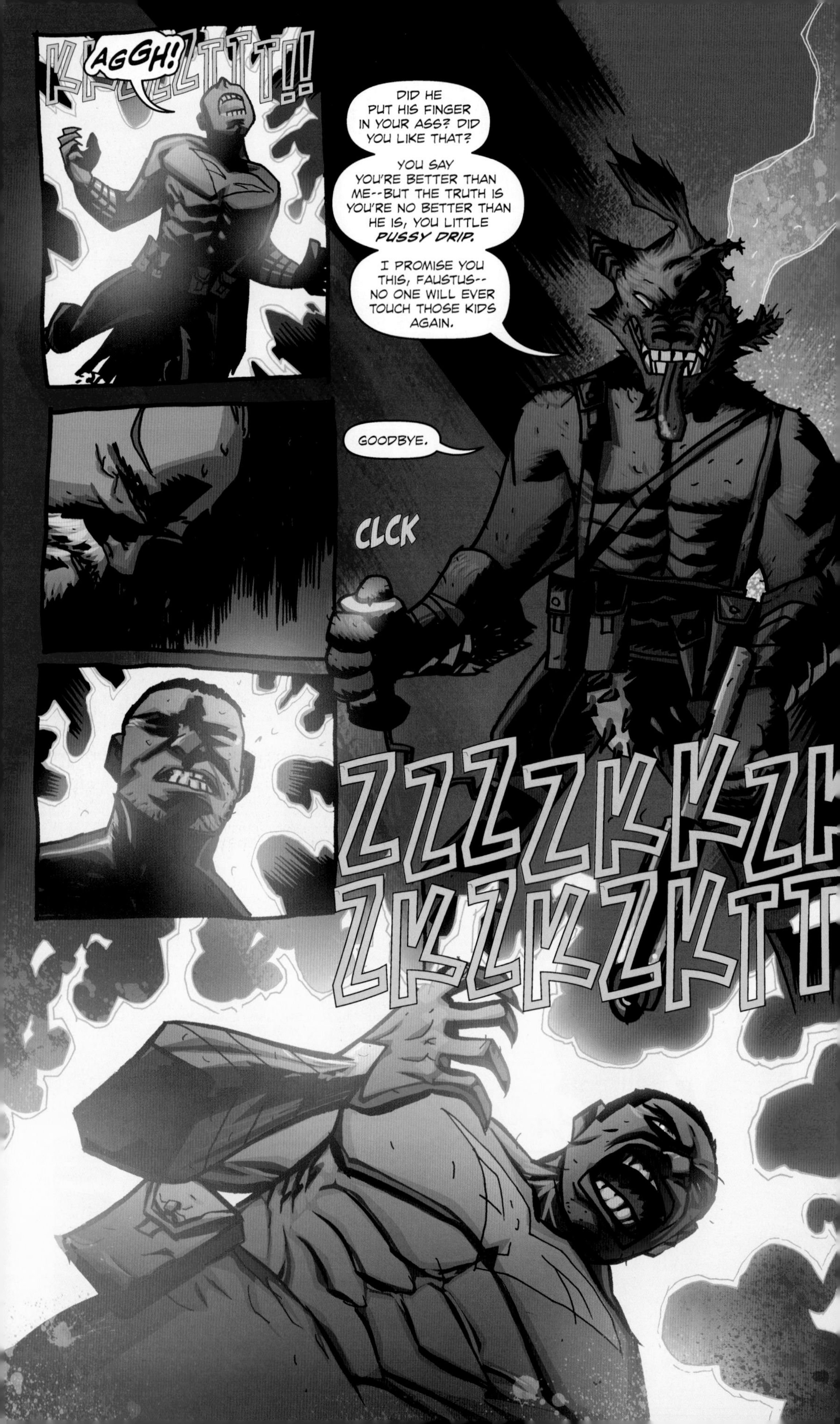
KRZZZTTTT!!
AGGH!
DID HE PUT HIS FINGER IN YOUR ASS? DID YOU LIKE THAT?
YOU SAY YOU'RE BETTER THAN ME--BUT THE TRUTH IS YOU'RE NO BETTER THAN HE IS, YOU LITTLE PUSSY DRIP.
I PROMISE YOU THIS, FAUSTUS--NO ONE WILL EVER TOUCH THOSE KIDS AGAIN.
GOODBYE.
CLCK
ZZZZKKZK
ZKZKZKTT

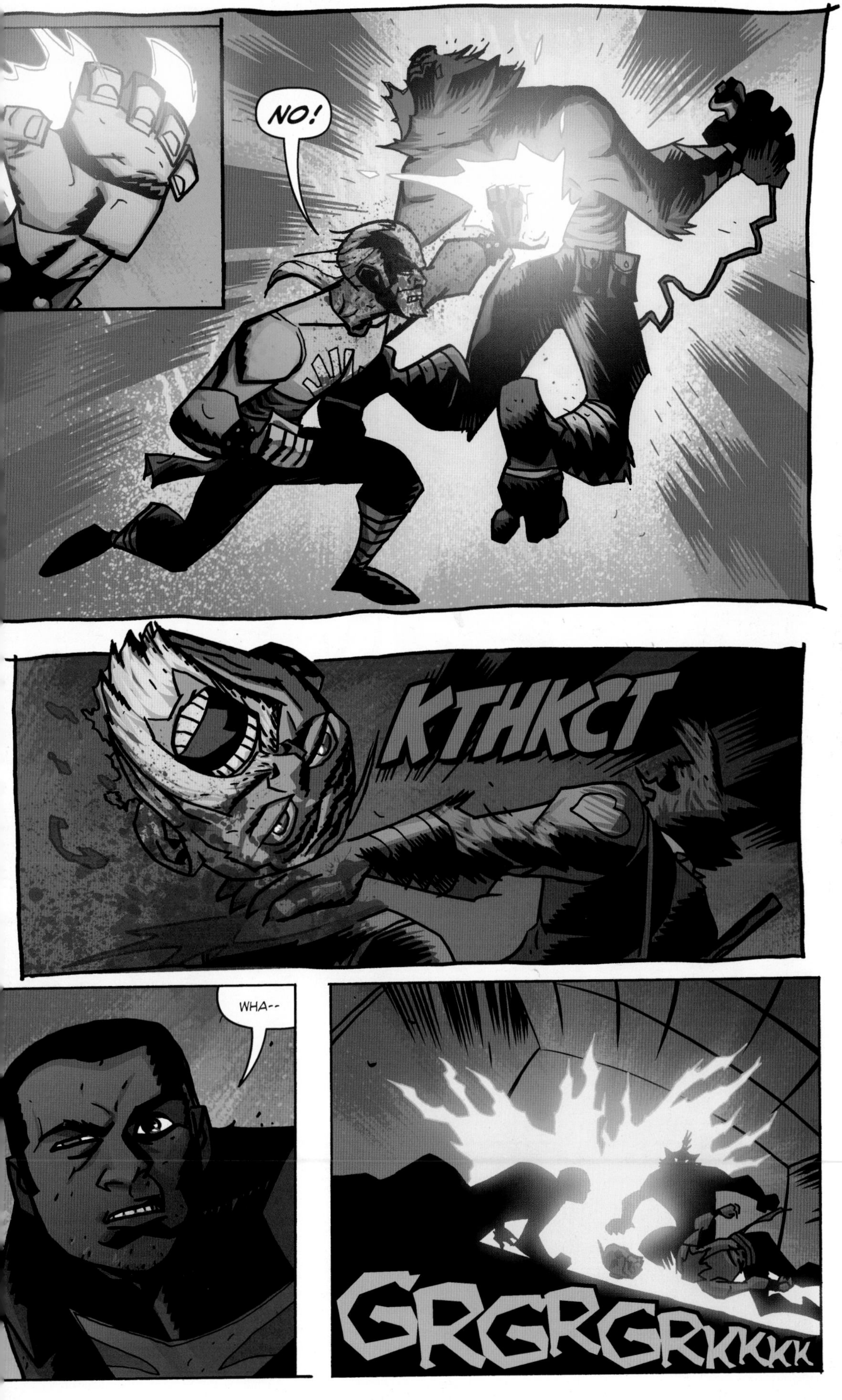
NO!
KTHKCT
WHA--
GRGRGRKKKK

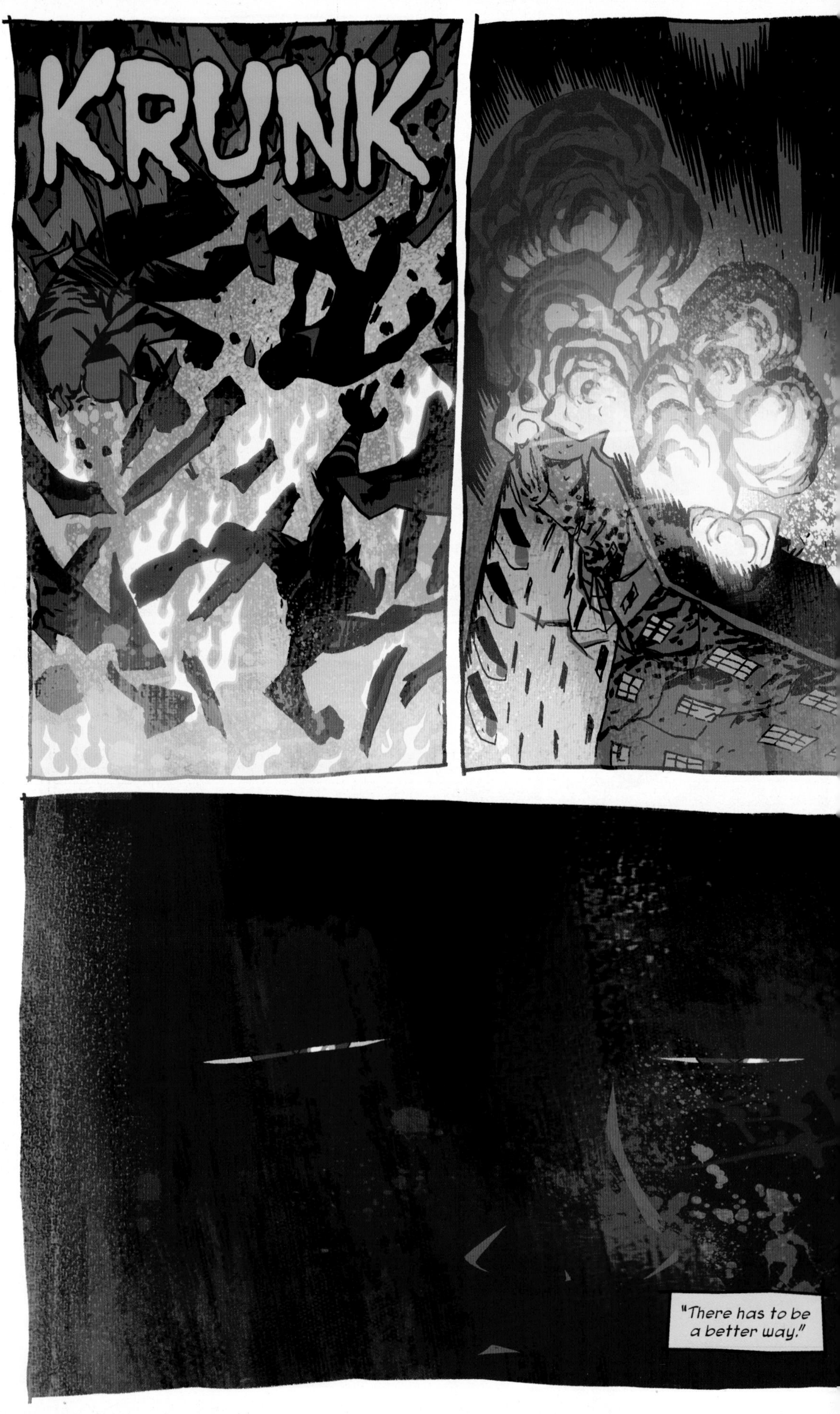
KRUNK
"There has to be a better way."

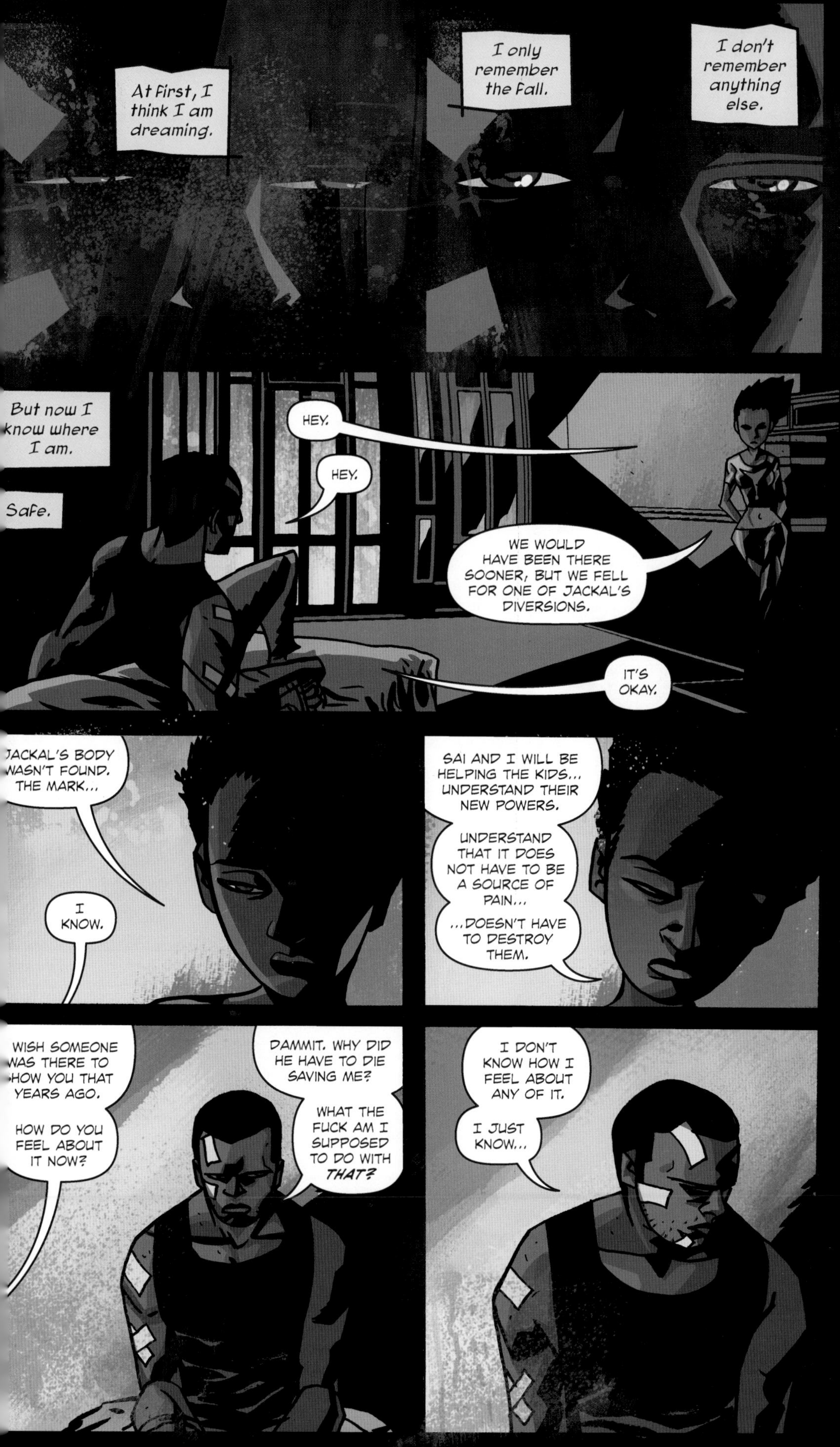

At First, I think I am dreaming.
I only remember the fall.
I don't remember anything else.
But now I know where I am.
Safe.
HEY.
HEY.
WE WOULD HAVE BEEN THERE SOONER, BUT WE FELL FOR ONE OF JACKAL'S DIVERSIONS.
IT'S OKAY.
JACKAL'S BODY WASN'T FOUND. THE MARK...
I KNOW.
SAI AND I WILL BE HELPING THE KIDS... UNDERSTAND THEIR NEW POWERS.
UNDERSTAND THAT IT DOES NOT HAVE TO BE A SOURCE OF PAIN...
...DOESN'T HAVE TO DESTROY THEM.
WISH SOMEONE WAS THERE TO SHOW YOU THAT YEARS AGO.
HOW DO YOU FEEL ABOUT IT NOW?
DAMMIT. WHY DID HE HAVE TO DIE SAVING ME?
WHAT THE FUCK AM I SUPPOSED TO DO WITH *THAT?*
I DON'T KNOW HOW I FEEL ABOUT ANY OF IT.
I JUST KNOW...

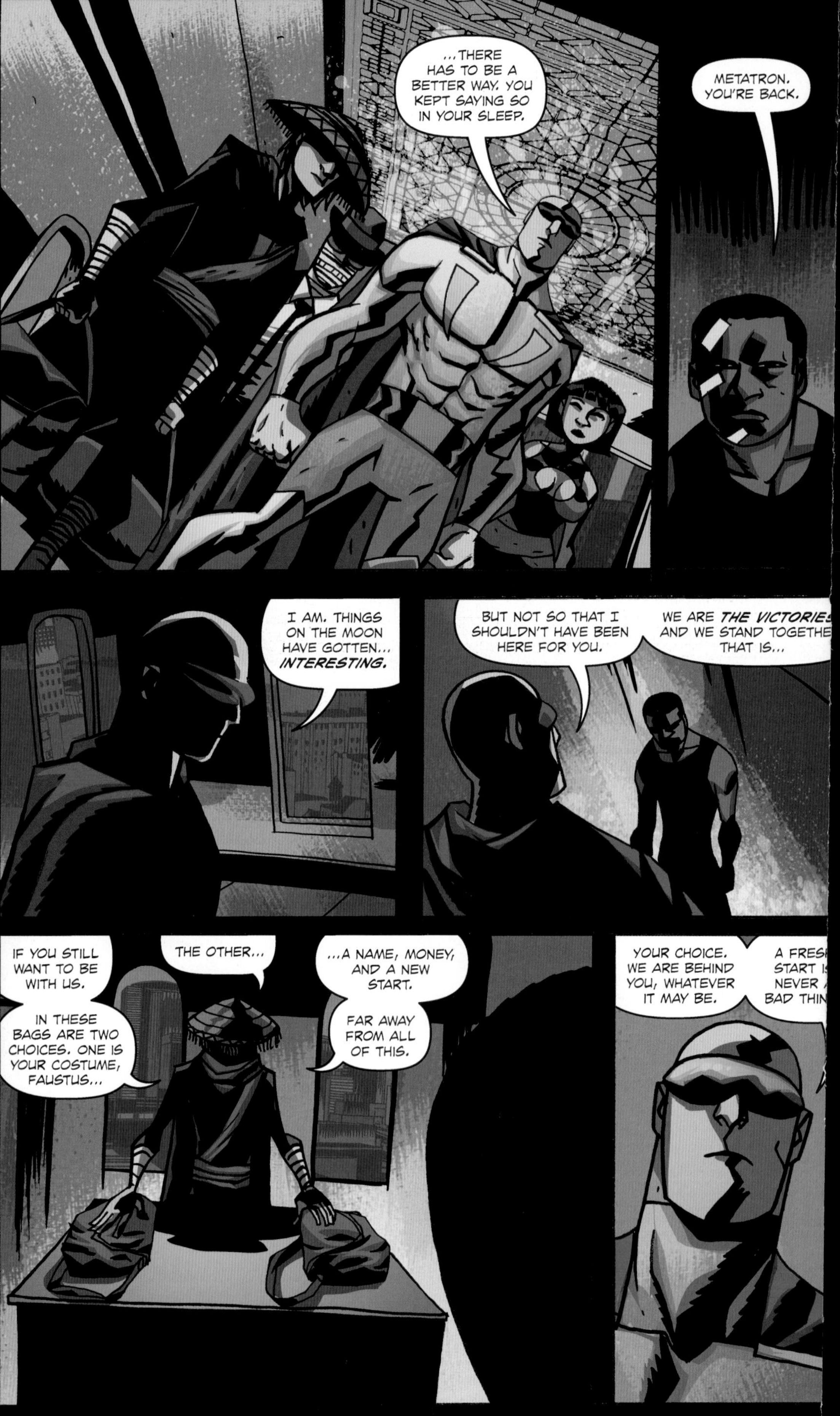
...THERE HAS TO BE A BETTER WAY. YOU KEPT SAYING SO IN YOUR SLEEP.
METATRON. YOU'RE BACK.
I AM. THINGS ON THE MOON HAVE GOTTEN... *INTERESTING.*
BUT NOT SO THAT I SHOULDN'T HAVE BEEN HERE FOR YOU.
WE ARE *THE VICTORIE* AND WE STAND TOGETHE THAT IS...
IF YOU STILL WANT TO BE WITH US.
IN THESE BAGS ARE TWO CHOICES. ONE IS YOUR COSTUME, FAUSTUS...
THE OTHER...
...A NAME, MONEY, AND A NEW START.
FAR AWAY FROM ALL OF THIS.
YOUR CHOICE. WE ARE BEHIND YOU, WHATEVER IT MAY BE.
A FRES START I NEVER BAD THI

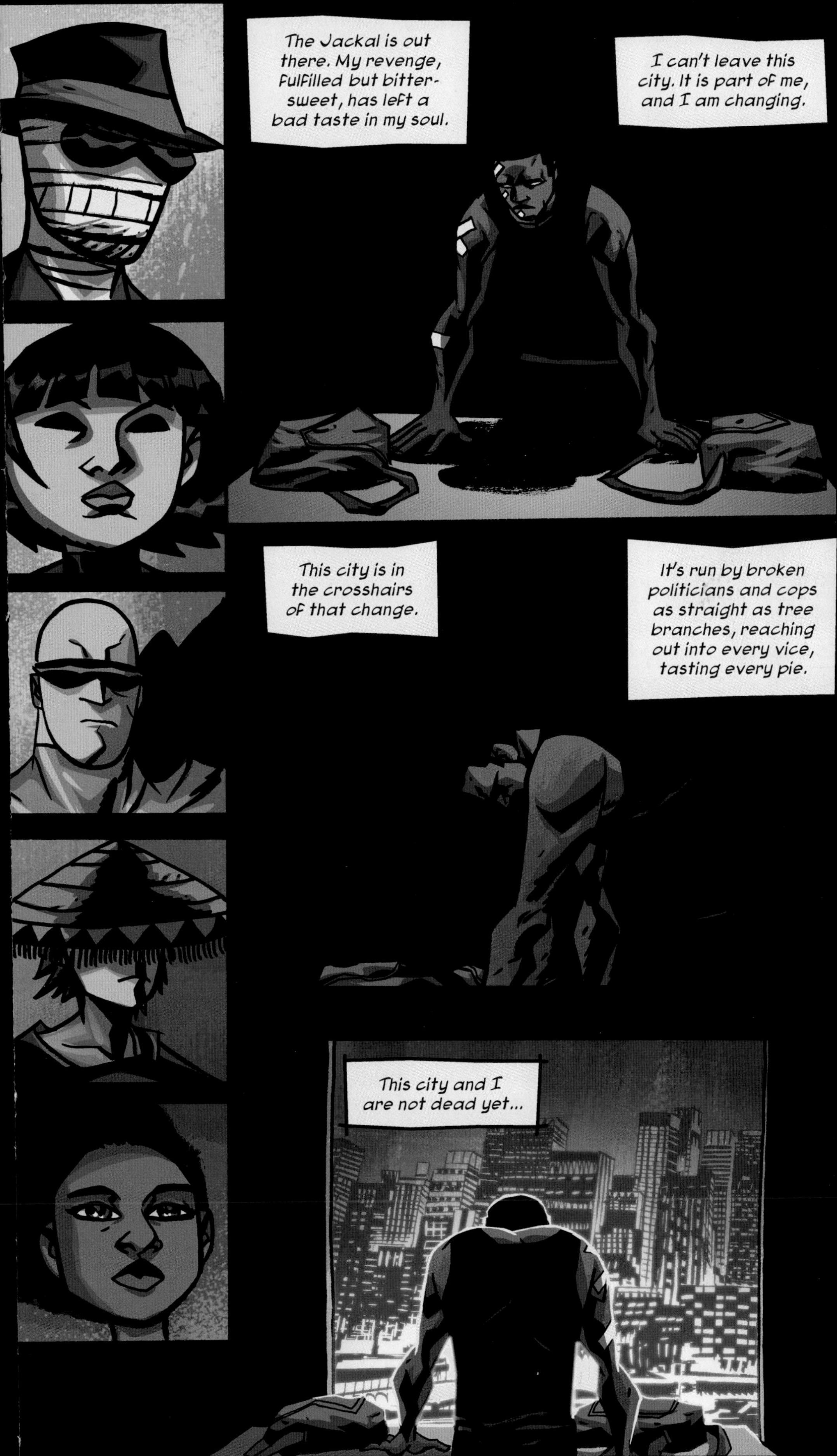

The Jackal is out there. My revenge, fulfilled but bitter-sweet, has left a bad taste in my soul.
I can't leave this city. It is part of me, and I am changing.
This city is in the crosshairs of that change.
It's run by broken politicians and cops as straight as tree branches, reaching out into every vice, tasting every pie.
This city and I are not dead yet...

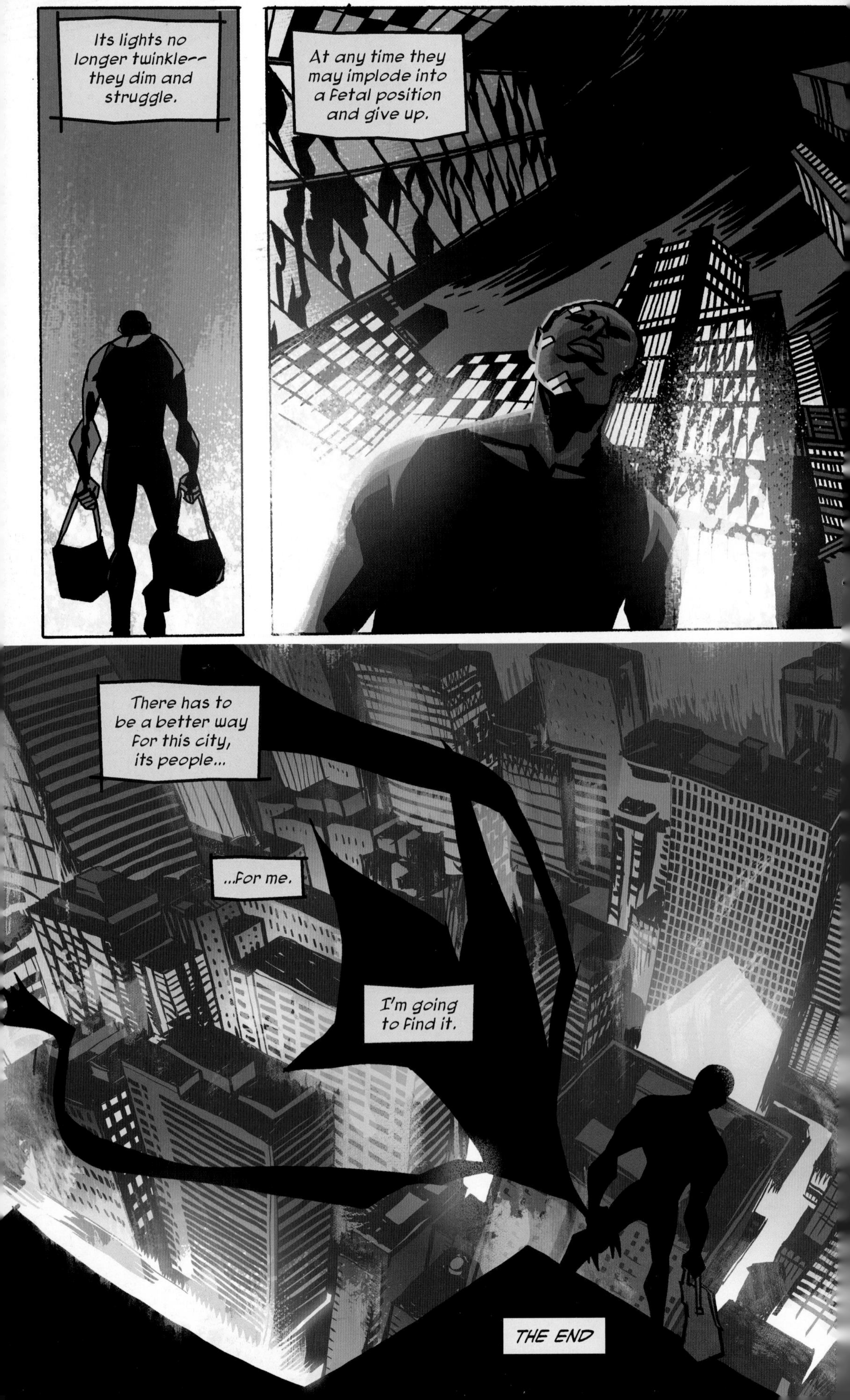
Its lights no longer twinkle-- they dim and struggle.
At any time they may implode into a fetal position and give up.
There has to be a better way for this city, its people...
...for me.
I'm going to find it.
THE END

SKETCHBOOK

Notes by Michael Avon Oeming

I've done more sketchbook work with *The Victories* than any of my other creator-owned works, including *Powers*, *Hammer of the Gods*, and *Mice Templar*. I began *Victories* (then called *The Touch*) during a time of heavy therapy. I was also working for the video-game company Valve Corporation full time, and not getting much comic-book work done, so sketchbooks became the outlet of everything artistic and anxiety driven within me. It was art therapy, and I wasn't even aware of it at the time.

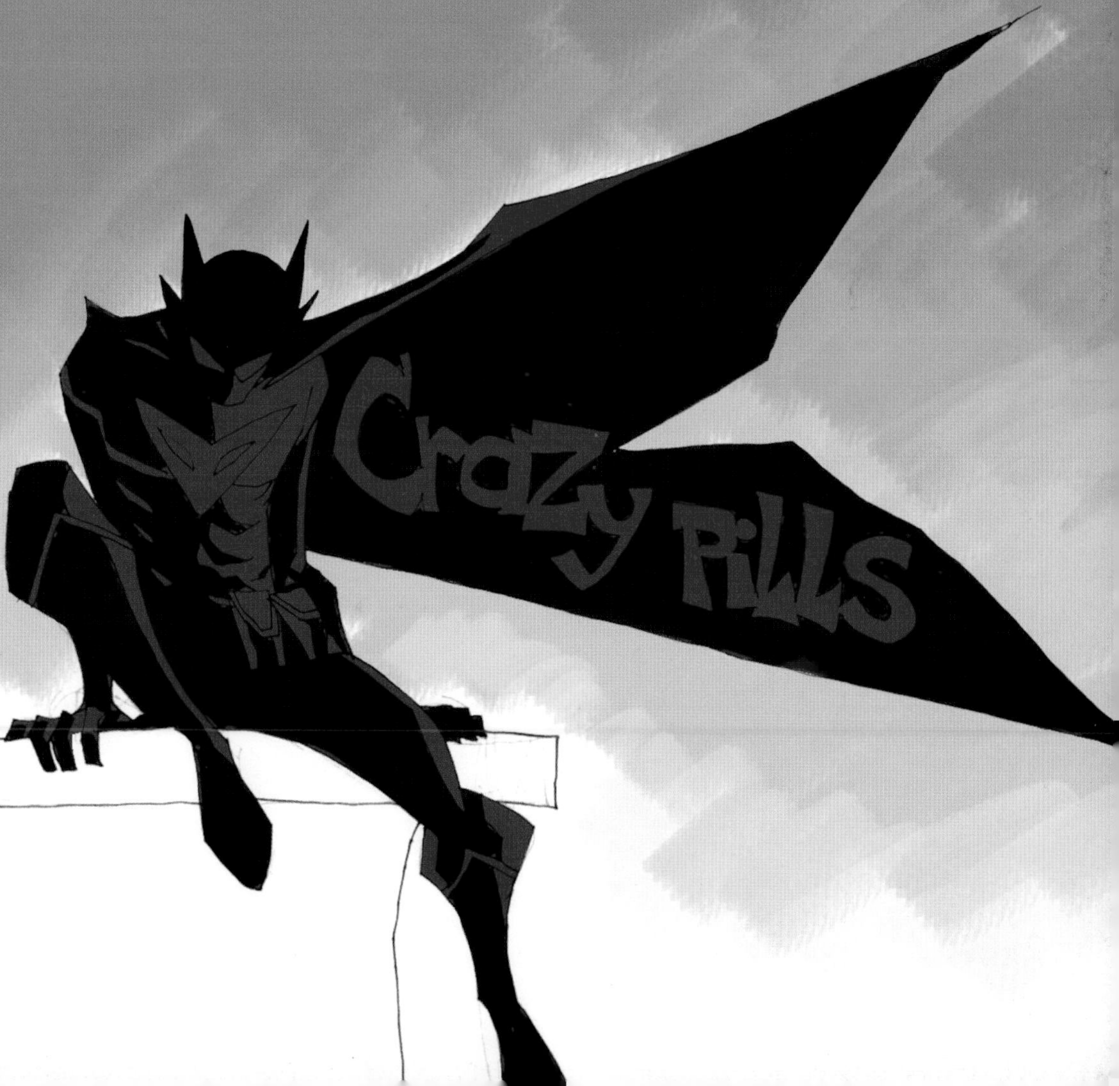
Crazy Pills

This one wasn't a sketch so much as it was practice. But it helped me define the character in a lot of ways.

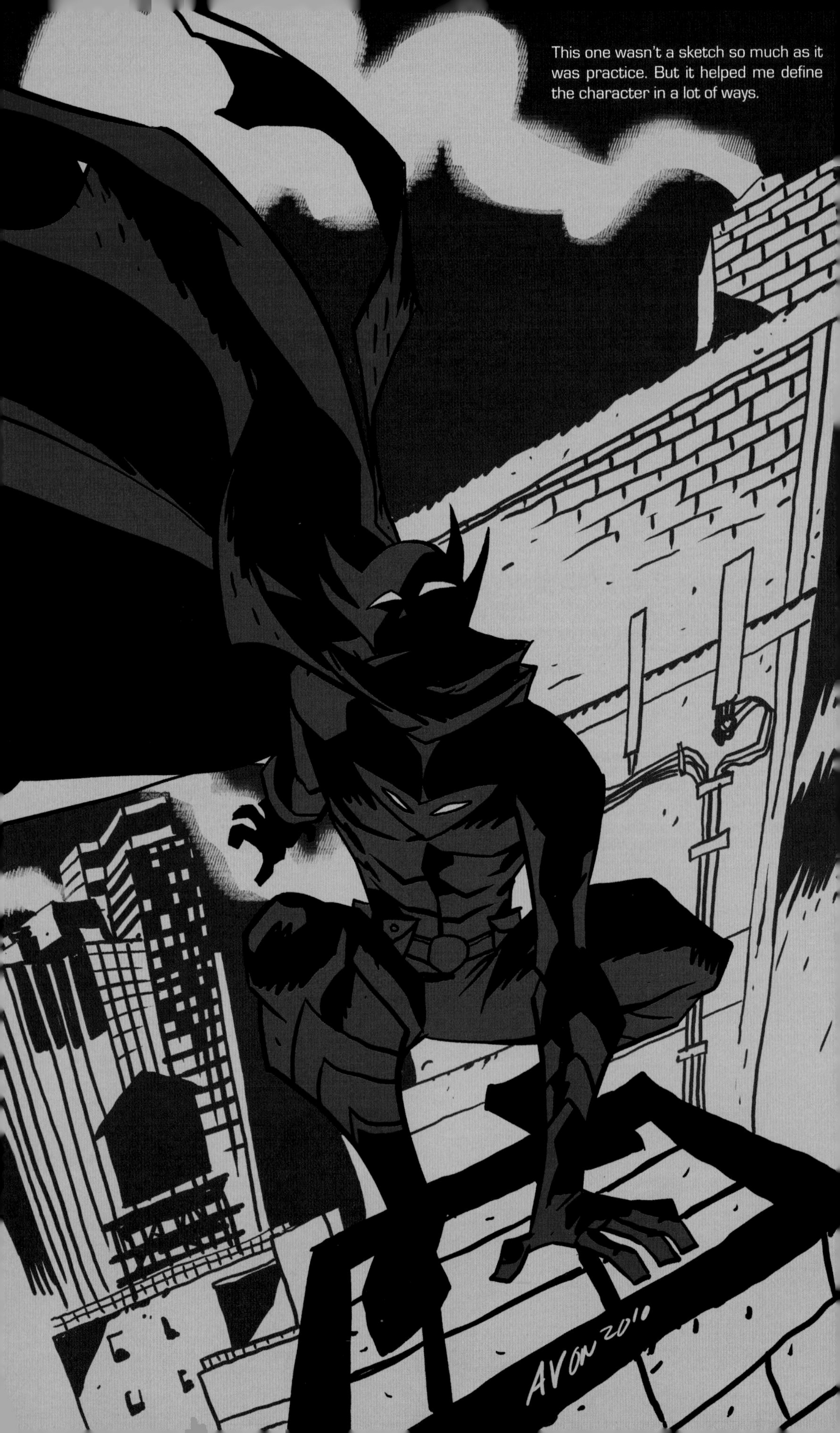
AVON 2010

These early character studies were as much about how Faustus would flow on the page as they were about his design.

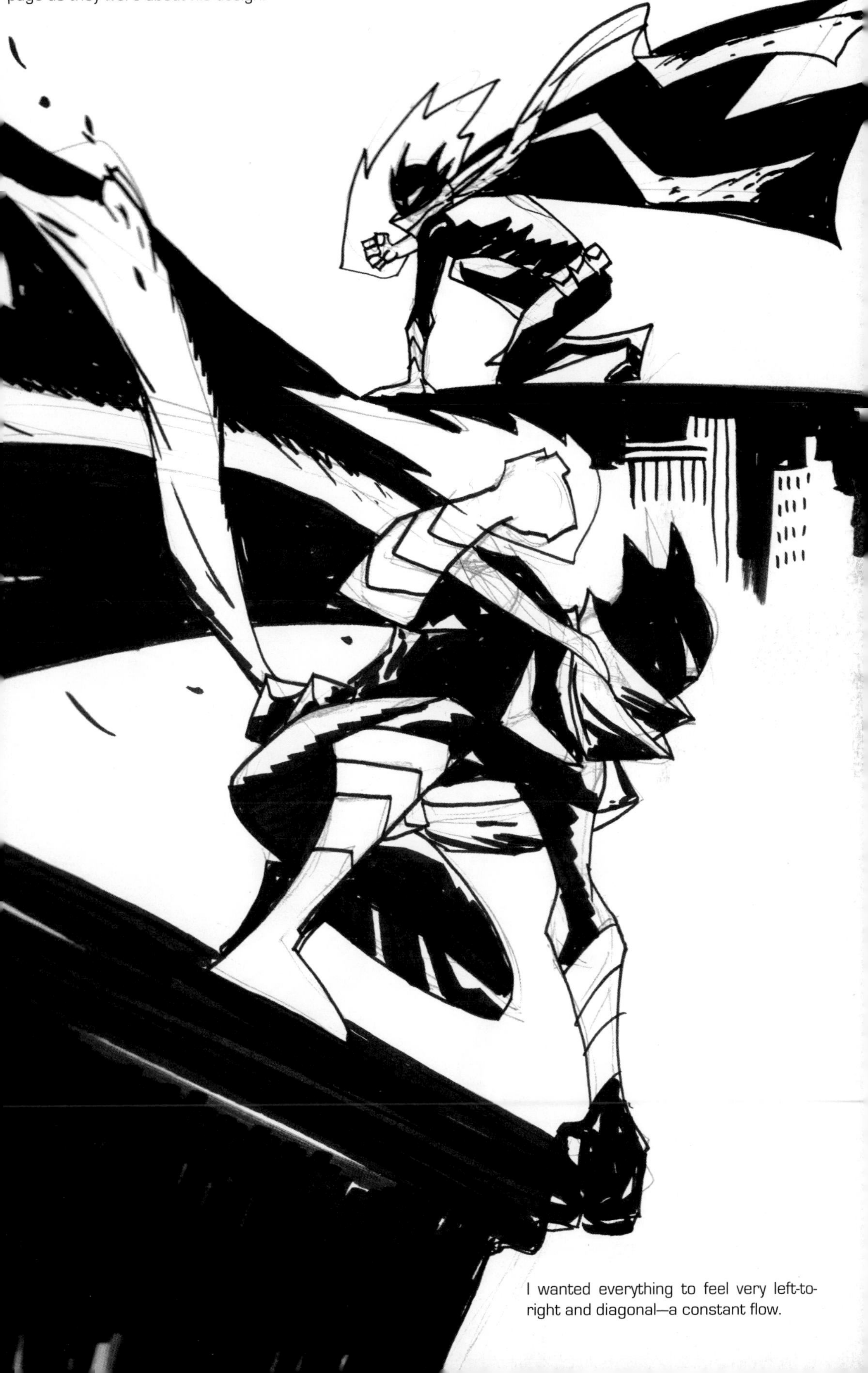

I wanted everything to feel very left-to-right and diagonal—a constant flow.

More pushing and pulling with Faustus. I like the bounce between these two poses.

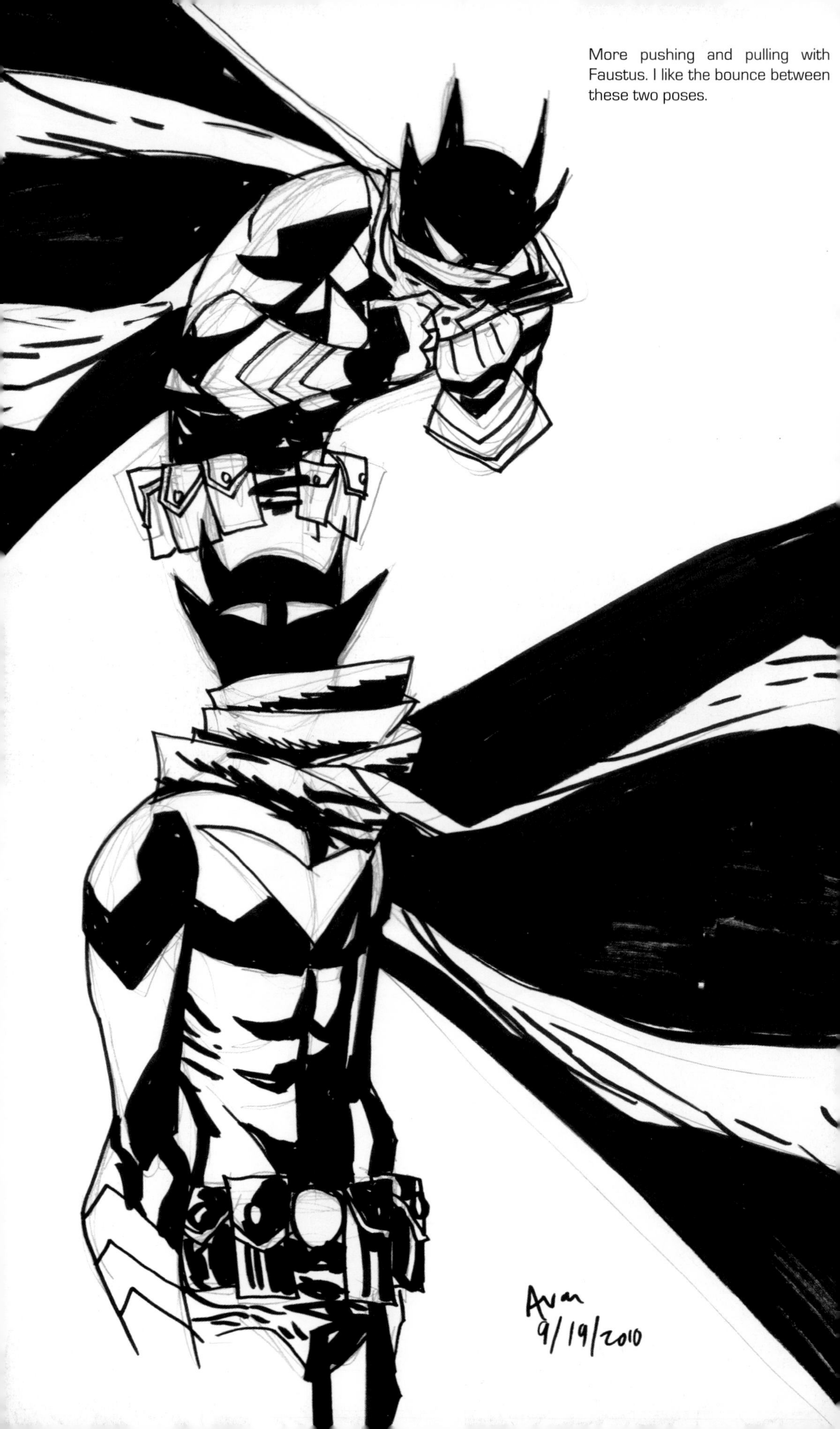
Avan
9/19/2010

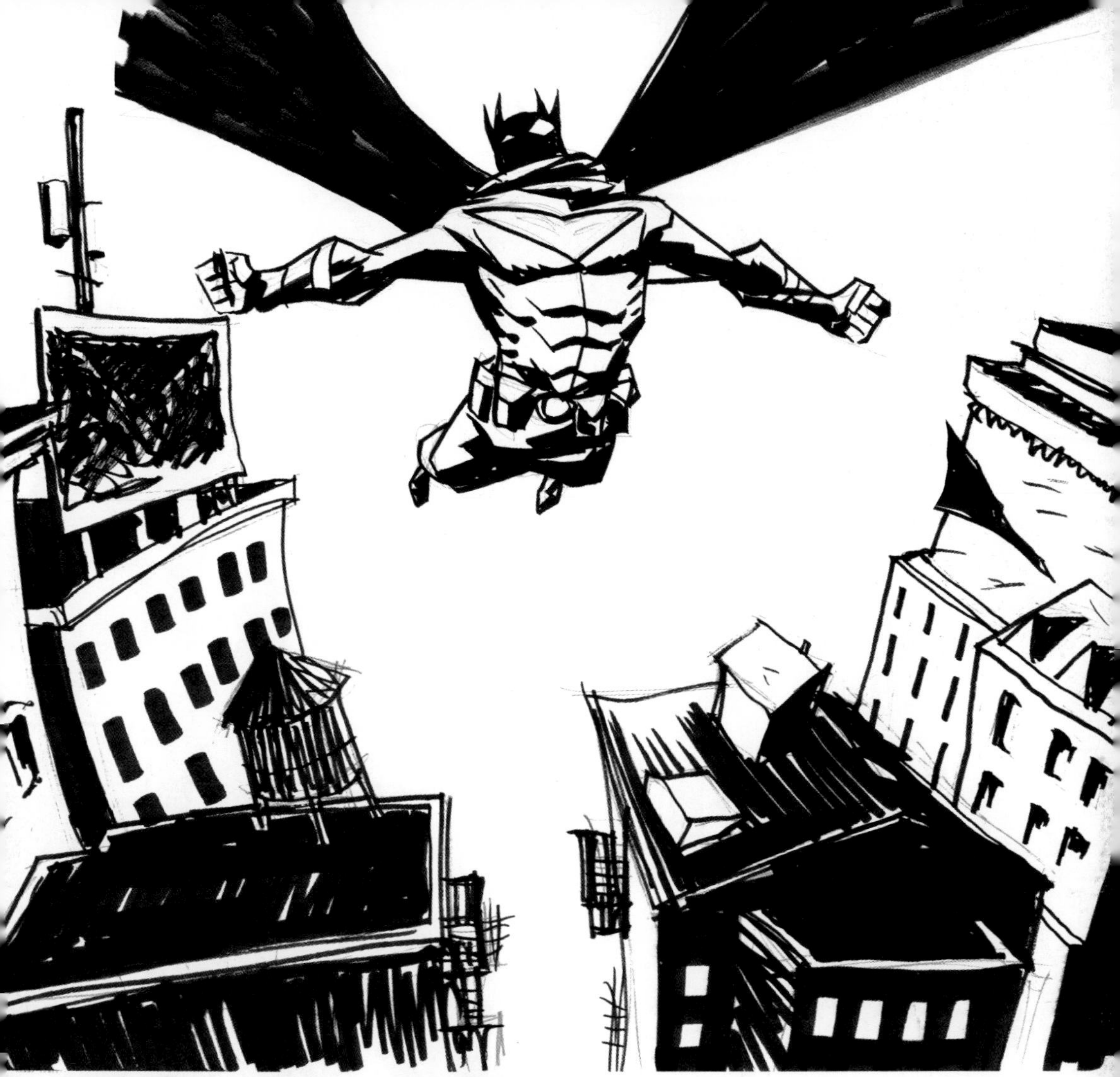

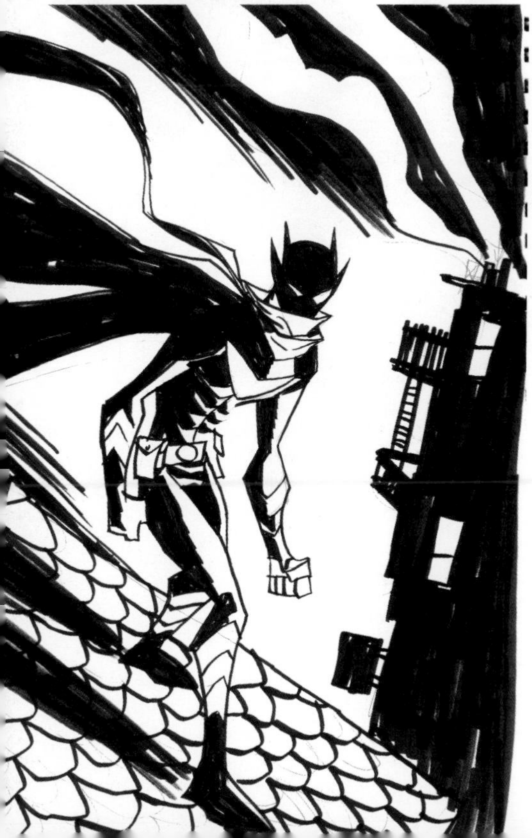

This was an experiment. I wanted to see if I could actually draw this in a sketchbook style, but it's a thin line between experiment and disaster . . . so I decided it would be better to play with styles depending on the emotional direction of the scene.

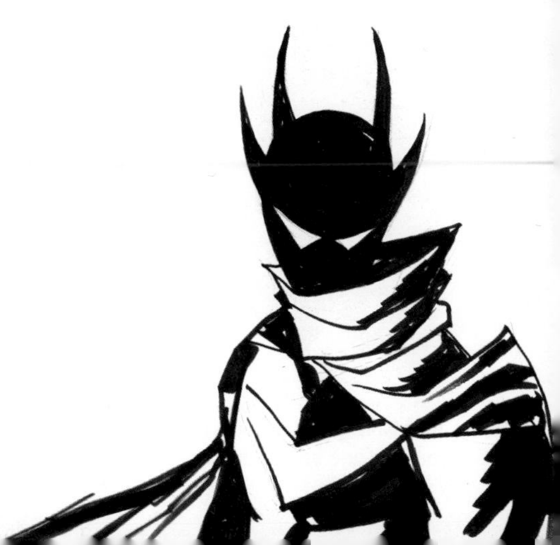

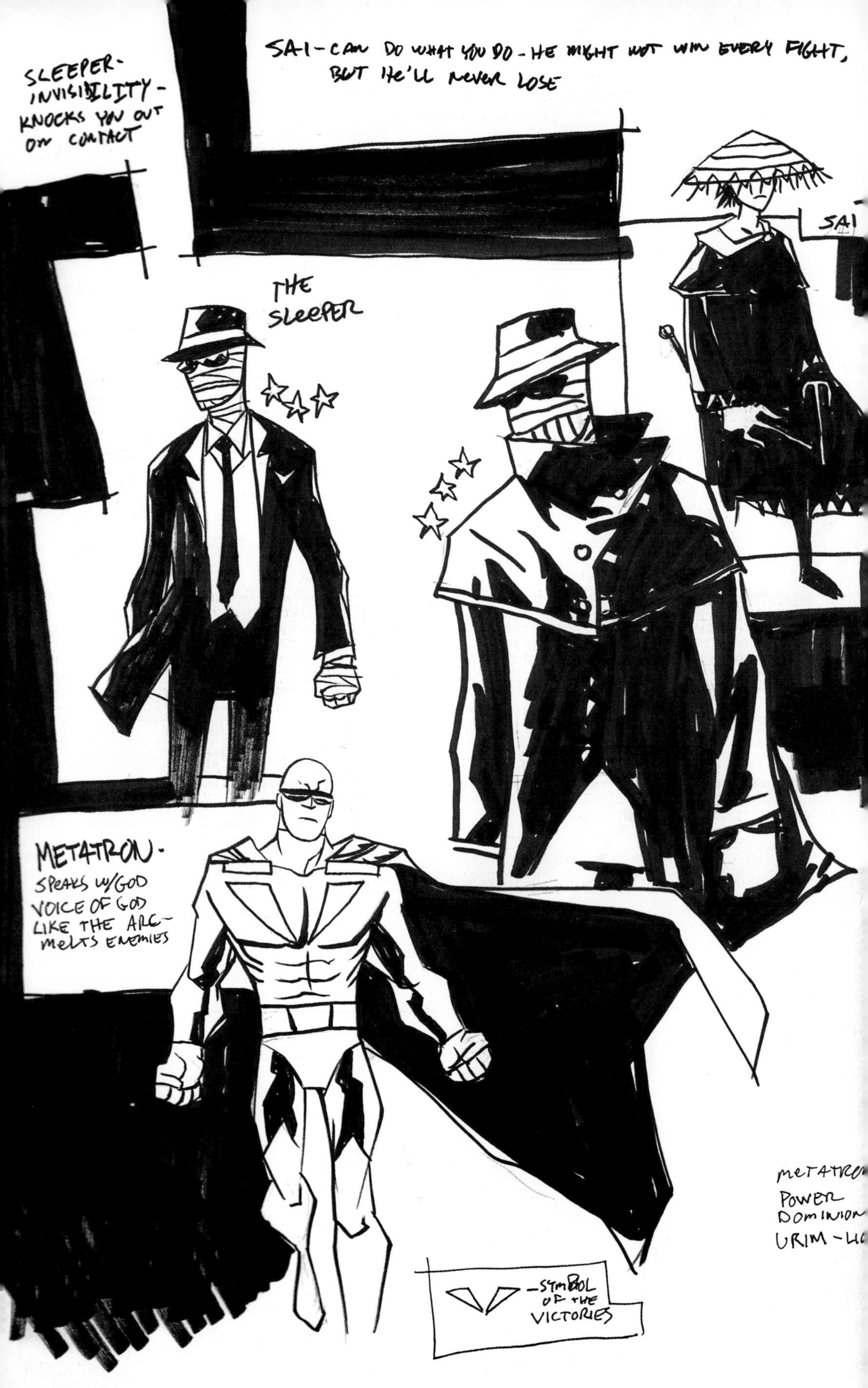
SLEEPER-
INVISIBILITY-
KNOCKS YOU OUT
ON CONTACT
SAI-CAN DO WHAT YOU DO-HE MIGHT NOT WIN EVERY FIGHT,
BUT HE'LL NEVER LOSE
SAI
THE
SLEEPER
METATRON-
SPEAKS W/GOD
VOICE OF GOD
LIKE THE ARC-
MELTS ENEMIES
METATRON
POWER
DOMINION
URIM-
-SYMBOL
OF THE
VICTORIES

The first shot at designing characters, and it pretty much stuck.
But you can see some ideas and names I wrote down that didn't.

Okay, you won't believe this, but originally the Jackal was going to have his dick out as part of his costume. It was meant to reflect his animal nature and to be a visual attack. The prospect of having to ship the book bagged because of this made me change my mind to a spiked codpiece.

When a review says *The Victories* is leaning on cheap shock tactics, they have *no* idea how much I actually hold back. But I'm glad I didn't do it, because this is all people would talk about.

I spent an afternoon editing out penises.

HYENA/JACKAL

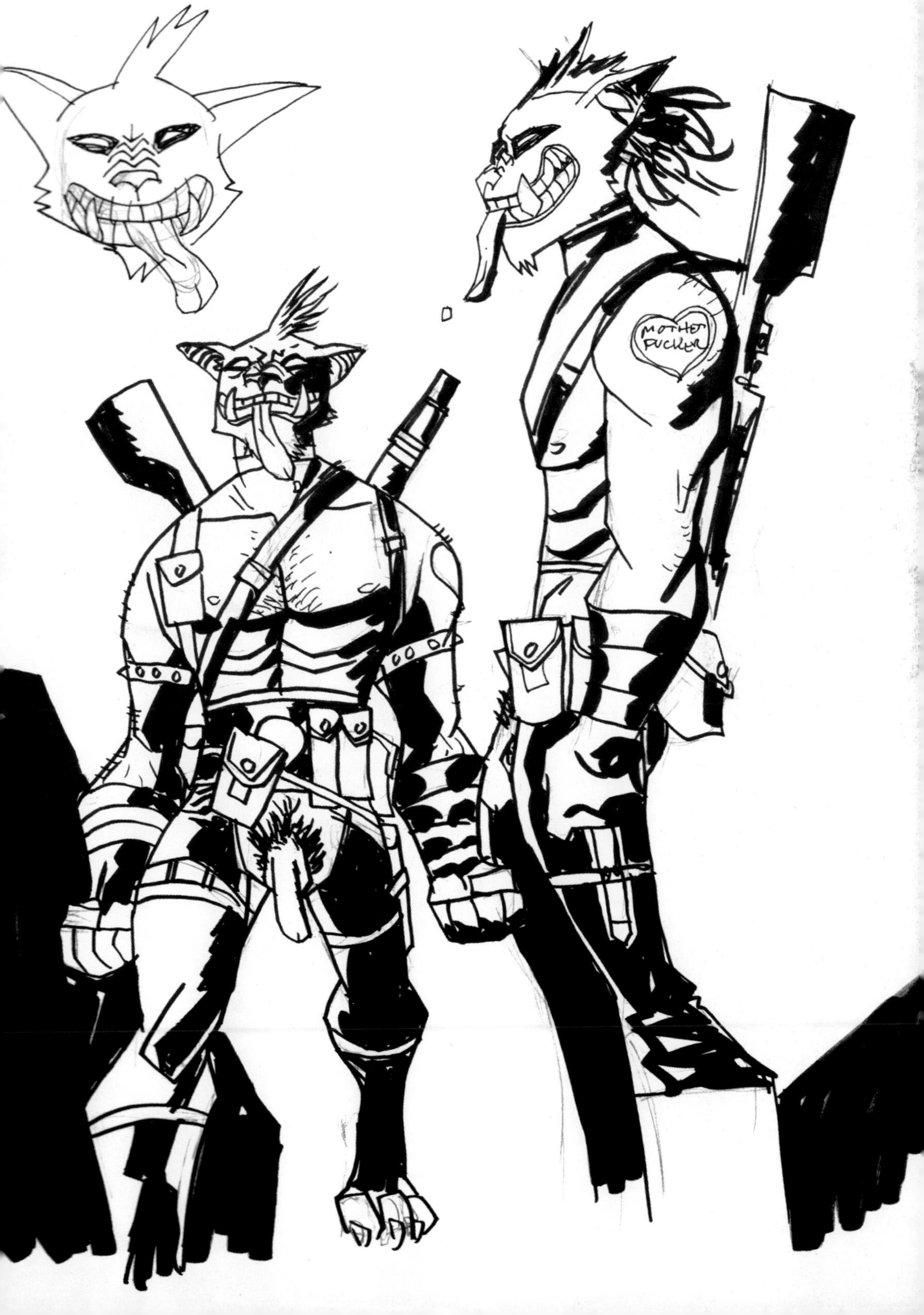
MOTHER FUCKER

I like how sad Faustus looks here. I've had a lot of rough nights of anxiety and feeling bad for myself that often manifested in sketches like these.

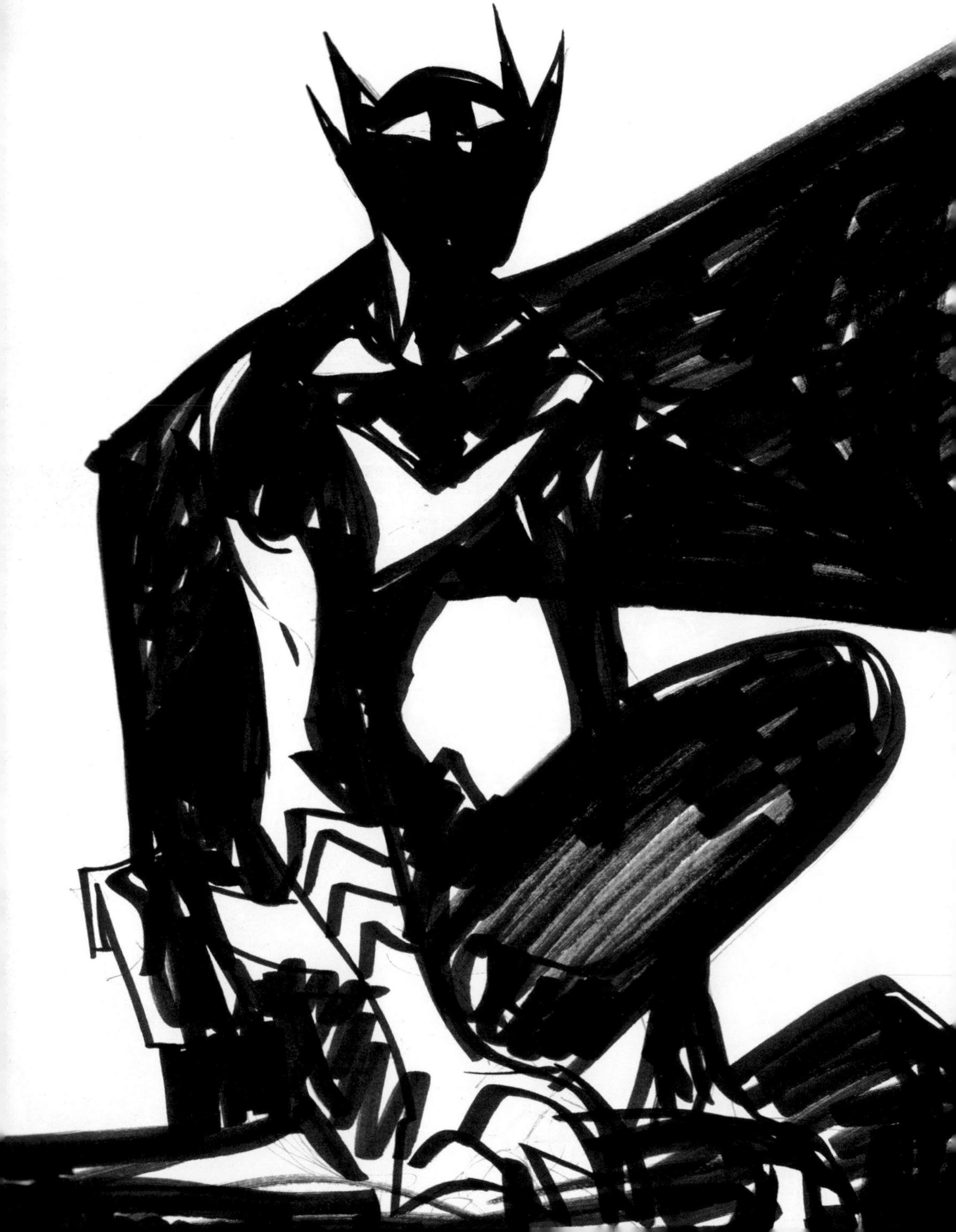

This is the very first image of Faustus *ever*. As you can see, I was going to arm him with a staff originally.

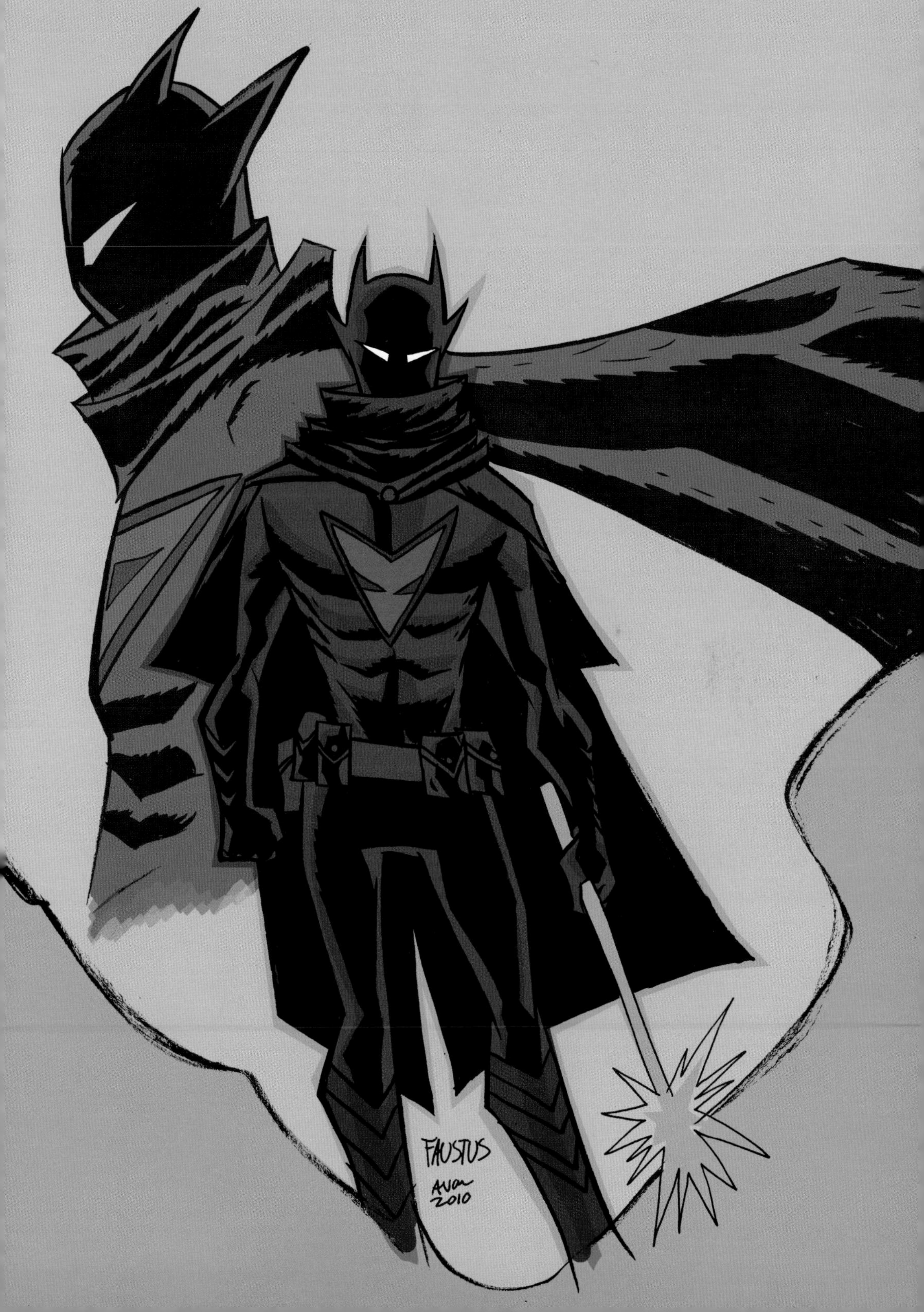
FAUSTUS
AVON
2010

I like this one. I drew this while feeling particularly shitty, and it really came out through the character.

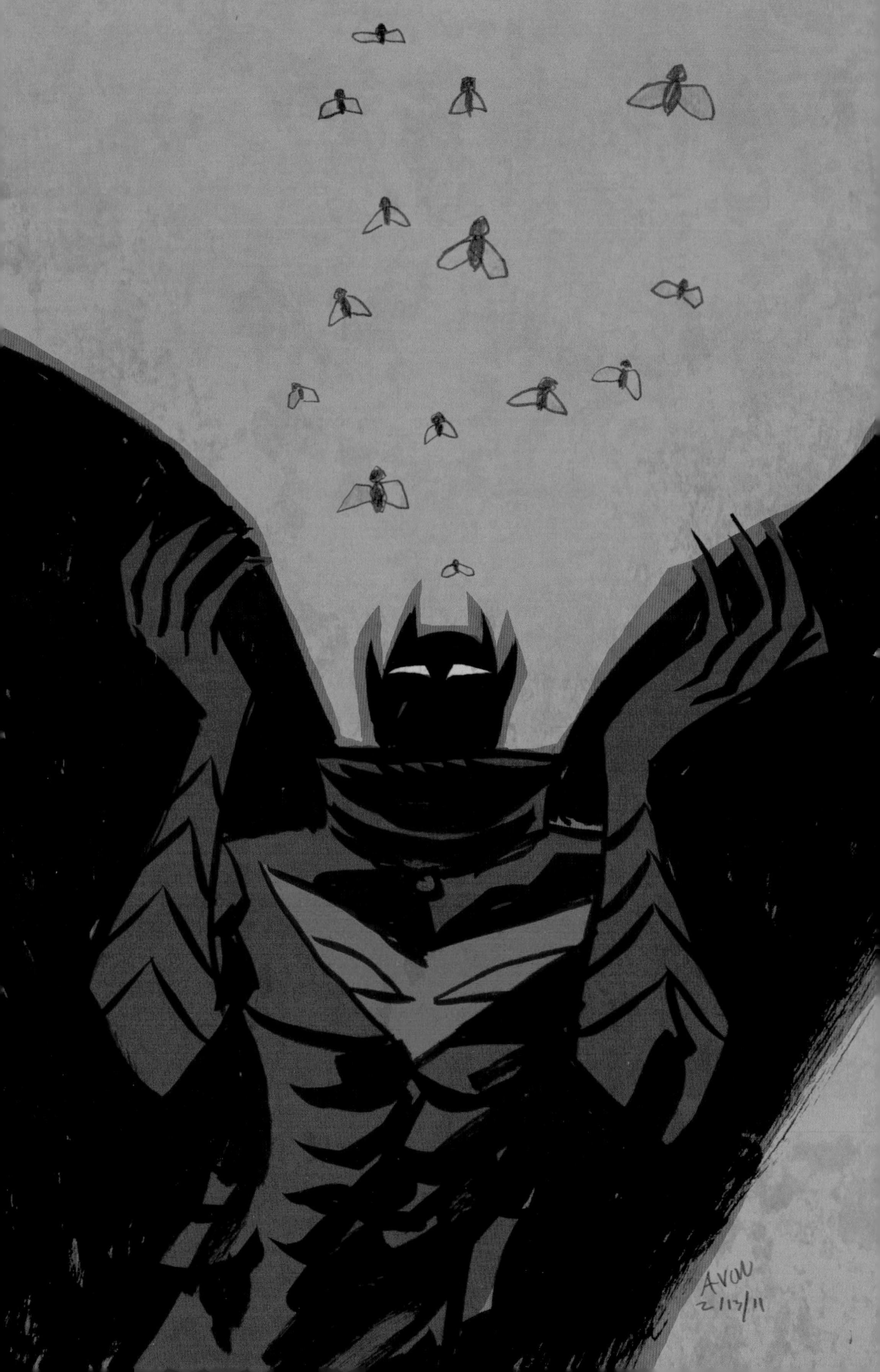
Avon
2/13/11

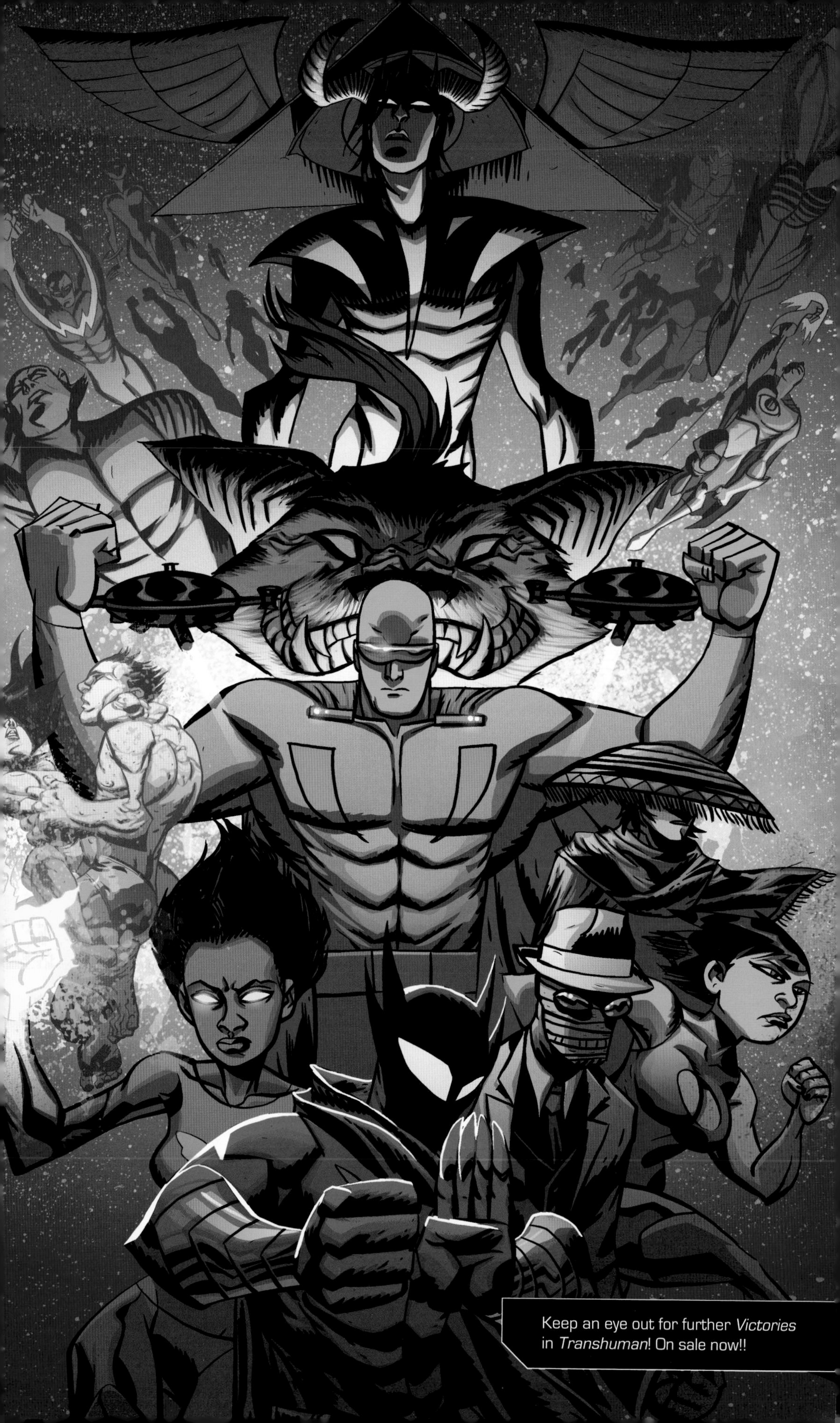
Keep an eye out for further *Victories* in *Transhuman*! On sale now!!

OTHER BOOKS BY MICHAEL AVON OEMING

TAKI SOMA • MICHAEL AVON OEMING
RAPTURE

RAPTURE
Michael Avon Oeming and Taki Soma

After warring for a century, Earth's greatest champions and villains suddenly disappear, leaving the planet decimated. Like a rapture, the Powers are gone and humanity is left behind to pick up the pieces. Amongst this wreckage, two lovers, Evelyn and Gil, find themselves separated by a continent and will do anything to find each other again. But when a strange being named "the Word" turns Evelyn into a champion with an angelic spear, she finds the force of her love for Gil clashing with her newfound power. Love and destiny collide in what will become the worst breakup ever!

$19.99
ISBN 978-1-59582-460-8

FROM THE PAGES OF HELLBOY
B.P.R.D.
PLAGUE OF FROGS 1
MIKE MIGNOLA GUY DAVIS
CHRISTOPHER GOLDEN TOM SNIEGOSKI RYAN SOOK GEOFF JOHNS
SCOTT KOLINS CAMERON STEWART MICHAEL AVON OEMING
AND MORE

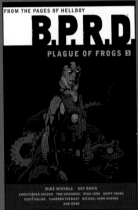

B.P.R.D.: PLAGUE OF FROGS
HARDCOVER COLLECTION VOLUME 1
Mike Mignola, Christopher Golden, Geoff Johns, Michael Avon Oeming, and others

In 2001, Hellboy quit the B.P.R.D., leaving Abe Sapien to lead Liz Sherman and a bizarre roster of special agents in defending the world from occult threats, including the growing menace of the frog army first spotted in *Hellboy: Seed of Destruction*.

$34.99
ISBN 978-1-59582-609-1

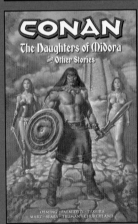

CONAN
The Daughters of Midora
and Other Stories
OEMING · PALMIOTTI · TEXEIRA
MARZ · SEARS · TRUMAN · CHURCHLAND

CONAN: THE DAUGHTERS OF MIDORA AND OTHER STORIES
Jimmy Palmiotti, Ron Marz, Michael Avon Oeming, and others

A must-buy for any Conan fan! Collects *Conan and the Daughters of Midora*, *Conan: Island of No Return* #1–#2, and stories from *MySpace Dark Horse Presents* #11 and *USA Today*.

$14.99
ISBN 978-1-59582-917-7

VALVE
PRESENTS
THE SACRIFICE
AND OTHER STEAM-POWERED STORIES

VALVE PRESENTS: THE SACRIFICE AND OTHER STEAM-POWERED STORIES
Michael Avon Oeming and others

Valve joins with Dark Horse to bring three critically acclaimed, fan-favorite series to print, with a hardcover collection of comics from the worlds of *Left 4 Dead*, *Team Fortress*, and *Portal*. With over two hundred pages of story, *Valve Presents: The Sacrifice and Other Steam-Powered Stories* is a must-read for fans looking to further explore the games they love or comics readers interested in dipping their toes into a new mythos!

$24.99
ISBN 978-1-59582-869-9